T0281592

The Map-Building and Exploration Strategies of a
Simple Sonar-Equipped Mobile Robot

Distinguished Dissertations in Computer Science

Edited by
C.J. van Rijsbergen, University of Glasgow

The Conference of Professors of Computer Science (CPCS), in conjunction with the British Computer Society (BCS), selects annually for publication up to four of the best British PhD dissertations in computer science. The scheme began in 1990. Its aim is to make more visible the significant contribution made by Britain – in particular by students – to computer science, and to provide a model for future students. Dissertations are selected on behalf of CPCS by a panel whose members are:

C.B. Jones, Manchester University (Chairman)
S. Abramsky, Imperial College, London
D.A. Duce, Rutherford Appleton Laboratory
M.E. Dyer, University of Leeds
G. Nudd, University of Warwick
V.J. Rayward-Smith, University of East Anglia
Ian Wand, University of York
M.H. Williams, Heriot-Watt University

THE MAP-BUILDING AND EXPLORATION STRATEGIES OF A SIMPLE SONAR-EQUIPPED ROBOT

An Experimental, Quantitative Evaluation

DAVID LEE
Department of Engineering Science
University of Oxford

CAMBRIDGE
UNIVERSITY PRESS

PUBLISHED BY THE PRESS SYNDICATE OF THE UNIVERSITY OF CAMBRIDGE
The Pitt Building, Trumpington Street, Cambridge, United Kingdom

CAMBRIDGE UNIVERSITY PRESS

The Edinburgh Building, Cambridge CB2 2RU, UK
40 West 20th Street, New York NY 10011–4211, USA
477 Williamstown Road, Port Melbourne, VIC 3207, Australia
Ruiz de Alarcón 13, 28014 Madrid, Spain
Dock House, The Waterfront, Cape Town 8001, South Africa

http://www.cambridge.org

© Cambridge University Press 1996

This book is in copyright. Subject to statutory exception
and to the provisions of relevant collective licensing agreements,
no reproduction of any part may take place without
the written permission of Cambridge University Press.

First published 1996
First paperback edition 2003

A catalogue record for this book is available from the British Library

ISBN 0 521 57331 9 hardback
ISBN 0 521 54215 4 paperback

Contents

Preface

This book is the product of my PhD research at University College London. I am grateful to the many people and organisations that have made my research both possible and enjoyable. I have benefited greatly from the companionship and support of all of my colleagues in the Computer Science and Anatomy departments during the course of this work. The following paragraphs can only recognise some of the more direct contributions.

Many thanks are due to Michael Recce for his enthusiastic and constructive supervision. Michael has been generous with his time, his ideas, and his lab space. I am also indebted to Michael for his careful reading of draft versions of this document and his valuable suggestions about its style and content.

Jim Donnett has made many much-appreciated contributions to this work, ranging from hardware design and debugging through to a detailed reading of the thesis. Jim's breadth and depth of knowledge have been invaluable, and his friendship and sense of humour have helped me through some trying moments.

I owe a great deal to Clive Parker for the construction of my robot, ARNE. Thanks to Clive's electronic and mechanical skills, a loose collection of components was transformed into an effective research tool.

David Brown of the Statistics Department kindly took the time to advise me about the statistical analysis of my results, despite having been 'volunteered' for the job. His insight and suggestions were most welcome.

John Greenwood contributed greatly to this work by forcing me to set deadlines during my writing-up and then carefully reading the chapters I produced.

Financial support is, of course, always welcome and I would like to thank the Engineering and Physical Sciences Research Council for their funding during this work.

This thesis is being published as part of the 1995 Distinguished Dissertations Scheme. I am very grateful to all of the judges for making this possible. My thanks are also due to Professor Keith van Rijsbergen, the series editor, and to David Tranah at Cambridge University Press for leading me by the hand through the preparations for publication.

Above all, I thank Melanie for more types of support and encouragement than I could possibly list here. Without her, this work would never have happened.

Chapter 1

Question, Context and Method

1.1 The Question - What is This Thesis About?

This thesis examines the process by which an autonomous mobile robot constructs a map of its operating environment. This process can be considered as two distinct topics. First, the robot has to interpret the findings of its sensors so as to make accurate deductions about the state of its environment. This is the problem of 'map-building'. Second, it has to select its viewpoints so that the sensory measurements contain new and useful information. This is the problem of 'exploration'. This thesis describes a practical and experimental investigation into both of these issues.

This document is structured as a large number of short chapters. This reflects the wide range of subjects which had to be examined in order to build an effective working robot for map-building and exploration experiments. For ease of reading, the chapters are grouped into three parts; Part I (Chapters 2 to 4) examines the principal areas of previous research upon which this thesis is built; Part II (Chapters 5 to 10) describes the components of the map-building system; and finally Part III (Chapters 11 to 20) reports on experiments to evaluate the effectiveness of a range of exploration strategies. The closing chapters of Part III summarise the results and conclusions and suggest directions for further research.

The remaining sections of this introductory chapter serve as an overview of the thesis and put the later chapters into context.

Section 1.2 begins with a brief review of the history of mobile robots and then describes some of the issues which are currently occupying researchers. Section 1.3 outlines the hardware and software which make possible the experiments described in this thesis and also explains some of the key implementation decisions. Section 1.4 summarises the contributions of this research.

1.2 The Context - Why Make Maps?

It can be difficult to devise watertight definitions of research topics. Take, for example, 'robotics'. Many researchers have suggested definitions, usually agreeing about the core of the subject but disagreeing about the inclusion of topics such as teleoperation and prostheses.

This thesis makes no attempt to provide a definition, but it may prove worthwhile to examine some views of the topic and to see what they have in common.

The fascination of robotics lies in its attempt to create machines which have something in common with human beings. The layman's idea of a robot is dominated by the fictional examples seen in films and on television, ranging from the first movie robot in 'Metropolis' in 1926 through 'C3PO' in 'Star Wars' to Data in 'Star Trek'. These machines not only have human skills such as language and reasoning but they also look like people. With this expectation it can be disappointing to visit a robot lab and see mobile robots that look more like dustbins on wheels.

If humanoid appearance is not important, then what is? Consider a few attempts at definition:

> A robot is a programmable, multi-function manipulator designed to move material, parts, or specialized devices through variable programmed motions for the performance of a variety of tasks. (Schlussel 1983)

> A robot is a machine which can be programmed to do a variety of tasks, in the same way that a computer is an electronic circuit which can be programmed to do a variety of tasks. (McKerrow 1991, page 8)

> Robotics is the intelligent connection of perception to action. (Brady 1985)

These definitions raise questions of course (Are mobile robots 'manipulators'? What does 'intelligent' mean? ...) but they share the requirement that a robot must be able to perform a variety of tasks. If a machine blindly repeats the same set of actions, with no possibility of variation, it does not qualify as a robot.

The first industrial robot began operation in the early 1960's. Since then robots have gained wide acceptance in the manufacturing industry, specifically in the manufacture of vehicles and electric machine tools. By 1988 the world population of industrial robots had grown to 280,000 (Kennedy 1993, page 88).

Early industrial robots operated in environments which were specifically designed around the robot. Each component was supplied to the robot in a predefined position and orientation so that the robot knew exactly where to find it. The robot could indeed be programmed to perform different tasks, but the changeover could be a costly and time-consuming process. As the range of potential applications has expanded over the last 30 years, there has been increasing interest in robots which are able to identify variations in their environment and to react to them without human intervention. It would, for example, be useful for an assembly robot to be able to pick up components from a conveyor belt, however they may be positioned. This interest in tolerance of variation has also been fuelled by the trend towards shorter production runs. A manufacturer may need to produce several products and may not be willing to incur the costs of frequent reprogramming and recalibration of a robot. For example, it was recently reported (Hallahan 1994) that these pressures led IBM to scrap the robots in an automated factory and to replace them with human workers. The result was an increase in productivity.

Environmental variation increases rapidly when robots become mobile. The appropriate action for the robot depends upon where it finds itself, it may be uncertain about its exact location, and it may have to share its environment with unpredictable human beings. In recent years, a growing amount of research effort has been invested in the problems peculiar to mobile robots. A rough indication of the rate of growth of this research effort can be obtained by counting the number of published papers about[1] 'robots' and 'mobile robots' in the last 10 years, according to the Bath Information and Data Services (BIDS). In 1983 there were 313 publications about robots, of which 5 were about mobile robots. By 1993 the total number of robot publications had grown to 775 (a factor of 2.5) of which 99 were about mobile robots (a growth factor of 19.8). By this measure 12.8% of robot research in 1993 was concerned with mobile robots.

Mobile robot research is generally taken to have started in the 1960's, although there were occasional earlier examples (e.g. Shannon's maze-runner in 1940 and Grey Walter's 'turtle' robot in 1953). The first mobile robot to use vision was Shakey, built in 1969 at the Stanford Research Institute. Its objective was to use its cameras to recognise objects, approach them, and perform an action such as pushing them over (McKerrow 1991, pages 4–6).

A successor to Shakey was the Stanford Cart (Moravec 1983). This again used vision, and built a world model which it used to plan paths whilst avoiding obstacles. Despite some successes, it was found to be unreliable (being confused by changes in the quality of daylight at different times of day) and was extremely slow.

Until the mid 1980's it was taken as axiomatic that a mobile robot should use its sensors to build a world model and then use the world model to plan its actions. Then several researchers, frustrated by the limited achievements of these robots, began to question the need for a world model. What types of behaviour could arise from a robot which simply reacted to its sensory inputs? 'Behaviour-based' robotics was born.

Early experiments with behaviour-based robots had impressive results. It was shown, by Brooks (1986) and others, that behaviour similar to that observed in simple animals, such as insects, could be produced by robots with very little, if any, internal state. Robots could avoid obstacles, approach targets, and follow walls by reacting rapidly to the input from their senses. An architecture, the subsumption architecture, was designed to make it easier to build these robots so that the most appropriate behaviour would be used at each moment.

Advocates of behaviour-based robots invoked evolutionary theory to support their cause. It clearly took much longer for nature to evolve the 'basic' skills, such as walking and avoiding threats, than the 'higher' skills, such as language and reasoning. Therefore, the argument runs, it makes sense to focus first on the acquisition of the simpler skills. Once these are mastered, cognition will be much easier. The use of evolution to support the cause is very much in keeping with a recent 'back to nature' trend. Supporters of artificial neural networks continue to cite neuroscience as their inspiration and justification; genetic algorithms evolve problem solutions in a Darwinian way; the new field of 'Artificial Life' is concerned with the study of artificial systems which exhibit lifelike behaviours.

The debate between the supporters of 'behaviour-based' robotics and the proponents of world models has been heated, giving the impression that the way forward would be *either*

---

[1]The selection was based simply upon the inclusion of the words 'robot' or 'mobile robot' in the paper's title.

behaviour-based *or* model-based. Although these extreme positions have helped to clarify the issues, opinion now appears to be settling in the middle ground. For example, at a recent workshop provocatively entitled 'Models or Behaviours - Which Way Forward For Robotics?', 12 of the 17 speakers favoured a hybrid approach. (AISB 1994)

World models are only useful if they continue to match the true state of the world. A model is then used to *predict* the state of the environment so that effective plans can be made. The value of a world model is therefore directly linked to the degree of predictability of the robot's environment. If the environment is completely under the control of the robot (an automated warehouse, for example), then a world model would be very useful. If, on the other hand, the robot has very little control over its environment (negotiating a busy high street, for example), then a world model would be much less useful than a quick set of reflexes. Most applications lie somewhere between these two extremes, suggesting the wisdom of a hybrid architecture in which the predictable features of the world are incorporated into a world model and the world model is used to *guide* the behaviour-based components.

The debate about the need for a world model has spawned discussions about the type of world model that is appropriate. In particular, a number of behaviour-based projects have decided to reject detailed metric maps in favour of distributed, topological maps. Chapter 2 reviews the different types of map which have been used by mobile robots and argues that the selection of a type of map depends strongly on the intended application of the robot. The different types of map are presented in a hierarchy, ordered by the 'strength' of the map. 'Strength', in this context, refers to the range of geometric properties which can be derived from the map. The categories are:

Recognisable Locations The map consists of a list of locations which can be reliably recognised by the robot. *No geometric relationships can be recovered.*

Topological Map In addition to the recognisable locations, the map records which locations are connected by traversable paths. *Connectivity between visited locations can be recovered.*

Metric Topological Maps This term is used for maps in which distance and angle information is added to the path descriptions. *Metric information can be recovered about paths which have been travelled.*

Full Metric Maps Object locations are specified in a fixed co-ordinate system. *Metric information can be recovered about any objects in the map*

The preceding discussion argues that the decision whether to use a world model and, if so, what type to use depends strongly on the intended application of the robot. One of the first steps in the research was therefore to choose an application. The selected application was *indoor delivery*. Examples of such an application could be office mail delivery, an intelligent wheelchair for disabled people, or even a domestic robot. Chapter 3 describes the properties of such an application in detail and argues that a full metric map would be needed.

The robot could get a metric map in two ways; a human operator could give it the map or the robot could build its own. Advantages of the latter solution include:

Changes in the Robot's Environment Over time the robot's environment will change. It could periodically re-map the world.

Matching the Map to the Sensors It is difficult for a user to predict which features of the world will be easily recognisable by the robot's sensors. A user-supplied map may therefore be of limited value to the robot.

Ease of Use It would be a more attractive commercial proposition for a purchaser of a robot to be able to put it to work without having to measure its new environment or otherwise obtain a map.

Level of Detail For some purposes the level of detail required might be higher than that obtained from a readily-available architectural drawing.

In the light of these advantages, it was decided to pursue the goal of autonomous map construction.

In all but the simplest environments, some objects will be hidden by other, nearer, objects. The robot will then have to move to gather knowledge about its entire work area. One is therefore left with the question of *how* it should move.

Exploration strategies have not been extensively examined in the literature. It is, however, possible to identify a number of categories into which the existing work falls:

Human Control Many researchers report the results of map construction while the robot was under the control of a human operator.

Reactive Control As mentioned earlier, supporters of behaviour-based robotics have, in situations in which some type of world model *is* needed, favoured topological maps. To obtain such a map, the robot will typically navigate under the control of a reactive algorithm, such as wall-following, which is well-suited to the behaviour-based architectures.

Approaching the Unknown A reasonable exploration strategy is for the robot to approach those regions of its environment about which it knows least.

Optimal Search Strategies Under the heading of 'terrain acquisition', researchers have provided mathematical analyses of strategies which are guaranteed to find all objects in the robot's environment. Emphasis is placed on minimising the length of the path travelled by the robot during exploration. This work typically makes simplifying assumptions about ideal sensors.

Chapter 4 describes previous exploration research in more detail and discusses a number of examples.

One of the objectives of this thesis is to provide quantitative comparisons between a representative sample of exploration strategies. In the light of the discussion of behaviour-based robotics, a key question is:

> How much should the robot use its developing map to guide the exploration? When, if at all, does the robot's map contain enough information to justify using it to guide further exploration, instead of using a reactive, representation-free strategy?

1.3   The Method - How Will the Question be Addressed?

Examination of mobile robot research shows two distinct approaches; simulation and implementation. Some researchers build computer models of the performance of a robot and then use the model to test theories and algorithms. Others choose to build a real-world robot. It was necessary to choose between these two approaches. Simulation has advantages. One can see the results of an algorithm much more quickly by applying it to a computer simulation than to the real robot. The researcher is able to test new ideas without the constraints of time and expense associated with using a real robot. In addition, simulations allow the researcher to focus more tightly on the precise aspect of the problem in which he or she is interested. If, for example, the research is centred on path planning there may be little value in worrying about the mechanical engineering problems of building a physical robot. But the advantages are outweighed by disadvantages. To build a computer model, the researcher has to abstract the essential features of the system being modelled. This abstraction necessarily involves some degree of simplification. In mobile robotics this is most often noticeable in the modelling of sensors. For example, analysis of terrain acquisition problems (Lumelsky, Mukhopadhyay, & Sun 1991) assumes a sensor which can reliably detect the boundaries of any object that falls within a given radius of the robot. This is a highly idealised model of a sensor. Research based on such simplifications may well produce useful results, but there is always the danger that, in the simplification process, one has ignored a vital property of the robot so that the results will not be valid when tested on a real robot. Another important disadvantage has been summarised as 'simulations are doomed to succeed' (Miller *et al.* 1989). Since the same person is modelling both the problem and its solution, it is very tempting to include into the model of the problem just those features which can be handled by the solution. This is not to suggest any dishonesty on the part of the researcher. It may simply be that the model and the solution are built upon the same set of assumptions. The work described in this thesis tests exploration strategies on a real robot. However, in order to keep the time savings of a simulation, a Trace/Replay mechanism was implemented. This meant that all the sensor and movement information which was generated during an exploration by the real robot could be stored and subsequently replayed at will. This was found to be extremely useful throughout the research. Whenever a new idea was being implemented, a large amount of authentic information was available for testing.

Recent research, especially that motivated by behaviour-based robotics, has emphasised the creation of completely stand-alone robots, shunning the use of 'umbilical cords' to connect the robot to a stationary computer. The approach adopted in this research was, however, just that. A small mobile robot was constructed with a serial cable link to a Sun workstation on which the map construction and exploration control were performed. The following points are given in support of this decision:

- A real-world robot was implemented to tackle two real-world problems which are often oversimplified in simulations: sensing and localisation. Neither of these problems is diminished by the presence of an umbilical cord.

- Given the objective of testing exploration strategies, the smaller the robot the better. If the robot were enlarged to be able to carry the equivalent power of the Sun workstation on-board, it would not only be much more expensive but would also need a larger area of lab space in which to create varied environments for exploration.

- In parallel with the communications cable, it was practical to supply constant power to the robot. This made it possible to have lengthy experimental sessions without having to worry about keeping batteries charged.

- The graphics workstation was ideal for the display of the generated maps and for the examination of the exploration paths selected by the robot. If the robot had been stand-alone, one would either have had to follow it around to examine the map or implement a periodic download to a static display.

- The separation of hardware mirrored a corresponding separation of function. The workstation operated with high-level commands such as 'Move Forward 1000 mm' or 'Turn Left 90 Degrees', leaving the robot to concern itself with the low-level details such as motor control and obstacle avoidance. The robot itself had no world model. With this separation it was straightforward to test the same high-level software with a different robot, and vice versa.

The robot, ARNE[2], is described in detail in Chapter 5.

A simple dialogue was defined for communication with ARNE. This could then be used for direct control, through a terminal for example, or for control by the exploration and map construction software. The dialogue is described in Appendix D.

A key choice was the type of range sensor to be used on ARNE. The most commonly used range sensors in mobile robotics are vision, laser rangefinders, and ultrasonic time-of-flight sensors (sonar). The use of each of these sensors is an active research topic. Ultrasound was chosen for ARNE partly because of its low cost (many delivery applications are likely to be at the cheaper end of the market) and also because of recent work which suggested that ultrasonic sensing had been under-rated. Many researchers, frustrated by problems of wide beam width and unwanted reflections, have decided that ultrasonic sensing is only suitable for short-range obstacle avoidance. However, recent work (Zelinsky 1991b; Leonard & Durrant-Whyte 1992; Curran & Kyriakopoulos 1993) has suggested that sonar's bad reputation may not be justified and that reliable range readings can be obtained from sonar if a realistic

---

[2]Autonomous Robot for Navigation and Exploration. Also named for Arne Saknussemm, Jules Verne's explorer who was first to reach the centre of the earth. (Pronounced 'Arnie').

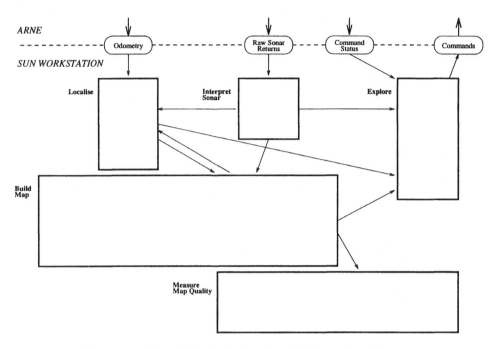

Figure 1.1: The Main Modules of the Workstation Software

The boxes represent the main software modules which were implemented on the workstation. The arrows
indicate data flow between the modules and the robot. The uneven size and spacing of the boxes is to
allow detail to be added as each module is explained. Path planning does not appear as a separate task on
this diagram because, as will be seen later, it plays a part both in exploration and in the map quality
calculations.

model of the sensor's behaviour is used. ARNE was therefore equipped with a Polaroid
ultrasonic rangefinder.

A suite of software modules was designed and implemented on the Sun workstation to perform the tasks listed below. The block diagram in Figure 1.1 summarises the communication
links among these tasks and between them and ARNE.

Interpret Sonar The range values generated by ARNE take the deceptively simple form
of an angle (relative to the robot's orientation) and a distance. Unfortunately the
sonar beam is wide and there is no guarantee that the object that caused the echo was
in the centre of the beam. Preprocessing of the sonar returns can reduce some of the
uncertainty. Chapter 6 describes some experiments to test the performance of ARNE's
sonar sensor and uses the results of the experiments to model the sensor's behaviour.

Build Map This is the core of the system software. Position and range information are
merged to generate a representation of the world which can be used to plan ARNE's
actions. The representation is formed in three layers; first the range information is analysed to suggest features which could have caused the given readings; these hypothetical

features are then gathered into mutually-supportive clusters to create 'confirmed' features; finally the confirmed features are used to construct a grid-based free-space map. The entire map-building process is described in detail in Chapter 7.

Plan Paths The free-space map can be used for path planning. The problem is to generate a sequence of movement commands which will, according to the map, move ARNE efficiently from a known starting position to a specified target position without colliding with any obstacles. A path planner is implemented using the technique of distance transforms. This is described in Chapter 8. The path planner is used in two places in this thesis. As one would expect, it is used to plan exploratory movements. It is also used when measuring the quality of the maps produced by these movements.

Localise To translate sensor readings into information about the world, it is essential to know where ARNE was when the readings were taken. This information comes from two sources. The first, and simpler, source is the odometry information returned by ARNE which converts measurements of the amount of wheel rotation into an estimate of the distance moved or the angle turned. Odometry is notoriously unreliable because of uneven floors or wheel slippage. It is therefore necessary to augment the odometry by measuring ARNE's position relative to known objects in the environment. Chapter 9 gives details of the chosen localisation method. It uses a Kalman filter to determine the best estimate of ARNE's position, given all the information available from odometry, range sensors, and the latest map.

Measure Map Quality The investigation described in this thesis has placed great emphasis on the need for practical experiments and quantitative, statistical, evaluation of the results. For this to be possible, it was essential to have a clearly-defined measure of map quality. The technique employed here is to define a set of 'benchmark' tasks and predict how successful the robot would be at performing those tasks if it used its latest map. Chapter 10 gives some background to the question of quality measurement and describes the metrics used in this thesis.

Explore How should the robot choose the next position from which to examine its environment? The majority of Part III of the thesis is concerned with this question. A range of exploration strategies are designed, implemented, and submitted to experimental evaluation.

1.4 Contributions

This thesis describes an experimental investigation into the complementary issues of map-building and exploration.

The novel contribution of this research consists of:

- The integration of a physical robot, a sonar model, map construction algorithms, and a localisation algorithm into an effective working system;

- The definition and implementation of a novel quantitative measure of map quality;

- A thorough quantitative and statistical evaluation of the map-building and exploration capabilities of the system, using the quality metric and a variety of exploration strategies. Each strategy is tested in a ránge of environments.

The system components and the quality metric have been outlined in the previous section and will be described fully in Part II of this thesis. The exploration strategies and the experimental results are described in Part III.

But first, Part I reviews the previous research upon which this thesis is built.

Part I

Starting Points

Chapter 2

Maps Used in Previous Research

Map construction is an essential component of the research reported in this thesis. This chapter examines the reasons why a mobile robot might need a map and reviews the variety of types of world model which have been devised and implemented by previous researchers.

Early research work into mobile robots (Moravec 1983; Crowley 1985) took it as axiomatic that an effective mobile robot would need an environment model. The process of control was viewed as two steps: first the robot uses its sensors to build a world model and then it uses the world model to plan and execute its actions. The details could vary (different sensor modalities, different data structures for the world model) but the underlying two-step process was not questioned.

In the mid-1980's a number of researchers, most prominent among them being Rodney Brooks (1986), became frustrated with the perceived slow progress in mobile robotics and began to search for an alternative approach to the 'traditional' dependence on environment models. The intention was to minimise the processing between sensing and action. Robots were built in which there was an almost immediate link between the robot's sensors and its actuators. (Braitenberg's excellent book 'Vehicles' (1984) describes, in the form of thought experiments, what could be achieved by such robots.) The robots were able to perform tasks such as approaching beacons, avoiding obstacles, and following walls. These behaviours were found to be very robust. Brooks's robots could operate in unmodified office environments, sharing their world with unpredictable humans. This contrasted starkly with the model-based robots which had operated in carefully constructed environments and were easily confused by people or moving objects.

The growth in 'reactive' robotics, as it came to be known, raised questions about the value of environment models. There were two main questions, which often become confused in discussions of this topic:

- Does a mobile robot need an environment model?

- If it does, what type of model is best?

The slogans adopted by the reactivists, such as 'Use the world as its own model' (Brooks 1991b, page 140) suggest that the robot does not need a model at all. Section 2.1 examines this position and discusses the circumstances in which a world model is useful.

Section 2.2 addresses the second question. It categorises the maps that have been used by previous researchers and considers the strengths and weaknesses of each type. The advantages and disadvantages of each type are very closely linked to the purpose for which the map is being used.

Discussion of the model used in this thesis is postponed until Chapter 3.

2.1   Is an Environment Model Necessary?

2.1.1   What is a model?

Precisely what is meant by 'an environment model'? If it is taken to mean a set of assumptions about the world which are used in the design and operation of the robot then, in a trivial sense, every robot can be said to be using an environment model. Take, for example, one of the simplest 'creatures' in Braitenberg's thought experiments (1984, page 6). The robot has two optical sensors on its front, one at each side. It is driven by two side wheels, each of which is connected to the sensor on the same side so that the brighter the light falling on the sensor, the faster the wheel turns. This very simple robot moves away from light sources. It is an implementation of the designer's world model, which included the facts that the world contains light sources and that it is beneficial to move away from them. This is clearly too broad an interpretation of 'environment modelling' for any useful discussion.

A more fruitful approach is to equate 'environment model' with 'environmental representation' in the mathematical sense discussed by Gallistel (1990, Page 15). Substituting robotics terminology for neuroscience gives:

> A robot is said to *represent* an aspect of the environment when there is a functioning isomorphism between some aspect of the environment and a robot process that adapts the robot's behaviour to it.

If, for example, the robot is modelling the occupancy of a region of its environment, there will be a one-to-one correspondence between the state of that region (occupied or free) and some portion of the state of the robot (1 or 0 in a cell of the map). The robot will use this correspondence to adapt its behaviour to the environment (for example, executing paths which avoid the occupied region).

It is in this sense that environment models will be considered in the remainder of this thesis.

2.1.2   The Significance of State

An environment model forms part of the internal state of the robot. (See (Gat 1993) for a full discussion of the role of internal state in mobile robots.) In any robot which has a time-delay between sensing and acting, this internal state is used to *predict* some aspect of the environment. If, for example, sonar is being used to prevent collisions with obstacles, there is a time-delay, albeit possibly very short, between the storing of the sonar reading which indicates the obstacle and the stopping of the motors. During this period, the internal state is acting as a prediction that the obstacle will still be there when the robot stops. In this example, the prediction is too short-range to be significant, but the prediction property is true whenever internal state is used.

There is clearly a danger with using internal state; the world may no longer match the prediction. This is especially true in rapidly-changing environments. It is in such environments that reactive, minimum-state, robots perform very well when compared with planning, model-using, robots. A key aspect of the robust behaviour of reactive robots in changeable environments is that they assume very little about their world. They operate on the basis that anything which needs to be known can be sensed immediately.

On the other hand, there is a wide range of robot tasks for which internal state is necessary. Consider the problem faced by a delivery robot which has to find a specific room in a large office building. Unless the building is extensively modified to make the robot's task easier, there will not be pointers to all offices at all corridor intersections. When the robot arrives at an intersection, it can not use its sensors to decide what to do. There must be some part of the robot's state which is accessed to tell it what to do. There is, of course, a risk that the world has changed between the acquisition of the state and its use (maybe a door which used to be open has now been closed), but the robot has no alternative but to believe its internal state until events prove that the state is incorrect.

In some situations, the robot can sense what it needs to do by examining the world *but only because the robot has made changes to the world for itself to find.* A comparable human example would be the technique of exploring a maze by unrolling a ball of string to show which alleys have been tested. Dudek *et al.* (1991), for example, describe the use of markers to indicate which paths have been explored while constructing a graph-based map. Sometimes the robot examines part of its own hardware to avoid the use of internal state. Connell (1990), describes his robot, Herbert, which, in an attempt to minimise the use of internal state, examines a gripper in order to determine whether the robot is outward or homeward bound. If the modification to the world is useful only to the robot and is not part of the robot's task, then the changes can be viewed as part of the robot's state. It has simply been stored externally or mechanically.

The value of stored internal state is directly related to the degree of constancy of the robot's environment. If the world is changing rapidly (an interactive video game, for example (Agre & Chapman 1987)), then there is little value in the predictive power of the model. If the world is essentially static (a deserted warehouse, for example), then the predictive power of the model gives great efficiency improvements.

There is a continuum of predictability, as represented in Figure 2.1, on which the previous examples are the extremes. Most applications lie somewhere in the middle. In recognition of this fact, there has recently been a growth of interest in hybrid systems which attempt to combine the rapid response of the reactive approach with the benefits of planning. The low-level, reactive components of the system effectively filter out the highly changeable aspects of the world, leaving the higher-level, model-based, components to deal with the constant or slowly changing features. An interesting research topic is the interface between the reactive and the model-based components (the region marked with question marks in the diagram). Connell (1992) has proposed the 'SSS' architecture (Servo, Subsumption, Symbolic) and defined interfaces between the three levels. Payton *et al.* (1991) propose 'Plan Guided Reaction', using internalised plans as additional sources of sensory input to

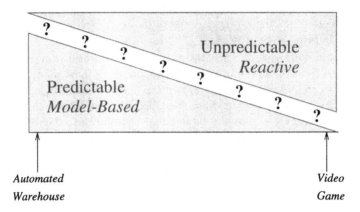

Figure 2.1: The Predictability Continuum

Robot applications operate in environments with a mixture of predictable and unpredictable features. The predictable features can be represented in a world model, and used as the basis for planning. Reactive behaviours can respond to the unpredictable features.

the real-time control behaviours. Slack (1993) uses 'navigation templates' to provide, as he says, qualitative guidance and quantitative control.

2.1.3   Robustness and Flexibility

The supporters of reactive architectures often cite 'robustness' as a strength of the approach. For example, reactive robots have operated successfully for long periods in unaltered, busy, office environments. This is contrasted with early model-based robots which operated in environments designed to suit the robot. It is useful to examine the idea of 'robustness' a little further.

Biology and evolution are commonly used as support for the reactive approach. Cognitive skills evolved much later than more reactive skills like locomotion and threat avoidance. Robots with very little internal state can perform insect-level tasks. Leaving aside discussion of the relevance of this comparison (Etzioni 1993, pages 8–9), the parallel suggests that the robustness of reactive robots arises from the fact that they are precisely matched to specific environmental features. Insects have evolved sensory apparatus and processing methods to detect and react to exactly those aspects of the environment which are essential for their survival. For example, moths have learned to detect light and to move at a constant angle to that light in order to fly in a straight line (Baker 1984, pages 92–94). This is a simple reactive technique which provides very robust behaviour *as long as the light source is far enough away*. However, the number of moths which circle and crash into porch lights is clear evidence that this is not a reliable technique in modern urban environments. Similarly, reactive mobile robots often employ a simple wall-following algorithm. This is a very effective technique *if the goal can be reached by following the current wall*. If a wall-following robot finds itself next to a free-standing pillar in the middle of an open-plan office, it is likely to circle it forever. The robust behaviour arises from a strict reliance on environmental cues. This reliance becomes a handicap when the cues are no longer present.

As a contrast, consider how a human being, equipped with a world model, would deal with the situations described above. Imagine a man trying to move in a straight line, maybe to escape from a forest. He can see a number of lights. Some are stars, some are man-made and much closer. Some might even be caused by a passing aircraft. He might make some experimental movements while tracking the position of each light source. An elementary type of dead-reckoning would enable him to determine which lights were close and which were distant (and which kept moving even when he was still). He could then adopt the moth's approach *but based on a world model that tells him which light sources to trust*. Similarly, imagine a woman who is trying to find the door in a pitch-black, closed room. Wall-following would be a good initial strategy. She could walk gingerly forward until she encounters a wall. She could then follow the wall by keeping her right hand in contact with the wall, checking for door handles as she goes. As she moves, however, she would be building a rough world model, based on her own estimates of distance covered. This would enable her to check whether she had completed a circular path around an object and returned to her starting point without finding the door. She could then decide to move away from the object, in search of another wall. The use of a world model makes the behaviours more robust, in that prior experience can be used to *interpret* and *validate* the sensory input, allowing the agent to be effective in a wider range of situations.

A world model also gives a robot additional flexibility. If the robot has an accurate world model, a human operator can specify the task he wishes the robot to perform. If objects in the environment have been identified and labelled, the user could say, for example, 'Go to the postroom' or 'Clean the living room floor'. Alternatively, if the objects have not been labelled, the user could indicate a location by pointing at the map (with a mouse, for example) or by specifying co-ordinates. Similarly the robot can use the map as a convenient way to return information to the user. The robot has the flexibility to perform any task from the large number that could be selected by the user. In contrast, reactive robots typically have one task to perform. From the moment they are switched on they go about their business, whether it be aimless wandering or collecting soda cans (Connell 1990). It would not be possible, for example, to ask the robot to collect specifically the soda can that was left in the post-room.

2.2   Model Types - The Strength Hierarchy

If the robot's objective and environment make a world model necessary, what type of model should be used?

Most mobile robot research aims to make robots more effective at a particular task. 'Task' typically refers to an aspect of the robot's competence (path planning, obstacle avoidance, localisation) but it is also important to consider the real-world application (office cleaning, planetary exploration, security patrolling). The choice of task and application strongly influences the choice of model. This section reviews the types of world model which have been studied and considers the applications to which they are best suited.

For the purpose of discussion, this chapter will categorise maps by their 'strength'. 'Strength is a geometric concept, stated by Gallistel (1990, page 105) to be 'the range of geometric relations among the mapped points that could in principle be recovered from the map'. The list of categories from page 4 is repeated here to introduce the following sections:

Recognisable Locations The map consists of a list of locations which can be reliably recognised by the robot. *No geometric relationships can be recovered.*

Topological Map In addition to the recognisable locations, the map records which locations are connected by traversable paths. *Connectivity between visited locations can be recovered.*

Metric Topological Maps This term is used for maps in which distance and angle information is added to the path descriptions. *Metric information can be recovered about paths which have been travelled.*

Full Metric Maps Object locations are specified in a fixed co-ordinate system. *Metric information can be recovered about any objects in the map*

Within these categories, there can be significant variation in the degree of precision with which the information is held.

The concept of map strength is used to organise the discussion of map construction techniques in the rest of this section.

The final section, Section 2.3, examines a number of research projects which use mobile robots as a test-bed for biological models of brain function. This work is discussed separately from the map strength categories because it includes many different types of map. In this work the objective is not so much to make a robot especially effective at a task, but to show that the robot can emulate basic animal skills with a biologically plausible technique.

2.2.1   Recognisable Locations

The recognition of landmarks is a fundamental navigational skill. Lynch (1960) provides experimental evidence of the extent to which people use landmarks when finding their way around cities. Piaget (1956, pages 3–9) shows that children represent space as *separate* places before they begin to add distance information. Several researchers have therefore investigated techniques which enable robots to recognise distinct locations.

Kuipers and Byun (1989) use the concept of *distinctive places*. Selected properties of the sensory input are defined to be *distinctiveness measures* and the distinctive place is found by a hill-climbing control strategy which is designed to maximise the distinctiveness measures. Distinctiveness measures could include the degree of symmetry or the amount of discontinuity in one or more sensors when a small step is made. The critical task is the design of effective distinctiveness measures, given the sensory capabilities of the robot. An attraction of the hill-climbing control strategy is that it counteracts the effects of cumulative position error by consistently returning the robot to the same position.

It is possible to use a combination of input from several sensors to recognise a location. Donnett (1992), for example, systematically placed his robot at a number of positions in its environment. At each position, the robot measured the properties (intensity, direction, range) of a variety of sonic, ultrasonic, and infrared beacons. The robot could then recognise its location on subsequent visits to the environment by matching its sensor readings against the stored properties. The matching is performed by a Bayesian process which effectively computes the probability of the robot being at each of the positions.

Locations can also be recognised by monitoring the movements made by the robot. Nehmzow and Smithers (1991) describe such a method. Range sensors are not used directly in the recognition process, although the robot's movements themselves are made in response to the sensory input. The robot adopts a simple wall-following navigation strategy and monitors the time taken by turning movements (such as small adjustments to the robot's direction) until a 'significant turn action' occurs. These significant actions correspond to corners in the environment. When these locations are detected, information about the most recent turn actions is used to train a self-organising neural network. After a few circuits of the room, this network is sufficiently trained to be able to recognise individual corners when presented with descriptions of the most recent turn actions. The network performs well, only becoming confused when the room contains multiple regions of similar shape.

Other researchers have also used self-organising maps to identify locations. Kurz (1993) uses the term *situation areas* to describe regions of space in which sensor data are similar. A self-organising map is trained to recognise these groupings of sensor data. An interesting part of this technique is the pre-processing that is applied to the sensor data before it is presented to the neural network. Dependencies on the orientation of the robot are eliminated by shifting the data as if the robot were facing in a standard direction. Different results are obtained if this standard direction is defined by an on-board compass or by pointing the robot in the direction with the most obstacles. For example, the former technique will distinguish left and right walls of a room whereas the latter will not.

Mataric (1990b) reports results in which a wall-following strategy is used and landmarks are defined as combinations of the robot's motion and its sensory input. (A corridor is a combination of straight movement and short lateral distance readings.) An on-board compass is used so that the orientation of landmarks can also be recorded (e.g. 'a corridor heading North').

If a robot is able to recognise landmarks, it can approach a chosen landmark and perform appropriate actions (e.g. connecting itself to a power supply). If all of its landmarks are constantly visible and not obstructed, then this may be all the robot needs. If, however, the robot needs to approach a landmark which is not currently visible, it may have to plan a route with a number of intermediate landmarks. It then needs to know which landmarks are connected by *paths*. A topological map gives this information. The information about connections between landmarks may also enable the robot to distinguish between landmarks which are otherwise indistinguishable. The next section examines topological maps.

2.2.2 Topological Maps

Most of the researchers whose landmark-detection techniques were discussed in the previous section subsequently link these landmarks to build a topological map.

A link on the topological map means that the robot can successfully travel between the two landmarks. A link can only be added to the map if the robot has made the corresponding journey.

In some instances the links are established at the same time as the landmarks are identified. Mataric's robot (1990b) navigates by wall-following and landmarks are discovered in a sequence which corresponds to their topological relationship. This makes the construction of the topological map straightforward. Kurz (1993), on the other hand, constructs the topological map in two stages. First the situation areas are identified and then the robot explores the environment, looking for transitions between situation areas. Each transition corresponds to a link on the topological map.

Dudek *et al.* (1991) report an interesting technique whereby a robot with very limited sensing capabilities can construct a topological map of its environment. The assumption is made that every time the robot arrives at a given landmark via a given path, it can enumerate the potential departure paths in a consistent sequence. No angular or distance information is available. The authors show that, in general, such a robot could not construct a topological map without one further crucial ability; *the robot can deposit markers at landmarks and can detect them on return visits*. One marker is sufficient, although the algorithm's efficiency can be improved by using multiple markers. Although a robot would typically have more powerful sensory capabilities, this algorithm provides an interesting 'base case'.

2.2.3   Metric Topological Maps

Topological maps are often extended by the addition of some metric information, typically including the estimated lengths of the paths between landmarks and the orientations of those paths. Benefits of the added information include:

Efficient Path Planning A purely topological map may include multiple routes between the same two landmarks. With the addition of path length information, the robot can select the shortest available route.

Additional Landmark Disambiguation Topological maps are often based on simple landmark descriptions (e.g. 'wall on left'). This description may not be unique across the whole environment. The connectivity between landmarks may be enough to remove any ambiguity (only one 'wall on left' is connected directly to a 'corridor'), but approximate metric information can be used to resolve any remaining uncertainties.

The source of the metric information is usually on-board odometry. This information is notoriously unreliable when attempting to construct a full metric map, but is usually adequate for the purposes described above.

It is common for metric topological maps to include the lengths and orientations of *paths* (Kuipers & Levitt 1988; Kurz 1993). However, an alternative approach is to focus instead on the metric properties of the landmarks themselves (Mataric 1990b). The landmarks might be chosen so that they are contiguous and there is no sense of a path between them. If, for example, the map represented walls as landmarks, there could be an immediate transition between two walls. In maps such as this, the odometry can be used profitably to measure the approximate dimensions of the landmark (e.g. the length of the wall). If the approximate size and orientation of each landmark are known, it is then possible to calculate the approximate position of each landmark.

2.2.4 Full Metric Maps

Topological maps are well-suited to environments with the following properties:

- Landmarks dominate the environment. Throughout the environment there are reliably recognisable distinctive locations. The robot's task is to move between these locations.

- Landmarks are linked by clear, unambiguous paths. If the robot knows that it is near one landmark and wants to approach another, there is a clear path that it must follow. The path can be followed by using a local navigation strategy such as wall-following.

As a contrast, imagine a robot operating in a large open space in which there are a number of obstacles (a large warehouse or a dock area, perhaps). The robot has to be able to move from any unoccupied place to any other unoccupied place, avoiding obstacles. There would be nothing about an individual location to make it distinctive, except its metrical relationships to objects in the environment. Landmarks could be used, but they would serve only as objects whose location was known and which could be sensed remotely (maybe as a basis for triangulation). The robot would not routinely approach the landmarks. The robot's path would be calculated to be as efficient as possible, while avoiding obstacles. This path could not be followed by using a local control strategy.

For such environments, the robot would need to be equipped with a map showing the full, metric relationships between all objects in the environment. This information can be stored compactly by describing objects and free space in terms of an external co-ordinate system. Cartesian co-ordinates are most frequently used.

Metric maps describe the environment by subdividing it in one of two ways:

By Feature The map consists of a list of primitive features (corner, wall, cylinder) and the properties of each (location, orientation, size).

By Area The environment is divided into a number of regions. These regions are typically square and usually of equal size. The properties of each region are then listed. Most frequently the only property of interest is the occupancy state of the region (free or occupied).

The choice of which type of metric map to use is not simple. Significant research work is continuing on both types. There are, however, some generalisations which can be made:

- Subdividing by area creates more compact representations of dense environments. If the environment contains a large number of obstacles, the storage space for feature descriptions may be much larger than that required for occupancy information. Conversely, a feature-based representation would provide a more compact description of a large open space with a small number of features.

- Area-based maps are typically used when the application is focussed on the use of free space. Area-based maps provide a natural representation for planning obstacle-free paths through space. By contrast, the user of a feature-based map would usually be paying more attention to the obstacles themselves. Feature-based maps are often used for robot localisation.

The following sections review previous research into each type of metric map.

Feature-Based

One of the earliest mobile robots to construct and use its own world model was the Stanford Cart (Moravec 1983). The Cart used stereo vision to determine the location of features in 3-D space, with associated ellipsoids to represent positional uncertainty. The polygonal obstacles in its environment thus appeared as clusters of overlapping ellipsoids. The Cart used this map to plan and execute a path to a user-specified destination. The system was unreliable, often failing to notice obstacles, and it suffered from, in Moravec's own words, 'excruciating slowness' (20 metres in 5 hours). It did, however, demonstrate the benefits to be gained by testing out one's theories of intelligence on a real-world mobile robot platform.

Research into map construction for mobile robots often makes the assumption that the world can be adequately modelled in 2 dimensions. Just as humans use 2-dimensional floor plans, the robot uses a map which projects all features into 2 dimensions. The complexity of the map is thereby greatly reduced. The simplification is often reasonable in practice, especially in man-made environments.

Crowley (1985) made the 2-D assumption and modelled the world as a collection of line segments. The robot analysed the data from a rotating sonar sensor and used a recursive line-fitting technique to extract line segments. These line segments were then matched with those which had been observed previously. A confidence measure was maintained with each line segment; the segments which were observed most frequently had the highest associated confidence. Early work used a discrete number of confidence levels. Later work (Crowley 1989) also recorded variances of, and covariances between, the properties of the segments (co-ordinates, orientation, length). He then used a Kalman filter to estimate the robot's position. (A Kalman filter will be used for the same purpose in this thesis. See Chapter 9 for details.)

Cox (1991) also chose to describe the world in terms of line segments, although his robot, Blanche, used an infrared rangefinder. The robot was given an *a priori* map of the environment. Its objective was then to match the sensor readings with the map in order to estimate its position. Unlike Crowley, Cox did not extract line segments from the sensor data, but chose to match the sensor readings directly against the given map. An iterative procedure was used which converged on a new position estimate. No attempt was made to update the robot's world model.

Leonard and Durrant-Whyte (1992) also assumed that the world could be effectively represented in 2 dimensions but extended the set of primitive features to include points, lines and arcs (although arcs were only discussed briefly). The subject of the research was localisation and they treated each of the features as a 'geometric beacon' (an object which could be reliably detected by the robot's sensors and tracked as the robot moved throughout its environment). Statistical measures were again associated with the features, to reflect the confidence which could be attached to each feature's properties, given the sensor data on which it was based.

It is common for the features in the map to correspond to objects in the environment, although this is not always the case. Najand, Lo and Bavarian (1992) propose an interesting representation in which the key features are *points in the middle of an area of free space*. A Kohonen self-organising map is trained using the co-ordinates of places which are known to be unoccupied. The network learns to represent points which are close to centroids of regions of open space. A nearest-neighbour technique can then be used to plan paths between these points.

Area-Based

Area-based maps appear under a variety of names, including 'Occupancy Grids' (Elfes 1989), 'Certainty Grids' (Moravec 1988; Cho 1990), 'Probability Maps' (Lim & Cho 1992), 'Histogram Grids' (Borenstein 1991) and 'Inference Grids' (Elfes 1991). In all of these examples, space is divided exhaustively into distinct regions and each region has one or more numbers associated with it. Each number represents a property of that region. (The property represented is usually 'occupancy'.) The differences between the methods arise from different answers to the questions:

- What shape should the regions be?

- What numbers should be stored for each region?

- How should the numbers be updated?

Most area-based maps use a grid of equal-sized square regions, since this provides a simple tessellation and is readily described by Cartesian co-ordinates. The requirement that the cells be of equal size does not, however, generate a compact representation of a sparse environment; too many cells are required to represent a large open space. Zelinsky (1992) and others discuss the use of 'quadtrees'. The quadtree is constructed iteratively. First, the entire environment is divided into 4 square regions. Each of these regions is then examined and is in turn divided into 4 *but only if it is partially occupied and partially free*. If a region is completely empty or completely occupied, no further processing is applied to that region. This process is continued iteratively until the smallest region is of a pre-determined minimum size. This provides a much more efficient representation for sparse environments. Zelinsky (1991a, Chapter 6) gives guidelines for when a quadtree should be used instead of a regular grid.

The numbers held for each region typically indicate the occupancy of the region. In his early work Elfes (1987) used a discrete occupancy status (unknown, empty, or occupied) and an associated 'certainty factor' in the range from zero to one. In his later work (1989; 1991; 1992) the certainty factors were treated more formally as occupancy probabilities. Lim and Cho (1992) adopted a similar approach but, in recognition of the difficulties caused by sonar signals reflecting from sloping surfaces, added an orientation probability for each cell. Borenstein (1991) was especially interested in high-speed obstacle avoidance and represented occupancy with a set of integer 'certainty values' in the range from 0 to 15. The robot could then avoid obstacles by summing a 'repulsive force' from each cell; the higher the certainty, the stronger the force. Zelinsky (1991a) includes an occupancy status and a 'confidence' value with each region of his quadtree. The confidence corresponds to the percentage of the region which has been visited during exploration.

Area-based maps are updated by merging the latest information received from the robot's sensors with the information currently in the map. If the map represents occupancy probabilities, it is important to have a probabilistic model of the sensors. The most commonly used sensor in this research is the sonar transducer, which has significant lateral uncertainty because the sonar beam width can be 30 degrees or more.

Various sonar sensor models have been proposed (Elfes 1987; Moravec 1988; Lim & Cho 1992; Elfes 1989; Cho 1990), each of which translates the sonar reading into occupancy probabilities of the grid cells within the sonar's range. These probabilities are based purely on the sensor reading and do not take into account the occupancy probabilities on the map. In early work (Elfes 1987), the new and old probabilities were merged by simple addition rules. This approach has recently been superseded by a more rigorous Bayesian update rule (Moravec 1988; Elfes 1989; Cho 1990; Lim & Cho 1992).

The process of merging the sensor data with the existing map is computationally intensive and may not provide adequate performance for rapid avoidance of obstacles. Borenstein (1991) therefore adopted a simplification which ignored the problem of sonar beam spread and updated only those cells which were directly in front of the sensor. (In common with Elfes and Moravec, he assumed that the probability of detection of an object was higher in the centre of the beam than at the sides. The cell that actually contained the object was therefore the most likely to be updated by this process.)

The probabilistic sensor models described above are designed to represent the uncertainty caused by the wide beam of the sonar sensor. Zelinsky (1991a) chose to minimise this uncertainty by examining obstacles at close range. His robot used a sonar sensor and a wall-following action to scan the perimeter of all obstacles it encountered. The obstacle description was then added to the map by adjusting the quadtree structure to describe the obstacle as a number of occupied regions.

2.3 Biologically-Inspired Models

This review concludes by looking at biologically-inspired research into map construction. This work varies greatly in the contribution made by biology. At one extreme there is work which, although motivated by general biological principles, makes no attempt to be biologically plausible at a detailed level or to contribute to biological knowledge. At the other extreme there is work whose primary motivation is to increase biological knowledge. Such work may use robots or computer simulations to test theories, but the research is focussed on understanding the mapping mechanisms of animals.

A large part of the research into neural networks falls into the first category. The growth of interest in neural networks in the 1980's (the work of Rumelhart and McClelland (1986), for example) was fuelled by their similarity to networks of neurons in the brain (large numbers of highly-interconnected processing units, each of which performs a relatively simple task). The impressive pattern-matching abilities of these networks led to their use in a wide range of research areas, including mobile robotics (as described earlier in this chapter). The emphasis is typically on the power of the application, not on the biological relevance of the solution.

Similarly, proponents of reactive robots refer to biology to support their position. Brooks (1991b, page 141) takes the history of evolution on Earth as evidence that researchers should concentrate their effort on the fundamental skills of mobility and survival before worrying about the 'pretty simple' issues of problem-solving behaviour, language, expert knowledge and its application, and reason. Brooks also invokes biology implicitly by calling his robots

'Creatures'. Again the emphasis is on the effectiveness of the robot, not on its similarity to a living creature.

There are, however, a number of research projects which use computer simulations of mobile agents to test specific neurological models. These models are, in turn, derived from numerous practical experiments. A widely-referenced model concerns the existence and function of place cells in the hippocampus of the rat. Extensive work by O'Keefe *et al.* (summarised by O'Keefe (1990) and Speakman (1987)) shows the existence of individual neurons in the hippocampus whose firing is restricted to a contiguous patch of the environment. These neurons are known as 'place cells'.

Mataric (1990b) draws parallels between place cells in the hippocampus and landmarks in her robot's world model. She associates an activation with each landmark in her topological map so that the robot's location is represented by a landmark with a high activation, analogous to the firing of a place cell. The research was not originally designed with the biological results in mind. The biological results have been subsequently enlisted to provide support for the choice of representation.

Hippocampal modelling was also performed by Sharp (1991). She describes experiments to simulate the behaviour of a rat in an experimental environment. The simulation is built on the assumption that, from any location in the environment, the rat can detect the angle and distance to a small number of cues. This information provides the input to a three-layer neural network each layer of which corresponds to a type of neuron (neocortical cells, entorhinal cells, and hippocampal cells). As the simulated rat moves about its environment, the 'hippocampal cells' show a pattern of activation similar to that observed in real place cells.

Prescott and Mayhew (1992) concern themselves with the ability of animals to construct a cognitive map which uses 'allocentric' (world-centred) co-ordinates (see also (O'Keefe 1990, page 304)). They suggest that the building-block of the map is a set of three visible cues (an 'L-trie'). When any particular set of cues is visible, the animal defines its location relative to them. The L-tries are assembled into a network in which the links are obtained by specifying the position of a landmark relative to each neighbouring L-trie. Target location and path planning are then performed by spreading activation through the net (a similar technique to that of Mataric (1990b)).

The idea that the cognitive map might be formed from a number of small pieces is attractive because it eliminates the need for large-scale localisation. (It is then only necessary to know your position within the current piece of the map.) Worden (1992) also proposes that the cognitive map consists of multiple small pieces, which he calls 'fragments'. However, unlike Prescott and Mayhew, he does not specify that each piece contains exactly three cues. He hypothesises that fragments include two to eight objects and the geometric relationships between them. There is a large fragment store and a number of separate processes, the 'fragment fitters', which dynamically select the sequence of fragments as the animal moves about its environment. He discusses in detail how such a technique could be implemented in the hippocampus and suggests practical experiments which would test his theory.

In recent work, Burgess, O'Keefe, and Recce (1993) have developed a computational model of rat navigation which builds on the results of the research on place cells. It starts from the known structure and connectivity of the hippocampus and then hypothesises roles which the various types of hippocampal neuron might play during navigation. In simulations the model has generated goal-seeking behaviour similar to that observed in rats. The model is currently being implemented on a mobile robot platform.

2.4   Conclusions

This chapter has summarised the types of map which have been used by previous researchers. It argues that the type of map needed by a robot depends upon its proposed application. Indeed there are many applications for which a map is not needed at all.

Maps have been grouped by the concept of 'strength', ranging from lists of recognisable landmarks through topological maps to full metric maps. Each increase in strength expands the range of tasks that the robot can perform, but the increased power comes at a cost. The more information that is held in the map, the more difficult the process of building and maintaining the map.

The next chapter describes the type of map that was chosen for this thesis, and explains the reasons for the choice.

Chapter 3

The Maps Used in This Research

Chapter 2 described numerous maps which have been used by mobile robots. This chapter considers which type of map to use in the current research.

The choice of map type is strongly constrained by the proposed application of the robot. In Chapter 1 a *delivery* application was chosen. Section 3.1 describes such an application in detail.

Section 3.2 uses the knowledge of the application to choose the maps to be used in this thesis. One of the most important choices was between probabilistic grid-based maps and feature-based maps. Section 3.3 explains why feature-based maps were selected. The chapter concludes in Section 3.4 by explaining why the robot will build its own map, instead of being given one by its operator.

The details of the map construction algorithm can not be described without knowledge of the robot and its sensors. This description is therefore postponed until Chapter 7 to follow the descriptions of the hardware and the sensor model in Chapters 5 and 6.

3.1 The Application

The choice of world model is strongly influenced by the proposed application of the robot. Indeed, as was discussed in Chapter 2, some applications do not require a world model at all. It is therefore vital to be precise about the intended application of one's robot before designing the world model.

This thesis addresses the construction of maps for use in an application with the following features:

1. The intended application is *delivery*. The robot will be required to carry a payload to a location in its environment. Typical applications include mail delivery within an office building, component transfer in a factory, or 'intelligent' wheelchairs to give increased mobility to the handicapped.

2. The robot will operate *indoors* in man-made environments. Such environments typically contain horizontal floors and vertical walls.

3. The environment will include *open regions*. The robot will have to select routes through regions of open space. Different routes will be taken through the same space, depending upon the locations of the starting position and the goal.

4. The environment will be dominated by *static* objects. Most features of the environment will either be stationary or will move infrequently.

5. The robot will function in an *unmodified* environment. Beacons or underfloor wires will not be added to make the robot's task easier.

6. The robot's target location for each delivery will be *user-specified*. The specification will be independent of the robot's position.

7. The robot will have to follow *many paths*. For each delivery, the goal location will be selected from numerous alternatives.

8. The goal location will be specified with a relatively *coarse resolution* (a few centimetres). If necessary, a local approach mechanism will be used.

9. The robot must follow *efficient paths*. The delivery must be made without unnecessary delay.

3.2   The Impact of the Application on the Choice of Map

What type of map, if any, should the robot use when performing the application described in Section 3.1? The following sections answer this question. (Numbers in parentheses refer to the application properties listed in section 3.1.)

3.2.1   The Robot *Does* Need a World Model

The robot must approach a specified location efficiently (9). To do this, it must predict the effects of its actions (e.g. to avoid wasting time by entering and leaving dead-ends). A world model enables it to make such predictions. Given the static nature of its environment (4), these predictions are likely to be correct.

The user will wish to specify goal locations in a way which is independent of the robot's location (6). The value of the robot would be limited if the user had to supply commands such as 'Move 1 metre to your left' instead of 'Go to Landmark 9' (for a topological map) or 'Go to co-ordinates (10,20)' (for a metric map). To interpret and act upon commands which are independent of the robot's position, it needs a world model in which to represent its location and the goal location.

It is not possible to modify the environment to remove the need for a world model (5).

3.2.2 The Robot Needs a Metric Map

The large number of potential starting points and destinations (7) implies that the robot will often be following a path which it has not followed before. Topological maps are useful when the environment consists of a number of distinct, recognisable locations with fixed paths between them. This would not be adequate in this application.

If the robot is to plan efficient paths across open space (9,3), it must be able to take 'short cuts'. Such behaviour is not possible with a topological map. If, for example, the robot has constructed a topological map of a room by following walls (Mataric 1990b) and is then asked to move from one corner of the room to the other, it will do so by following the walls along two sides of the room, in preference to the more direct diagonal route.

When the robot is in an open space (3), its location can only be defined in terms of metric relationships. These could be the angles and distances to known objects or they could be expressed in a co-ordinate system.

3.2.3 The Robot Needs a Free-Space Map

The delivery application (1) means that the robot's primary concern is free space. It needs to know where it can safely go without collisions. Goal locations are specified using the co-ordinate system of the metric map. The identity of objects is therefore not important; their only significance is that they occupy space which would otherwise be free.

3.2.4 The Robot Will Use a 2-Dimensional Map

This work uses a 2-dimensional projection to model the obstacles in the robot's environment. This simplifying assumption is usually acceptable in man-made environments (2).

3.2.5 The Free-Space Map Will Use a Regular Grid

Grid-based maps have resolution limited to the size of the smallest represented area. The application is well-suited to a grid-based representation because it requires only a limited resolution (8).

There are well-established techniques for planning efficient paths on a grid-based map (9). (Latombe 1991, Chapter 6)(McKerrow 1991, pages 462–472)

Zelinsky (1991a, Chapter 6) examined the use of quadtrees instead of regular grids. He compared path planning efficiency in environments of various sizes (compared to the selected resolution) with various numbers of obstacles. He found that quadtrees were more efficient if the map area was greater than 128 by 128 cells. Delivery applications which cover a wide area (e.g. office delivery) or which require high precision (and therefore would benefit from a small grid) would need maps that large, whereas others (e.g. intelligent wheelchair) would probably not. For simplicity it was decided to use a regular grid.

3.2.6   The Grid-Based Map will be Derived from a Feature-Based Map

A common way to construct grid-based maps is to use occupancy probabilities. Since this seemed at first to be an attractive idea, the techniques of Elfes (1989) and Lim and Cho (1992) were implemented and tested. A probabilistic sensor model was used to build an occupancy grid, using Bayesian updating rules. After testing these algorithms, it was decided instead to construct a feature-based map first and then to derive a free-space map from it. The reasons for this decision are discussed in full in Section 3.3.

3.3   Probabilistic Grid Maps and Feature Maps

Section 2.2.4 described two distinct types of metric map, feature-based and area-based, and reviewed the considerable research effort which has been invested in each type. It was necessary to decide which map-building techniques to use in this research.

Probabilistic grid-based maps (PGMs) (Elfes 1989; Moravec 1988; Cho 1990; Lim & Cho 1992) appeared to be attractive at first because they use a representation which is very similar to that ultimately needed by the robot. (The robot needs a grid-based free-space map. This can be derived from the PGM by selecting only those cells with a low occupancy probability.)

The implementation and testing of a PGM raised a number of issues which cast doubt on the value of the probabilistic approach and ultimately led to its replacement by the construction of a feature-based map. These issues are listed below and then expanded in later sections. These concerns led to the decision to use a feature-based representation for the primary map and then to derive the free-space map from the features.

The following observations were made about the probabilistic maps:

Ambiguity about the meaning of probability. Repeating a sensor reading from the same location gives unreasonable results, due to a confusion about the type of uncertainty which is being represented by the probabilities.

Premature use of probability. Probability is being used when it would be possible to extract more information with a better model of the sensor.

No modelling of data dependence. Some unreasonable results arise from the assumption that the occupancy probability of a cell is independent of those of its neighbours.

Premature loss of precision. Data precision is lost early in the construction of a PGM, making tasks such as localisation unnecessarily difficult.

3.3.1   Ambiguity About The Use of Probability

When the robot was creating a PGM, it was observed that the measured probability of a particular cell being occupied could be increased by repeating exactly the same sensor reading from the same location. For example, assume that the robot takes one sensor reading in a static environment and updates its map. The new map might show an increased occupancy probability for a cell 1 metre directly in front of the robot. If, without moving, the robot now repeats the sensor reading and updates the map, the occupancy probability of that cell will increase. The robot's confidence in the occupancy of the cell will continue to increase each time it repeats the sensor reading. This is unrealistic since, in practice, the sensor reading is almost totally determined by the physical environment around the robot. One would expect repeated readings to be very similar, with a very small unpredictable variation in range. The additional information gained by repeated readings should be minimal.

The difficulty here arises from an ambiguity about the type of uncertainty which is being modelled by probability. The difference is best illustrated by the following 'thought experiments'.

1. Imagine that you have a box. I ask you whether there is something in your box. Before answering, you roll a die. If the die lands on a 6, you lie to me. Otherwise you tell me the truth.

2. Again you have a box and I ask my question. Now, however, you decide whether to lie by looking at my position when I asked the question. (You could imagine, for example, that the floor is marked in a way that only you can interpret.) The effect is that for one sixth of my possible positions, you will lie to me.

In the first case, I can use standard Bayesian update techniques to estimate the probability that the box is full. (See the work of Moravec (1988, pages 70–73) for an example of the application of these techniques to PGMs.) It would be beneficial for me to stand in one spot and repeat my question over and over. Probability is being used to represent an uncertainty in *how you answer the question*.

In the second case, I can still use Bayesian techniques to obtain my estimate, but I would be wasting my time to repeat my question from the same spot; the answer will always be the same. It is, of course, a good idea for me to ask my question from multiple locations. In this case the uncertainty is related to *how I ask the question*.

The 'increasing probability' result that was described at the beginning of this section arises because probability is being used primarily in the second way in PGMs, to represent an uncertainty in how the question is being asked.

Feature maps, on the other hand, often use probability in the first way. For example, the localisation scheme in Chapter 9 uses a probabilistic representation of the unpredictable variation in sonar range readings.

3.3.2 Premature Use of Probability

There are two complementary ways to model a physical process; physics and probability. Some aspects of the process can be well described and predicted by physical laws. Other aspects may fall outside the realm of physics. The physics may not yet be well understood or the process may be too complex for physical modelling to be worthwhile. These latter aspects of the process are commonly modelled by probability.

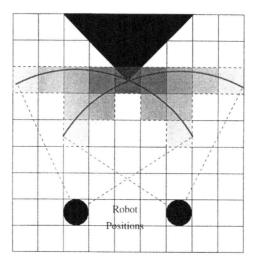

Figure 3.1: Interpreting Sonar Returns in a PGM

The convex corner at the top of the diagram has been detected by sonar scans from the two positions at
the bottom of the diagram. The dotted lines from the robot's positions mark the edges of the sonar beam.
The shading of the grid cells near the corner represents their occupancy probability - the darker the cell,
the higher the probability. The highest probability is assigned to the cell which actually contains the
corner, but increased probabilities are also assigned to all of the cells at the measured range from the robot
positions.

A variety of models have been used to describe sonar sensors. These models vary in
the balance between physics and probability. Some build on a thorough understanding of
ultrasonic energy propagation and the behaviour of transducers. Probability is used, if at all,
to model less-significant details such as the variation in range reading due to air currents.
Others describe the sensor almost totally in probabilistic terms. The probabilistic model
may be based on some elementary physical knowledge of the sensor, but in this work the
balance has swung firmly towards probability and away from physics.

The better the physics of a sensor is understood, the more information can be extracted
from that sensor. The premature application of probability limits unnecessarily the amount
of information that can be obtained from the sensor.

To construct a probabilistic map, one needs a probabilistic sensor model. The models used
here are therefore from the 'low physics, high probability' class and suffer from the limitations
described above. As an example consider the situation in which two sonar readings have
been taken near a convex corner of two walls. A probabilistic model, such as that of Cho
(1990) would increase the occupancy probability in a number of cells at the measured range
from the sensing positions (see Figure 3.1).

Each reading would be processed separately in this way. The end result would be a higher
occupancy probability in the cell in which the arcs intersected (a reasonable result) together
with increased occupancy probabilities in a number of other cells (a less reasonable result).
By contrast, a feature extraction technique such as that of Leonard and Durrant-Whyte

(1992) uses a more detailed physical knowledge of the sensor to hypothesise the existence of an object which could have caused the two readings that were obtained. The end result of this method is a single hypothesised point object. This object may yet need to be confirmed by subsequent readings, but more precise information has been extracted from the two sensor readings.

3.3.3 No Modelling of Data Dependence

The probabilities which are recorded in the cells of a PGM are usually treated as independent. A number of difficulties were observed to arise from this assumption:

Unrealistically Low Compound Probabilities To calculate the probability that a robot can move forward 1 metre, it is necessary to examine all the cells through which the robot would have to pass. Each cell contains the probability p of that cell being full. The probability of all of the cells being free is then $\prod(1 - p)$. In practice this continued multiplication of probabilities leads to unrealistically small results.

Dependence on an Arbitrary Cell Size The number of cells involved in the calculation described above depends on the size of the cells. A smaller cell size would require more probabilities to be multiplied together. Unless the probabilities were in some way related to the cell size, the resulting probability of being able to move forward 1 metre would be smaller. This is nonsense since the choice of cell size is arbitrary and can not change the probability of achieving a result in the world.

Difficulty in Choosing Initial Probabilities The robot starts with no knowledge of the objects in its environment. Each cell in the grid map must, however, be given an initial probability value. A tempting approach is to look at typical environments in which the robot will find itself and to estimate what fraction of the floor space is covered with obstacles. If, for example, the value was 0.20 an initial occupancy probability of 0.20 could be assigned to all the cells. Such an approach generates the same starting probability for all sizes of cell, leading to the problems of low compound probabilities and dependence on an arbitrary cell size.

No Concept of the Scale of the World Imagine two environments, 'box world' and 'needle world'. In 'box world', objects are typically about 1 metre wide and the gaps between objects are of a similar scale. In 'needle world' the objects and the gaps are about 1 millimetre wide. Prior knowledge of which of these worlds a robot was in would clearly be very useful when interpreting sensor readings and making plans. These are, of course, extreme cases but it does seem to be an omission that there is nothing in the prior information or the update rules to tell the robot that it is operating in a human-scale environment.

Most of these problems can best be understood by observing that the occupancy probabilities of individual cells *are not independent*. If a specified cell is known to be empty, this increases the probability that its neighbours are also empty. Likewise, if the first and third cells in a line are known to be full, then it is more likely that the intermediate second cell is also full.

The degree of dependence between cells would vary with the choice of grid size and on the 'scale' of the world. Modelling the interdependence between cells could eliminate the changes in real-world probabilities when changing the grid size.

Elfes (1989) notes that his occupancy grids are Markov random fields of order 0 (independent) and states that it would be possible to use 'computationally more expensive estimation procedures' for higher-order Markov fields. No examples of such higher-order PGMs appear to have been published.

3.3.4 Premature Loss of Precision

The robot does not need high precision in its free-space map. It is therefore reasonable to construct a grid-based free-space map which can be used for efficient path planning. However it is important to recognise that the map is being constructed from data with a higher precision, such as sonar returns with a precision of 1 cm. Information is being lost when the low-precision map is generated from the higher-precision data. A good rule of thumb is that this loss of information should be delayed as long as possible, within the constraints of the available storage space.

PGMs are constructed by reducing the data precision as soon as the sensor return is processed. Once the sonar reading has been used to update the map, the reading is discarded and the only remaining information is limited to the precision of the grid map. By contrast, features in a feature-based map are described with a precision which is limited only by the precision of the computer which is storing the map.

The loss of precision is especially apparent when one considers the use of the map for robot localisation. Using a PGM, localisation becomes a problem of seeking the best correlation between the robot's local map (a grid) and the larger map (also a grid). The precision of the localisation is limited by the precision of the grid (Elfes 1989). On the other hand a feature-based map can be used for localisation by seeking the position which minimises the error between the robot's current sensor readings (high precision) and the previously measured positions of features (also high precision). Chapter 9 shows how such a method was used in this thesis.

3.4   Why Build Maps?

The previous sections of this chapter have argued that ARNE will use two maps, a feature-based map and a grid-based free-space map which will be derived from the features. It is a goal of this thesis to investigate techniques by which ARNE can construct these maps autonomously. It is reasonable to consider whether this is a worthwhile aim. Why not simply give the robot maps which have been obtained by hand measurement, or from architectural plans? A number of researchers have indeed adopted this approach (Cox (1991), for example). There are, however, some drawbacks with giving the robot a pre-constructed map:

- First, the environment of an operational robot will often change. Over a period of days or weeks, objects will be moved (furniture will be changed, office walls may be added or removed). If the robot is working from user-specified maps, the user will often need to provide corrections. This could soon become tedious. Why not let the robot re-map the world itself periodically?

- Second, it is difficult to generate by hand a map which will correspond reliably with the world that the robot will experience via its sensors. It is, for example, difficult to predict which objects in a room will be most significant for a robot that uses sonar.

- Third, from a commercial point of view it would be better to give users a robot which can immediately be put into operation without the user having to create or obtain a map of the robot's new environment.

- Fourth, for some purposes the level of detail required might be higher than that obtained from a readily-available architectural drawing.

For these reasons it was decided to make ARNE build its own maps.

Chapter 4

Approaches to Exploration

Published work shows a variety of approaches to exploration for mobile robots, ranging from disregarding the issue completely through to detailed mathematical analysis of exploration algorithms. This chapter reviews this work in the context of the recent debate between 'reactive' and 'model-based' robotics (as discussed in Section 2.1).

Many of the published papers on the map-building and navigation of mobile robots do not consider the question of exploration at all. This is, of course, often just a choice of research focus; effort is expended on the mechanics of map construction from sensor data without worrying about how the sensing positions were selected. On the other hand there are theoretical reasons why some researchers have chosen not to study exploration. A robot will not need to explore if its application is such that it does not need a map (Brooks 1990, pages 8–9) or if the map is to be supplied by the operator (Crowley 1985; Drumheller 1987). Neither of these arguments apply in the context of this thesis. Section 2.1 argued that a map *was* needed for the proposed delivery application and Section 3.4 explained the reasons for allowing ARNE to build its own maps.

Some researchers (Engelson (1992), for example) have adopted a strategy of 'passive' mapping, in which the map is built while the robot carries out its normal activities. In contrast, the current research proposes an initial exploration period during which the robot's objective is simply to learn about its environment. In a practical delivery application such exploration would take place before the robot began its operational duties. The robot could then be effective as soon as it began work instead of, for example, spending its first day delivering mail very slowly because it had to build its map at the same time.

The debate between the 'reactive' and the 'model-based' camps has its echoes in the area of exploration. Reactivists like their robots to have the minimum of internal state and to respond rapidly to their sensed environment. Therefore in circumstances in which they concede that some form of world model is useful, they still prefer an exploration strategy which emphasises the current sensor readings when making its choices. On the other hand, the modellers focus on the value of a world model for prediction and planning. It is then natural for them to define exploration strategies which lean heavily on the information in the world model, adding some extra processing if necessary to deal with situations in which the information coming from the sensors doesn't match the predictions of the model.

By far the most widely-used exploration strategy to emerge from the reactive camp is wall-following. Section 4.1 analyses the reasons for its popularity and gives examples of its use.

Model-based exploration strategies vary with the type of model being used. However, although they may superficially appear to be very different, these strategies are usually based on the same underlying idea: *go to the least-explored region*. Section 4.2 compares a number of these methods.

Section 4.3 builds on the review of the individual research projects to give a preview of the investigation of exploration that will be described in Part III of this thesis.

4.1   The Wall-Following Boom

Wall-following is a navigation method which became popular among roboticists as the interest in reactive robotics grew in the late '80s. To illustrate the idea with the simplest case, imagine that the robot is next to a long, straight wall. To follow the wall, it simply has to move forward whilst maintaining a fixed distance from the wall. If its range sensors tell it that it is too far from the wall, it turns towards the wall; if it's too close, it turns away from the wall. Such a strategy can be implemented either step-by-step (move, look, turn ...) or in a tight real-time control loop.

Such an approach seems fine for long, straight walls but robot environments are typically more complex. For example, how does wall-following cope with corners? If the robot is only sensing the distance to an object on one of its sides, then corners are indeed a problem. But this can be overcome by a simple extension: let the robot take a complete 360° scan and assume that the shortest range reading corresponds to a wall. If the robot then turns so as to keep this hypothetical wall to its side and moves to maintain the ideal distance from it, then it will manoeuvre successfully along straight walls *and* around both convex and concave corners. This is a good example of the way in which apparently complex behaviour can result from the application of simple rules. This property of *emergence* is a strength of the reactive or behaviour-based approach to robotics (Brooks 1991a, page 3).

Wall-following requires very little internal state. Each navigational decision is made on the basis of the robot's latest sensor information only. The robot's internal state is only used to keep the range readings until the decision has been made.

The lack of internal state makes the behaviour of a wall-following robot easy to predict. When the robot encounters a set of objects in its environment, its behaviour is determined by those objects, not by some mysterious internal state. The robot will therefore make the same choices each time it encounters those objects. If a robot goes around a room several times it will follow approximately the same path on each circuit[1]. There will be no sense of the 'drift' associated with accumulating odometry error. Such a robot has little use for odometry during navigation; it does not care where it is on a global map, only how far away it is from the objects that it can sense.

The predictability of wall-following can be put to good use even if one's robot *is* building a map. As will be seen in Chapter 13, a predictable path can be an asset when testing the parameters of the localisation process.

---

[1]The paths will be only *approximately* the same because of minor differences in sensor readings and small differences in the positions from which the sensor readings are taken.

There are many examples of wall-following robots in the literature. For example, Connell's robot, Herbert, (Connell 1990) was designed to minimise the use of internal state and used wall-following as it searched for soda cans. Van Turennout (1992) has investigated the accuracy of sonar-controlled wall-following. He describes a controller which maintains the ideal distance from the wall, to within a few millimetres as the robot moves at a constant speed of 0.4 m/s.

Koza (1991) has recently demonstrated the possibility of evolving wall-following behaviour by Genetic Programming. Using a simple fitness function and random mutations, his system evolved a LISP program which, in simulation, successfully guided a robot around the edge of an irregular room. The intent of Koza's work is to show that such an evolution is possible, not to develop a high-quality wall-following algorithm. It is unlikely that an evolved program will outperform one written by a human with a full understanding of the robot and the objective.

Section 2.1 argued the case for world models in predictable environments. After experimenting to see what robots can achieve with no internal state, some researchers (such as Mataric (1990b)) began to investigate how these achievements can be enhanced by the addition of maps. Reactive robotics began as a movement against complex metric world models, which were viewed as an unnecessary bottleneck. When world models were added to reactive robots it was therefore natural that models from the lower end of the strength hierarchy were selected. Topological maps were an attractive choice.

The growth in interest in topological maps added further to the popularity of wall-following. A topological map does not record *how* the robot travels between linked nodes on the map. The map simply indicates that there is *a* path between the nodes. The predictability of the path selected by wall-following is attractive in these circumstances. Imagine that, while mapping a static environment, the robot began wall-following at Node A and subsequently found itself at Node B. If it later finds itself at Node A and again begins to follow the same wall, it will again find itself at Node B. Wall-following therefore continues to be an effective navigation strategy when the robot is using a topological map.

Although odometry does not influence the movements made during wall-following, it may still prove useful to record the odometric information gathered during wall-following exploration. Mataric, for example, (1990a) uses approximate metric information, derived from odometry, to distinguish between nodes of the topological map.

The work of Nehmzow and Smithers (1991) used wall-following in an unusual way. The robot learned to recognise places by monitoring its own movements as it followed the walls of its environment. (See page 19 for details.) The idea of allowing the robot to behave reactively while another process monitors its behaviour is an interesting one. The strategy of 'Supervised Wall-Following', which will be introduced in Chapter 14, uses a similar idea.

Wall-following has a number of attractions as an exploration strategy. First, it is easy to implement; a few simple rules can generate effective behaviour in a wide variety of circumstances. Second, the behaviour is robust; a wall-following robot isn't misled by a faulty world model into making bad choices. (It either has no world model at all or it ignores it when choosing its next movement.) Third, it recovers well from temporary distractions. If a moving object passes close to a wall-following robot, the robot may change its behaviour, possibly treating the object as a wall to be followed, but once the object goes away the robot will doggedly return to its wall-following.

On the other hand, this very doggedness can also be viewed as a weakness, possibly generating a fruitless path through a fully-mapped region. If a robot has some, albeit partial, knowledge of its environment, other researchers have argued that the exploration should be controlled by that knowledge. This view has motivated the research that is discussed in the next section.

4.2   Go Where It's Interesting

This section examines some of the research into exploration strategies which base the exploration decisions totally on the latest map.

Examination of the map-based strategies reveals that they are mostly variants on a simple idea: *examine the regions of space about which least is currently known*. Such a strategy will systematically reduce the uncertainty in the robot's map. Within this shared approach, however, individual researchers differ in the details of their implementations. As the following review will show, different researchers have chosen different ways to answer the following questions:

- How does the robot decide which areas are the least known? Different types of map suggest different ways to measure the extent to which a region is 'known'.

- How should the next unknown region be selected for examination? It may be that the robot should always choose to examine the least-known region, regardless of the difficulty of reaching a point from which to make the examination. Alternatively, it might be more efficient to examine partly-explored regions first if they are easier to reach.

- How should the robot move to examine a particular region? A common strategy is to make the robot move *into* the unknown region in order to examine it. This may be appropriate if the robot is equipped with only short-range sensors, but long-range sensors might make it more appropriate to examine the unknown region from a distance.

To start with an example of the use of exploration to build a non-metric map, consider the work of Dudek *et al.* (1991) on the construction of topological maps by a robot with minimal sensing capability. In it there is an explicit separation between the explored and unexplored edges of the graph. An edge is considered to be unexplored until the robot has established correspondences between both ends of the edge and vertices in the explored graph. Before exploring the edge, the robot knows where the edge starts but not where it finishes. This work has a simple, binary, knowledge measure. The edge is either explored or it is not.

It is common for an exploring robot to choose a single region of the map upon which to focus its attention. The work of Dudek *et al.* is unusual in that the algorithm requires the robot to select several unexplored edges at once. The robot is equipped with a number of distinguishable markers and it places a single marker at the unknown end of each unexplored edge. It then searches the entire explored graph to see whether any of the markers are actually at known nodes. For efficient exploration, it is important that a set of unexplored edges is selected so that they can all be covered in a short path. A search algorithm is used to find the shortest path between the 'known' ends of a set of unexplored edges. This work shows that efficient exploration strategies can be defined for robots with elementary sensory abilities. It is, however, not applicable to a robot equipped with long-range sensors or to the construction of a metric map.

The projects described in the remainder of this section have all used full metric maps. More information can be extracted from a metric map than, say, a topological map and this information can then be used in a variety of ways to focus the robot's attention on the next region to be explored. Among the different types of metric maps, grid-based maps are convenient for the investigation of exploration strategies. The environment is already divided into discrete regions; the key problem is then to decide which region is the best candidate for exploration.

In some of the early work with probabilistic grid maps, Moravec (1988) proposed a knowledge metric which could guide exploration. The mapping algorithm starts by assigning to each cell in the grid a default probability, P_d, that it contains an obstacle. These probabilities are then adjusted (up or down) during exploration, to give a value P_x for each cell. Moravec suggested that a function such as $\sum (P_x - P_d)^2$ should be computed over an appropriate-sized window to determine how well-known a region is. Such a function measures the total amount by which the information about a region differs from the default assumption. Moravec then suggests that the 'lowest-knowledge' region should then be explored by going directly to it.

In later work Elfes (1991), still using probabilistic grids, put Moravec's intuitions on a sounder theoretical basis. He proposed a similar measure to Moravec's, but using the concepts of information theory. The *entropy* of a cell on the map is defined as:

$$E = - \sum_{s_i} P(s_i) \log_2 P(s_i)$$

where the summation is over the possible states, s_i, of the cell (empty or occupied) and $P(s_i)$ is the probability of that state. The cell entropy can then be summed to give the entropy of a region. A region is then a candidate for exploration if it has high entropy. (Allowing for a change of sign, this measure is similar to Moravec's function with $P_d = 0.5$.) Elfes also proposed two other theoretical concepts, 'Observability' and the 'Locus of Interest'. The Observability of a cell is the highest probability of being able to detect an object in that cell, across all possible viewpoints. It takes into account not only the probability that an object will be detected from a viewpoint but also the probability that the robot will be able to *reach* that viewpoint. The 'Locus of Interest' defines a region of the grid which is relevant to the task in hand; if the robot is exploring, the Locus of Interest is taken to be the entire map. Regions within the Locus of Interest can then be selected for exploration if they have high average entropy and high average Observability. Because path difficulty is bundled into the definition of Observability, the robot will therefore choose first the region that it can examine most easily. Although it is not stated explicitly, Elfes' interest in Observability would suggest that the robot would not necessarily move *into* the chosen region but to a viewpoint from which it could be examined.

Thrun (1993) was also concerned with building grid-based maps by autonomous navigation but he chose quite different techniques to estimate the occupancy of the cells and the confidence associated with the estimates. Two neural networks were used. The first, the sensor interpretation network, was trained to predict the occupancy of a cell, given a set of sensor readings from a nearby location. The second, the confidence network, was trained to predict the likely error in the results of the sensor interpretation network. The confidence values served two purposes. First, they could be used as multiplicative weights when combining the occupancy predictions from multiple viewpoints, giving an aggregate occupancy prediction for each cell. Second, and more important in the context of exploration, the confidence values from multiple viewpoints could be combined to give a *cumulative confidence* value for each cell in the grid. The lower the confidence value, the more attractive the cell as a target for exploration. Thrun then proposed an unusual way to select the next region for exploration. To determine the path that the exploring robot should follow, each cell was assigned an *exploration utility*. This was initially set to the negative of the cumulative confidence value. All the exploration utility values were then updated by an iterative method similar to that used in distance-transform path-planning (as described in Chapter 8). In Thrun's procedure the utility of each cell is adjusted to be the maximum utility of its neighbours, less a cost associated with moving from the cell to its neighbour. The robot can then plan exploration paths by following paths of steepest ascent in utility. This is an attractive way to combine exploration control and path planning. Unfortunately the environments in the published work had reasonably simple shapes, making it difficult to determine the effectiveness of the strategy. In practice the results appeared superficially similar to those obtained by wall-following.

Zelinsky (1992) uses grid-based maps which take the form of quadtrees (see page 23). He also considers a robot which has only tactile sensors; the only way that the robot can know that a region is free is to have visited the region and not touched anything. He therefore defines a measure of 'confidence' in a map quadrant to be the fraction of the area of the quadrant which has been visited by the robot. This confidence measure is applied only to quadrants in which no obstacle has been detected. The regions with the lowest confidence values can then be selected as interesting regions for exploration. The choice of exploration path has two parts. First, Zelinsky proposes a variation on the distance transform method of path planning to favour paths which pass through regions with a low confidence of being empty. He then selects low-confidence regions as goals. (If the distance transform method is given multiple goals, the planned path will go to the goal which is easiest to reach.) The robot then approaches the most accessible low-confidence area by an 'adventurous' path. This is an imaginative approach but it is not applicable to robots which are equipped with long-range sensors.

The previous examples have used a grid-based map and the attention has focussed more on free space than on obstacles. If, on the other hand, the robot is building a feature-based map, it can monitor the extent to which each individual feature has been explored. For example, Moutarlier and Chatila (1991) describe the behaviour of a 'curious' mobile robot which investigates new objects which appear on its feature-based map. If line segments are detected which correspond to an incomplete object, the robot moves to viewpoints from which it can discover the complete outline of the object. There is no sense of *degree* of uncertainty in this work; an object is either complete or not. Although this appears to provide the basis for an exploration strategy, there are questions left unanswered. For example, how should the robot choose between multiple incomplete objects? And does exploration terminate when there are no remaining incomplete objects? (Might there not still be unexplored regions in which no objects have yet been detected?)

Iijima (1989) also proposed that the robot should aim to complete the boundaries of observed objects but he extended the exploration strategy by constructing a free-space grid map from the feature-based map (a similar technique to that implemented in this thesis). The free space map serves two main purposes. First, it enables the robot to select viewpoints from which to continue its examination of an incomplete object. Second, it is used to control exploration when there are no further incomplete objects on the map. The robot will then approach the nearest unknown region on the free-space map. (If there are no incomplete objects *and* no unknown regions, then exploration is deemed to be complete.)

With the exception of Dudek's work, the strategies discussed in this section so far have had a practical focus, usually being tested on real robots. The authors have made no attempt to perform any mathematical analysis of the effectiveness of their strategies. A much more mathematical approach is adopted in the study of 'Terrain Acquisition'. Researchers in this area design algorithms which are guaranteed to detect all of the objects in a robot's environment. Mathematical expressions are then derived which link the cost of the exploration (usually in terms of the distance covered by the robot) to, for example, the total number of objects in the environment. The focus of the research is on designing strategies with small upper bounds on the cost of planning or executing the exploration. A common criterion is to minimise the exploration path length.

To make the mathematics tractable, terrain acquisition research has to make some simplifying assumptions about the robot and its environment. Lumelsky, Mukhopadhyay, and Sun (1991), for example, require that the robot be able to detect exactly the boundaries of any unoccluded object within a limited 'radius of vision'. (Shieh (1992) makes a similar simplification but, for most of his work, also assumes that the radius of vision is greater than the maximum distance that would be encountered during exploration.) A laser range-finder might go some way towards meeting this ideal, but it is certainly not an assumption which can be used about an ultrasonic sensor. He also requires that the robot have perfect localisation. This assumption is shared by many other researchers (Zelinsky, for example) and may not be unreasonable in practice. One could imagine, for example, a beacon-based localisation system giving enough positional accuracy for the algorithm to be effective. An assumption which does *not* appear in Lumelsky's work (unlike the research of Iijima, for example) is that the objects must be polygonal. All that is required is that the perimeters form simple closed curves.

Lumelsky proposes two different terrain acquisition strategies: the 'Sightseer' and the 'Seed-Spreader'. The 'Sightseer' strategy is similar to some of the strategies discussed earlier in that the robot circumnavigates objects in order to 'acquire' their complete boundaries. After completing the boundary of an object, the robot then moves to the nearest visible incomplete object. Under the assumptions of the research, the upper bound on the exploration path length can be shown to be linear in the number of obstacles.

One of the assumptions of the 'Sightseer' strategy is that the obstacles are mutually visible; any pair of obstacles are connected through a sequence of obstacles that are visible from each other. Since no constraints are imposed on the overall size of the environment, this assumption is essential to allow the algorithm to terminate. If all detected obstacles have been circumnavigated, then the exploration is complete. If the mutual visibility criterion is relaxed then it is necessary to impose another restriction; the environment must be within known size limits. The 'Seed-Spreader' strategy is designed to operate in these circumstances.

To use the 'Seed-Spreader' strategy, the robot's environment is divided into a number of parallel rectangular strips and the robot then moves backwards and forwards along the edges of these strips. If an obstacle is encountered which crosses the edge of a strip, the robot has to circumnavigate the obstacle before continuing its path along the edge of the strip. If, on the other hand, the robot detects an obstacle which does not cross the edge of a strip but which is not completely visible from the edge of the strip, then it must deviate from its standard path and circumnavigate the obstacle before returning to its path along the edge of the strip. The upper bound on the exploration path length for this algorithm can be shown to be *quadratic* in the number of obstacles (compared with the *linear* performance of the 'Sightseer'). This would suggest that, in situations in which both strategies could be used, the 'Sightseer' would be a clear favourite. Lumelsky emphasises, however, the worst-case nature of the upper bounds and shows that the 'Seed-Spreader' can compete well with the 'Sightseer' if, for example, most of the path generated by the 'Sightseer' is used in circumnavigating objects.

Shieh (1992) provides a detailed mathematical analysis of the problem of selecting viewpoints so that a patrol robot could see all of the free space in a given environment. He starts from the case in which the environment is completely known and moves on to the case in which the environment has to be explored. The difference is that, in the second case, viewpoints are selected to examine the *unexplored* regions instead of the free regions. Perhaps the most significant difference between this work and Lumelsky's is that the focus is on minimising the time required to *plan* the optimum set of viewpoints instead of the time (or path length) required to *execute* the exploration. Lumelsky's criterion appears to be the more practical.

Sankaranarayanan and Masuda (1992) build on Lumelsky's work by introducing the possibility that the robot can interrupt its circumnavigation of one obstacle to go and visit another. They introduce a parameterised algorithm in which a single parameter controls the likelihood that such interruptions will occur. By choosing the parameter value so that interruptions never occur, Lumelsky's 'Sightseer' strategy emerges as a special case of this more general algorithm. They propose the idea of 'Hierarchical Map Making' in which the control parameter is gradually modified so that the robot first builds a coarse, approximate, map and subsequently fills in the details.

The terrain acquisition research proposes some interesting exploration strategies but they are not directly applicable to the problems of exploring with ARNE. A single sweep of a sonar sensor does not reveal the boundaries of all obstacles within a given 'radius of vision'.

This section and the previous one have described a variety of ways in which researchers have investigated the exploration problem. The next section makes some general observations about this body of work and uses these observations to motivate the investigations which will form Part III of this thesis.

4.3 The Approach in this Thesis

The research papers described in the last two sections do not show the results of many practical exploration experiments. This is of course to be expected in the case of the terrain acquisition research which is mathematical and abstract. But even those papers which include experiments do not present many results. For example, Moutarlier and Iijima each give one experimental result and Thrun gives two. Nehmzow does evaluate the map quality several times during circuits of a test room, but the reported results are still limited to a single room. Elfes shows the likely targets for exploration at a single moment during exploration but does not present a complete exploration.

Even when results are presented, they are usually not quantitative. Iijima and Moutarlier each show a single picture of the viewpoints that the algorithm selected and the resulting map. In both cases a single object has been successfully identified, but there is no measure of the quality of the rest of the map or the efficiency of the exploration path. Although Nehmzow does use quantitative measures of recognition success, he makes no attempt to measure the cost of exploration. Thrun presents his results purely visually. Elfes, although proposing quantitative measures of map quality, does not present any examples of their use.

The shortage of quantitative experimental results makes it impossible to gain an impression of the relative strengths of alternative exploration strategies.

The research presented in Sections 4.1 and 4.2 shows a clear correlation between the type of map a robot has and the exploration strategy it uses. Wall-following is used by robots with no map or with topological maps. If the robot has a full metric map, wall-following is rejected in favour of a totally map-based strategy. This rejection seems to be unreasonable given that wall-following is reported as being easy to implement and robust. An incomplete map might also contain inconsistencies and default assumptions (see, for example, Section 7.4.3). A strategy which is based completely on the developing map could generate inefficient explorations. Perhaps better results could be obtained by a mixture of reactive and map-based strategies.

These observations have led to the following decisions which have motivated the research described in Part III of this thesis.

- Exploration strategies will be evaluated *experimentally*.

- Strategies will be tested in *multiple environments*.

- Strategies will be tested from *multiple starting positions* in each environment.

- Strategies will be evaluated *quantitatively*, using clearly-defined measures of map quality and exploration cost.

- The value of alternative strategies will be compared *statistically*.

Finally, which exploration strategies will be tested? Given the reports of its ease of implementation and robustness, wall-following is clearly a strong candidate. Wall-following will therefore be used as a 'base case'. Other strategies will be introduced to make increasing use of the robot's incomplete world model. The research focus will be to determine how much the use of a partially-formed world model can improve the effectiveness of a robot's exploration.

Part II

System Components

Chapter 5

The Robot

Figure 5.1: ARNE

Figure 5.1 shows ARNE, the mobile robot that was developed during the research reported in this thesis. This chapter describes ARNE. Section 5.1 describes ARNE's physical construction, sensors and electronic hardware. Section 5.2 then examines the on-board control software.

5.1 Hardware

ARNE's key physical component is a 300 mm diameter disc which supports the control electronics and the rotating sonar sensor. Below the disc is a chassis which holds the motors and shaft encoders to control the two drive wheels.

ARNE has a drive wheel on each side of the chassis and a low-friction castor at the back. It moves holonomically, turning the wheels in the same direction to move forward or in opposite directions to rotate on the spot. Shaft encoders with a precision of 1024 steps per revolution determine the distance travelled by each wheel to a precision of 0.2 mm.

At the lowest level, the wheel movements are controlled by two dedicated HCTL-1100 motion control chips (Hewlett-Packard 1992, pages 1-77 to 1-115) which generate and execute trapezoidal velocity profiles. The length, acceleration and peak velocity of these movements are specified by the on-board CPU, a 68000-compatible 'Mini-Module' micro controller from PSI Systems Limited (PSI 1991).

ARNE's only range sensor is a single rotating Polaroid ultrasonic rangefinder (Polaroid 1991) which can be seen in Figure 5.1 on top of the box which houses the CPU and other control electronics. The transducer is rotated by a stepper motor with a minimum step size of 1.8°. A full 360° scan is performed in twenty 18° steps.

Section 1.3 explained the decision to connect ARNE to a stationary workstation. A 9600-baud connection to the Mini-Module's RS485 serial port was used for this purpose. The cable was suspended from the ceiling of the laboratory and ARNE was given a long vertical 'tail' to avoid the cable hanging in front of the sonar sensor. The tail obstructs the sonar measurement which looks directly backwards. The remaining 19 measurements are unaffected.

The time between the emission of the sonar pulse and the triggering of the echo threshold is measured by an 8-bit timer and passed to the digital I/O ports of the Mini-Module. (See Section 6.1 for a full description of the sonar rangefinder.) A range precision of 1 cm is used, giving a maximum range of 2.53 m[1]. The minimum range that can be measured is 21 cm. (After the transmission of the pulse, there is a 'blanking period' during which no echoes can be detected. This gives the transducer time to settle before listening for the echo. The minimum range is a function of the blanking period.)

Power is supplied to ARNE by cable from a mains power supply. An on-board 6V battery supplies the short bursts of high current required by the ultrasonic transducer and is kept charged by the remote power supply.

ARNE has one more sensor, in addition to the sonar and the shaft encoders. A piezoelectric bumper around the circumference of the main disc is used to detect collisions. The interrupt mechanism of the Mini-Module is used to stop ARNE as soon as a collision is detected.

The next section reviews the way in which ARNE's actuators and sensors are co-ordinated by the on-board control software.

---

[1]The theoretical maximum range from the 8-bit counter would be 2.55 m. Calibration of the sensor required a 2 cm fixed offset, giving a practical maximum of 2.53 m.

5.2   Software

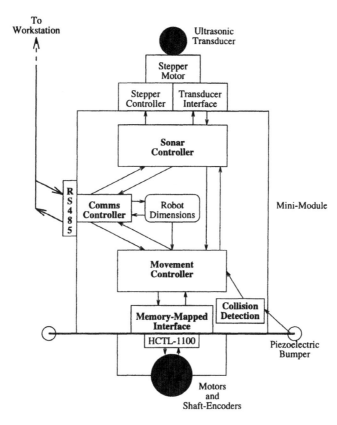

Figure 5.2: A Schematic Representation of ARNE's Control Architecture

Figure 5.2 is a schematic representation of ARNE's control architecture. It shows a number of modules, implemented on the micro-controller, which communicate with the remote workstation and with the electronics dedicated to the sensors and actuators. These modules also communicate with one another. The arrows in Figure 5.2 show the main lines of communication.

The processes on the mini-module comprise about 1500 lines of Modula-2 code. The remainder of this section considers each of the modules in turn and reviews the decisions which were made during their design.

5.2.1   Communications Controller

This module accepts commands and issues responses through the RS485 serial port. For most of the research a Sun workstation was on the other end of the line. However, the dialogue was designed to be easily readable so that an operator could communicate directly with ARNE through a dumb terminal.

Appendix D lists the key commands understood by ARNE. There are, in addition to these, commands to configure the system and to provide help and debug information to an operator.

The data transfer rates necessary during ARNE's operation are low enough that it was not necessary to compress the data. The longest message (the response to the request for an ultrasonic scan) is at most only 209 bytes long.

The Communications Controller parses the incoming commands and forwards requests to the Sonar Controller or the Movement Controller. It then formats the results of the requested operations and writes them back to the serial port.

5.2.2 Sonar Controller

This module is responsible for both the sonar transducer and the motor that changes the transducer's direction.

Requests for sonar information come from two sources; the Communications Controller may request a scan in response to input from the serial port or the Movement Controller may require the sonar sensor to look out for obstacles during a movement.

Standard electronics which detect the sonar echo were purchased with the transducer. A signal from this threshold detector is used to stop a timer, giving the delay between the transmission of the pulse and the detection of the echo. This delay is passed to the Sonar Controller which then converts the time into a range reading. This conversion was calibrated experimentally.

Sonar scans alternate their sense of rotation to prevent broken transducer wires.

5.2.3 Movement Controller

The Movement Controller is the largest component of ARNE's control software. It has to co-ordinate the action of the sensors and actuators during a movement.

The movement is initiated by writing the target 'final positions' for each wheel to the Memory-Mapped Interface to the motion controllers. These positions are expressed not in metric units such as millimetres but in steps of the shaft encoders. The Movement Controller therefore has to use knowledge about the dimensions of the robot (wheel size, encoder steps per revolution, distance between wheels ...) to convert from millimetres to steps.

Before beginning a forward movement, ARNE uses the sonar sensor to check whether the movement is safe. The same check is performed repeatedly during the movement to prevent collisions. A full sonar scan would not be useful here because it would waste time looking behind ARNE during the forward movement. It is important to focus attention in the direction of the movement. It is, however, also important to check to the sides to prevent glancing collisions with smooth walls which are almost parallel to the direction of movement. (The front readings could all be reflected away from the transducer.) Figure 5.3 shows the scan pattern which was implemented. This pattern was found to be effective at avoiding collisions.

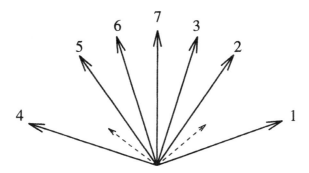

Figure 5.3: The Sonar Scan Pattern During Forward Movements

As ARNE moves forward, the sonar sensor scans for obstacles. This figure shows the sequence in which readings are taken. The sensor rotates in steps of 18°. Reading 7 is looking directly ahead. Readings 1 and 4 are included to detect walls which are approximately parallel to the direction of motion.

Tolerances for the range readings during these obstacle checks were determined experimentally. (How close must an object be before the move is abandoned?) The tolerances are strongly dependent on ARNE's speed; the faster the movement, the greater the safety margin that is needed. Reasonable values were found to be 350 mm for the front readings and 300 mm for the two side readings.

If an obstacle is detected, ARNE must stop immediately. Emergency stops were difficult to implement with the trapezoidal velocity profile mode of the HCTL-1100 motion controllers. Once the movement has started, it can only be interrupted by an emergency stop which releases control of the wheels, allowing them to drift. To compensate for this drift, the Movement Controller was designed to measure the positions of both wheels just before the emergency stop and then to bring ARNE back to that position. Although this is not an ideal solution, the results were good enough to prevent major localisation errors on the rare occasions that emergency stops were necessary.

After an emergency stop, the Movement Controller repeats the scan five times to verify that the obstruction is still there, and was not, for example, someone crossing ARNE's path. If the obstacle has disappeared, the movement is continued. Otherwise, the movement is abandoned.

When the movement has been completed or abandoned, the Movement Controller returns a status code to the Communications Controller, indicating whether the movement was successful and, if not, why not. It also reads from the Memory-Mapped Interface the actual distance travelled (in steps), converts it into millimetres and passes it to the Communications Controller.

Turn movements are simpler in that there is no need to check for obstacles before or during the turn. The required and actual turn angles are specified in degrees.

5.2.4   Memory-Mapped Interface

The HCTL-1100 motion control chips use a bi-directional multiplexed address/data bus. The Memory-Mapped Interface was designed to hide this complexity from the Movement Controller. It emulates the mechanism, often implemented in hardware, which enables a higher process simply to write values to, and read values from, specific memory locations without being concerned about the low-level protocols.

5.2.5   Collision Detection

The Collision Detection module is interrupt-driven. If the piezoelectric bumper detects a collision, the current movement is stopped immediately. It was found necessary to limit the sensitivity of this mechanism; in early experiments the inevitable vibration which occurs during movements was interpreted as a collision.

Chapter 6

Modelling the Sonar Sensor

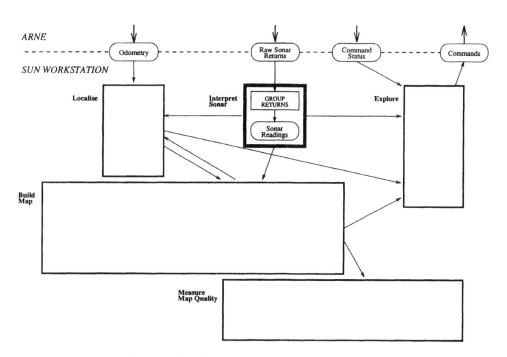

Figure 6.1: The Sonar Interpretation Module

This chapter presents the sonar sensor model that was developed in this research. Figure 6.1 shows that the model is used to interpret the raw sonar returns from ARNE before the information is passed on to the the other modules on the workstation.

Section 6.1 outlines the operation of the Polaroid ultrasonic rangefinder used by ARNE. Section 6.2 then describes initial experiments to measure the range to a smooth wall in the test environment. The experiments highlight two key features of the sonar sensor: its wide beam and its uneven signal strength. Section 6.3 proposes a sonar model to mitigate the effect of these features by grouping neighbouring range readings. Section 6.4 then describes

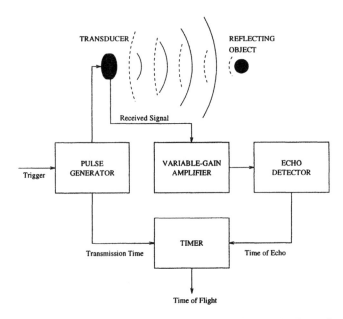

Figure 6.2: The Operation of the Polaroid Ultrasonic Transducer

experiments to verify that the model will be applicable when measuring the range to the variety of objects that ARNE will encounter in the test environment. Section 6.5 then summarises the model.

6.1 The Polaroid Ultrasonic Sensor

Time-of-flight sonar is used in this thesis; distance information is derived from the time taken for a pulse of sound to travel to an object and be reflected back to the sensor.[1]

Figure 6.2 is a simplified diagram of the rangefinder. Voltage pulses are sent to the transducer, which emits 16 cycles of square wave sound at about 50 kHz. As the sound begins, a timer is started. For a short period after transmission, the transducer is disabled (to give enough time for the vibration to die away) and it is then used to listen for an echo. When an echo is detected, the timer is stopped and the time-of-flight is measured. This time-of-flight can then be multiplied by the speed of sound in air to obtain a measurement of the round-trip distance to the object that caused the reflection. The most difficult, and potentially error-prone, part of the process is the detection of the echo. This is achieved by waiting until a signal is detected whose strength exceeds a predefined threshold. This is, however, complicated by the loss of strength of a sound signal as it passes through air; the further the signal has had to travel, the weaker it will be. To compensate for this, the

---

[1]There has been recent work on the construction of more 'intelligent' sonar sensors which analyse the shape of the waveform of the echo. This work is reviewed in Section 20.3.

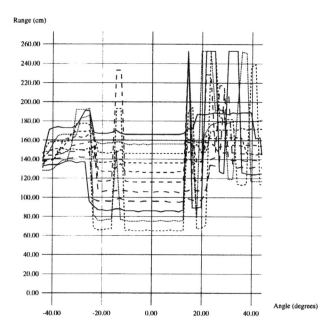

Figure 6.3: Sonar Returns from a Smooth Wooden Wall

Sonar scans with a step of 1.8° were taken at several distances from a smooth wooden wall. An angle of 0° is directly in front of the robot. Notice the sharp increase in range reading at about −22° and +22°. There are also transient increases at about −15° and +15°.

rangefinder electronics include an amplifier the gain of which increases over time.

6.2 Experimental Evaluation

This section presents the results of experiments to determine the behaviour of the sonar sensor when confronted with a smooth wooden wall.

The robot was placed roughly 1.5 m from the wall, approximately facing it. The robot then performed a complete 360° scan, using the smallest available step size between sonar returns. This produced 200 returns at steps of 1.8° (although some of the returns behind the robot were obstructed by its 'tail'). The robot then moved 100 mm forward and performed another scan. This step-and-scan process was repeated a total of ten times to test the behaviour of the sensor at a variety of ranges. (The same technique was used when testing other objects in Section 6.4.)

Figure 6.3 shows the returns from 40° either side of the robot's centre-line. Points to note include:

- All of the scans show a flat central region from roughly −10° to +10°, in which the

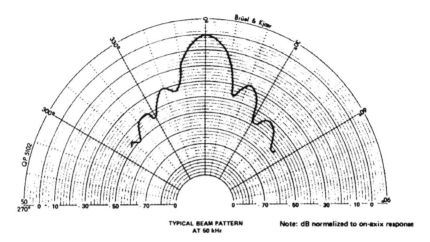

Figure 6.4: Typical Signal Strength of a Polaroid Ultrasonic Transducer

The signal strength is greatest directly in front of the transducer (in the centre of the graph). It reaches a
local minimum at about 15° either side of centre before increasing again to create weaker 'side lobes'.
(Polaroid 1991)

range reading changes very little. This is consistent with the findings of Kuc (1991)
and others that the measured range is actually the normal distance from the sensor to
the wall.

- To either side of the central region, at about ±15°, the measured range increases. In
  some instances the increase is substantial, causing the obvious 'spikes'. In other cases
  the increase is only a few centimetres.

- Beyond the regions of increased range, between 18° and 22° and between −17° and
  −23°, there are additional flat regions. The range in these regions appears to be slightly
  higher than in the centre of the beam.

Figure 6.4 helps to explain these results. It shows the significant variation in signal strength
at different angles from the centre of the ultrasound beam. The results in Figure 6.3 showed
that the wall can be detected through a total angle of about 45°. The wall can therefore be
detected by the strong central lobe and by the first side lobes. Contact is then lost as the
strength of the side lobes decreases beyond ±25°.

The transient overestimates are caused by the low signal strength between the central and
side lobes. The very long readings arise when the echo is too weak to exceed the threshold.
The detection mechanism then times out, returning a maximum reading, or is triggered by
a multiple reflection, giving a long false reading. Leonard and Durrant-Whyte (1992) have
shown that the smaller overestimates occur when the signal is still strong enough to trigger

the detection mechanism, but too weak to trigger it promptly. The echo detection hardware relies upon the charging of a capacitor. A weak signal takes longer to charge the capacitor, causing an overestimate of range.

These experimental results have shown that the ultrasonic sensor has a wide beam and can overestimate the range if a weak echo is received. These two properties both contribute to the positional uncertainty associated with a sonar return. The next section examines techniques to lessen this uncertainty.

6.3   Proposed Sonar Model

A number of researchers have shown that the position of an object can be measured with greater precision by combining the results from *multiple* ultrasonic range readings. Some (Nagashima & Yuta 1992; Peremans, Audenaert, & Van Campenhout 1993; Wilkes *et al.* 1993) use more than one transducer and make multiple time-of-flight measurements simultaneously. Others (Leonard & Durrant-Whyte 1992) use a single rotating sensor to make multiple measurements sequentially. Since ARNE is equipped with a single transducer, the latter approach has more relevance to the current research.

Leonard and Durrant-Whyte (1992) used dense sonar scans (with only 0.588° between readings) and looked for flat regions like those in Figure 6.3, which they called 'Regions of Constant Depth (RCDs)'. An RCD was defined to be a contiguous set of sonar returns which differed no more than 1 cm. By imposing a minimum width on these RCDs (typically 10°) they guaranteed that the returns all came from the strong central lobe of the beam. This eliminated the problems caused by weak returns. They were also able to decrease the angular uncertainty by using the multiple returns in the RCD to constrain the possible direction to the object.

The creation of RCDs has been shown to be an effective way to eliminate the problem of weak returns. The practical limitation of the method is the scanning time. Each dense scan in Leonard and Durrant-Whyte's work took roughly 2 minutes, which they admit to be 'a very impractical length of time'. They propose to overcome this problem by using multiple 'tracking sonars' each of which focuses its attention on a single feature of the environment. This option is not available to ARNE, with its single sensor. This section therefore considers how the positional uncertainty can be reduced by intelligent interpretation of the returns from a sparse scan (in which a full set of 19 returns is obtained in 3 seconds).

With the limited amount of data in a sparse scan, it is impossible to eliminate weak returns entirely. If an object is detected by only one return it is impossible to tell whether that return was strong or weak. It is, however, possible to increase the quality of the sensor data whenever an object is detected by more than one return. One can then decrease the likelihood of a range overestimate by taking the minimum range of all the returns. The angular uncertainty can also be decreased because the detected object must be in the area in which all of the sonar beams overlap. Both of these techniques will be explained further in this section.

Returns are taken to have been caused by the same object if they are adjacent in the scan and their ranges differ by no more than a threshold value. To discuss the grouping of adjacent sonar returns, it is necessary to define some terminology. In this thesis, the word *return* will be used to denote the numeric value returned by a single firing of the sonar sensor, whereas a *reading* will be taken to mean the result of grouping together one or more adjacent returns.

The threshold for grouping the returns can be determined from the results that were presented in Figure 6.3. They show that the range readings in the flat regions (during which an echo is being detected from the wall) differ by no more than 4 cm. This value can also be supported by calculation. The sonar pulse consists of 16 cycles at 50 kHz. Leonard and Durrant-Whyte (1992, page 34) report that a strong return triggers the echo detection mechanism after 3 cycles. The greatest overestimate would therefore occur if the mechanism were triggered by the 16th cycle, 13 cycles too late. Taking the speed of sound in air to be 343 m/sec, this delay corresponds to an overestimate (in metres) of:

$$\frac{13 \times \frac{343}{50000}}{2} = 0.045$$

The experimental results also showed that the returns from the strong central lobe often overestimated the range by 1 cm. With this in mind, the threshold for grouping returns was set to 3 cm. The grouping procedure then erred on the side of caution, including fewer rather than more returns into a reading. This was found to be useful to prevent the unrealistic narrowing of the effective beam width.

Each reading is assigned a range value equal to the *minimum* range of its component returns, thereby eliminating the overestimates from weak returns. Notice that the angular difference between the weak returns on either side of the beam is at least 20°, which is greater than the 18° step between adjacent returns, and that the width of each weak region is less than 10°, which is much less than the step size. These two properties make it impossible for two adjacent returns *both* to be weak. Therefore if a reading is formed from at least two returns, any overestimates from weak returns are guaranteed to be eliminated.

Figure 6.3 showed a difference of about 45° between the extreme angles at which the sensor could detect the smooth wall. This difference is known as the *visibility angle* of the object. This is the amount of angular uncertainty in a single sonar return from the wall. If a reading is composed of multiple returns, the directions of the returns and the visibility angle of the object can constrain the direction to the object. This has the effect of narrowing the effective beam width of the reading.

Figure 6.5 illustrates the calculation of the effective beam width for a reading formed from three returns. In general, the effective beam width $w(v, s, c_{read})$ is given by:

$$w(v, s, c_{read}) = v - (c_{read} - 1)s \tag{6.1}$$

where v is the object's visibility angle, s is the angle between adjacent returns (18° in this implementation) and c_{read} is the number of returns in the reading.

The effective beam of the reading is symmetrical around the average direction of the returns. The average direction is therefore taken as the direction of the reading.

All of the results in this chapter so far have been concerned with one type of object, a smooth wall. The next section considers the other types of object which ARNE will encounter in the test environments.

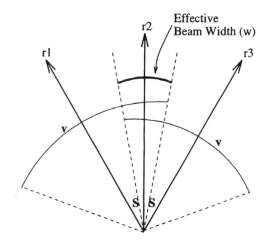

Figure 6.5: Effective Beam Width for a Reading of 3 Returns

Three sonar returns (r1,r2,r3) are grouped into a reading. The angle between adjacent returns is s, giving an angle of $2s$ between the extreme returns. If the object's visibility angle is v, then the direction to the object must lie within the central overlap region (indicated by the thick arc). The effective beam width, w, of the reading is therefore given by $w = v - 2s$.

6.4   Other Types of Object

ARNE's test environment was designed to be heterogeneous. As Bozma and Kuc (1992) have pointed out, sonar experiments typically use *either* smooth surfaces *or* rough ones. The environment used in this research has some smooth walls (constructed from card or smooth wooden board) and some rough painted brick walls. Thin cylindrical pillars[2] were used as free-standing obstacles. The test environments are described in Appendix B. This section repeats the experiment from Section 6.2 for each type of object to determine each object's visibility angle and to check that the proposed sonar model can be applied in all of these circumstances.

As a first example, consider the convex edge[3] formed by two walls meeting at 90°. Figure 6.6 shows the results. The central flat region is much narrower than for the walls. In this case the flat region extends from approximately -10 to $+10$ degrees. The region becomes a little wider as the robot approaches the edge. For this object it is clear that the echo can only be detected if the signal comes from the powerful central lobe of the beam. The edge is more difficult to detect than the smooth wall because the echo from the edge is diffuse whereas the echo from the wall is specular (Hallam 1986; Kuc & Viard 1991). The strength of the diffuse echo decreases more rapidly than that of the specular echo, making it harder to trigger the detection mechanism. This effect becomes

---

[2]actually sand-filled potato chip cartons 7 cm in diameter

[3]In this thesis, unless otherwise stated, an 'edge' should be taken to refer to a *convex* edge and a 'corner' will be a *concave* corner.

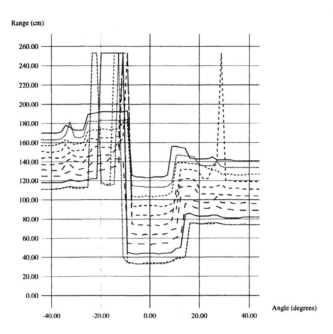

Figure 6.6: Sonar Returns from a Convex Edge

Sonar scans with a step of 1.8° were taken at several distances from a 90° convex edge. An angle of 0° is directly in front of the robot. Notice the sharp increase in range reading at about ±10°.

more pronounced at greater ranges, causing a slight narrowing of the flat region at greater ranges.

The returns from the smooth corner (Figure 6.7) show, with two exceptions, a flat central region between −12 and +12 degrees. Throughout this region the ultrasonic signal reflects specularly from both walls before returning to the transducer. This central region is delimited by range increases (either 'spikes' or small increases) corresponding to the troughs in signal strength at the side of the central lobe. After this, at about −22° and 20°, the range drops to about 70% of its central value as the side lobes begin to measure the normal distance to the side walls. The exceptions are the scans taken at 160 cm and 100 cm. Both of these scans show a more gradual change from the central value to the side value. This behaviour is similar to that of a corner between rough walls (see later in this section), indicating that the sensor may have detected some surface texture on one of the walls.

Figure 6.8 shows the test results with the cylindrical object. A specular reflection occurs at the point at which the surface of the cylinder is normal to the transducer (Hallam 1986). Once again there is a flat central region between approximately −10° and +15°. Beyond that the sensor fails to detect the echo. The only exception occurs when the robot is close to the cylinder and an echo from a side lobe is detected.

All of the experimental results presented so far have been very similar, the main difference being in the visibility angle of the object. The proposed model describes the operation of

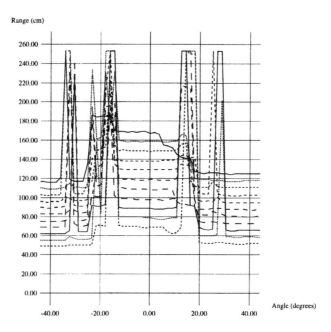

Figure 6.7: Sonar Returns from a Smooth Corner

Sonar scans with a step of 1.8° were taken at several distances from a 90° concave corner formed by two smooth walls. An angle of 0° is directly in front of the robot. Sharp increases in range reading occur at about ±12°. After these 'spikes' the range drops as the sensor begins to measure the distance to a single wall instead of to the corner.

the sensor well in all of these cases. The last two objects to be examined, the rough corner and the rough wall, generate noticeably different results which merit discussion.

The results from the rough corner are shown in Figure 6.9. This graph is strikingly different from the others in this chapter, all of which showed a pattern of a shorter range reading in the centre with longer readings further away from the centre. These results are the opposite. The sensor is actually measuring the distance to surface features of the rough wall, each of which is generating diffuse echoes. The experiments with the convex edge earlier in this section showed that the diffuse echoes could only be detected from the central lobe. In a rough corner the sensor is therefore in effect measuring the distance to the wall along the shorter side of the central lobe. For illustration, consider the arrangement shown in Figure 6.10.

Figure 6.11 compares the range values predicted by Figure 6.10 (with d set to 75 cm and β set to 6.6 degrees) with the values obtained by experiment. The model matches the observed results well. (A narrow beam width is reasonable in this case since a very strong signal would be necessary to detect the weak diffuse echo.)

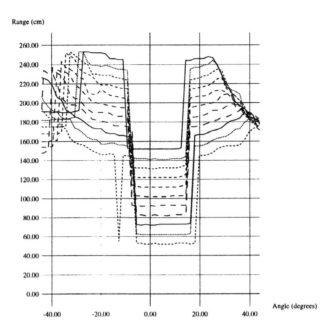

Figure 6.8: Sonar Returns from a Thin Cylinder

Sonar scans with a step of 1.8° were taken at several distances from a 7 cm diameter smooth cylinder. An angle of 0° is directly in front of the robot. Sharp increases in range reading occur at about −10° and +15°. (The exact position of the flat region varies as the robot moves nearer to the object because the cylinder was not exactly in front of the robot.)

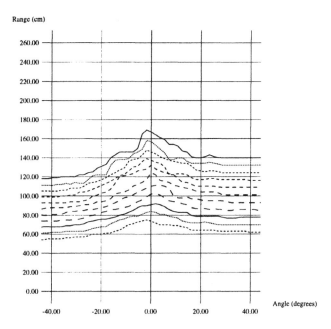

Figure 6.9: Sonar Returns from a Rough Corner

Sonar scans with a step of 1.8° were taken at several distances from a concave 90° corner formed by two rough walls. An angle of 0° is directly in front of the robot. The measured range decreases as soon as the sensor turns away from the corner.

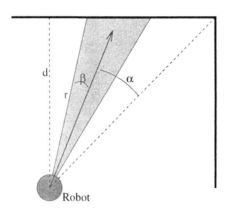

Figure 6.10: An Idealised Sonar Sensor in a Rough Corner

The robot takes a return at an oblique angle from a rough wall. The direction of the centre of the beam is shown by the arrow, and the shaded area represents the beam width. The length of the short side of the beam is given by $r(\alpha, \beta, d) = d \sec(45 - \beta - |\alpha|)$ where α is the angle between the sensor and the mid-line of the corner, β is half the beam width (all angles in degrees) and d is the normal distance to the wall.

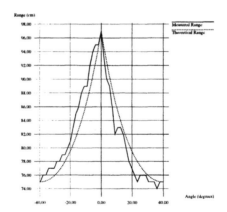

Figure 6.11: Theory and Practice of Range Readings from a Rough Corner

A comparison of the actual measured range to a rough corner (solid line) and the range predicted by the method shown in Figure 6.10. The model matches the observations closely.

These results show that the rough corner can not be treated as a single object which can be detected by sonar from a variety of angles. The sonar will instead detect surface features in the vicinity of the corner. The rough corner will therefore be excluded from any further discussion of visibility angles.

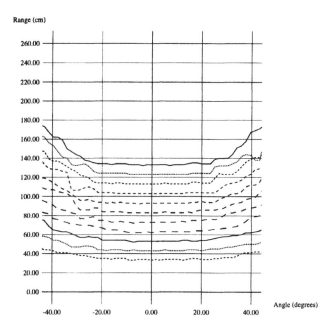

Figure 6.12: Sonar Returns from a Rough Brick Wall

Sonar scans with a step of 1.8° were taken at several distances from a rough wall. An angle of 0° is directly in front of the robot. The measured range shows a flat region between about ±25° with a gradual increase to the sides. The range increase is sharper the further the robot is from the wall.

The final object to be tested is the rough wall. Figure 6.12 shows the results. As with the smooth wall, there is a flat region in the centre of the graph. The most striking difference from the earlier results is the absence of 'spikes' corresponding to the troughs in signal strength at about ±15°. It seems likely that, when the sensor is oriented so that the normal reflection would be too weak to be detected, the central lobe detects some surface features at an oblique angle. (The range to the detected features is not very much greater than the normal distance.) As the sensor turns more, the normal echoes again become strong enough to be detected. The range finally begins to increase significantly as the sensor turns beyond about 25° and the normal echo again becomes too weak to be detected. The central lobe then begins to detect surface features which are much further away than the normal distance.

The difference between the results from smooth and rough walls may help to resolve a difference of opinion which appears in the literature about ultrasonic rangefinding. Some researchers (Brown 1985; Kuc & Viard 1991) report that sonar measures the normal distance to a wall, whereas others (Crowley 1985; Song & Chang 1993) state that sonar measures the distance along the short side of the beam. It may simply be that the first group is using smooth walls and the latter group is using rough walls.

Object Type	Mean Visibility Angle	Standard Error	Max. Visibility Angle
Convex Edge	18.0°	0.57°	21.6°
Thin Cylinder	23.4°	0.24°	25.2°
Smooth Corner	25.2°	0.29°	27.0°
Smooth Wall	43.2°	0.97°	45.0°
Rough Wall	54.0°	1.46°	61.2°

Table 6.1: Visibility Angles by Object Type

Table 6.1 lists the mean visibility angles from the experiments in this chapter. The objects fall into two groups. The edge, corner and cylinder have similar visibility angles, whereas the two types of wall both have much larger visibility angles. This grouping corresponds to the way the objects will be represented on the feature map to be described in the next chapter. The objects in the first group will all be represented as point features and the second group as line features.

The map building algorithm uses a single visibility angle for each of the two types of feature. To prevent the rejection of valid readings, the *maximum* mean visibility angle of the objects in each group was used. A visibility angle of 25.2° was therefore used for point features.

Preliminary map-building experiments used a visibility angle of 54.0° for line objects. This led to the rejection of a large number of valid readings from close to rough walls. At close range the transition from the flat central region to the increasing side regions is difficult to detect, allowing more returns to fall within the 3 cm limit. This problem was overcome by using the *maximum* visibility angle of a rough wall instead of the mean. A visibility angle of 61.2° was therefore used for line features.

6.5   Summary

Using the data element names from Tables A.3 and A.4 in Appendix A, the procedure for grouping sonar returns into readings can be summarised as:

1. Returns with range (r_{raw}) equal to the maximum range of the sensor (2.53 m) are discarded. These returns have little value because they mean only that the nearest object is *at least* 2.53 m away.

2. The remaining returns are scanned for groups of adjacent returns whose range values differ by no more than 3 cm. Each group forms a *reading*. The range of the reading (r_{read}) is set to the minimum range of the returns, the direction of the reading (a_{read}) is set to the average angle of the returns, and a count (c_{read}) is kept of the number of returns which formed this reading.

The effective beam width is $v - (c_{read} - 1)s$ where v is the object's visibility angle, and s is the angle between adjacent returns (18° in this implementation).

A visibility angle of 25.2° will be used for point features and 61.2° for lines.

The model described in this chapter is similar to Leonard and Durrant-Whyte's (1992) RCD work, and was indeed inspired by it. There are, however, a number of important differences:

- Weak returns are deliberately *included* in the groupings in order to decrease the angular uncertainty. Grouping them with strong returns also prevents the use of the overestimated range readings.

- This is an opportunistic approach, grouping returns wherever possible. However, *all* of the sonar returns are used, even if they have not been included in a group. The only exception is that maximum-range returns are discarded.

- Different visibility angles are used for different types of object. Leonard and Durrant-Whyte used the same visibility angle for all objects.

- ARNE's sparse sonar scan is 40 times faster than the dense scan that is used to generate RCDs.

This model of the sonar sensor can now be used as a starting point for the map-building described in Chapter 7.

Chapter 7

Map Construction

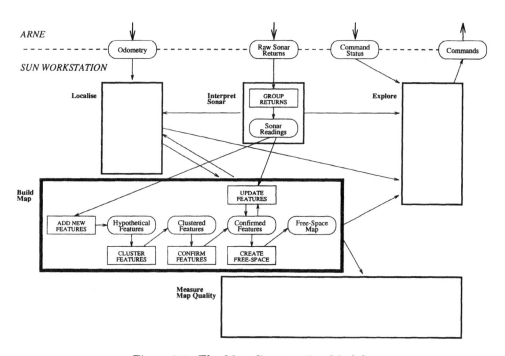

Figure 7.1: The Map Construction Module

This chapter describes the map-building algorithms which were designed and implemented in this research. Figure 7.1 shows that the sonar readings (as described in Chapter 6) and knowledge of ARNE's position are combined to generate a sequence of feature-based representations and a free-space map.

The sensor model that was developed in Chapter 6 showed that positional uncertainty in the sonar returns could be decreased by grouping multiple returns from the same viewpoint. But uncertainty, especially angular uncertainty, still remains. The objective of the algorithms in this chapter is to reduce the uncertainty further and build an accurate representation of the environment.

More value can be derived from a sensor reading by examining it in the context of pre-existing information about the world. This information comes from two sources; either the latest map or sensor data which has not yet contributed to the map. As an example of the first type, imagine that the current map shows that there is a wall directly in front of the robot. If a sensor reading is then obtained which is consistent with a sonar reflection from that wall, the range reading can be used to update the estimated position of the wall. The uncertainty due to beam width has been eliminated and the new range reading can be averaged with the existing knowledge to limit the impact of unpredictable errors.

Unfortunately map-building is not quite this simple. First, there is the 'bootstrap' problem of gathering enough initial information so that sensor readings can be matched with known objects. This problem can be addressed by seeking matches *between* sensor readings, without reference to known objects. Section 7.1 describes the process by which these matches are used to generate potential features and Section 7.2 then explains how these features become confirmed when they have been observed repeatedly. The second difficulty is the *correspondence problem*; how does the robot determine which features have caused the readings that it is obtaining? Section 7.3 explains how these correspondences are established and how the properties of the confirmed features are updated. Finally, Section 7.4 describes how a grid-based free-space map is constructed from the set of confirmed features.

7.1 Detecting Potential Features

In this section we examine the process of creating new features on the map. This has to be done whenever a sensor reading is obtained which can not be associated with any of the known features. This will usually be because the feature is being observed for the first time. It is also possible that the feature *has* already been observed, but not enough times for it to have been confirmed.

To build a feature-based map, one has to decide what features to use to describe the robot's environment. It is necessary to choose a set of features which can be reliably detected by the robot's sensors.

Hallam (1986) defined a set of six 3-dimensional echo sources which can be detected by ultrasonic sensors: concave corners, concave linear sources, planar sources, cylindrical sources, spherical or ellipsoidal sources, and convex linear or corner sources. In this thesis the environment is modelled as a 2-dimensional projection, thereby restricting the set of features to those which are orthogonal to the horizontal plane on which the robot moves. These features are a vertical plane, a vertical cylinder, a concave vertical corner, and a convex vertical edge. The 2-dimensional projections of these features are the line (plane), arc (cylinder) and point (concave corner or convex edge). Many researchers have used only line segments (Crowley 1985; Drumheller 1987; Nagashima & Yuta 1992; Song & Chang 1993; Zelinsky 1991b). Others have built maps containing lines *and* points (Kuc & Viard 1991; Leonard & Durrant-Whyte 1992; Peremans, Audenaert, & Van Campenhout 1993). Arcs are rarely included in the feature set. Whereas two sonar readings are usually[1] enough to

---

[1]If the angular uncertainty in the readings is high enough, there may be two mirror-image interpretations.

determine the position of a point or the position and orientation of a line, three readings are required to describe an arc of unknown radius. For this reason only lines and points have been used in this thesis. In this representation, thin cylinders can be approximated as points. Cylinders of larger radius can be approximated as a set of tangential line segments.

It is not possible to use a single time-of-flight sonar reading to distinguish between lines and points or to measure the precise direction to the feature from the robot. A number of researchers have therefore recognised the need to combine sonar readings from multiple viewpoints. The viewpoints can be obtained from multiple transducers on the robot (Nagashima & Yuta 1992; Peremans, Audenaert, & Van Campenhout 1993; Brown 1985) or by moving the robot between readings (Leonard & Durrant-Whyte 1992; Zelinsky 1991b). The second method has been used in this thesis because ARNE has only a single sensor. The feature extraction algorithms described in this thesis are modelled on the work of Leonard and Durrant-Whyte (1992).

There is value in combining multiple readings if the readings are caused by the same object. The angular uncertainty in the readings can then be eliminated and the position of the object can be determined. In work with multiple transducers (e.g. (Nagashima & Yuta 1992)) there is usually an implicit assumption that the echoes received at the transducers have all come from the same object. This assumption may be reasonable in practice because the transducers are close together and facing in the same direction. If, on the other hand, the robot has moved a significant distance between the readings, one has to adopt a more tentative approach and *hypothesise* the existence of features to explain multiple readings. These hypotheses can then be tested by subsequent readings. In this implementation the hypothetical features are sought by examining the readings in pairs.

In the search for explanations of pairs of readings, one could consider trying to match each of the most recent readings against *all* of the readings from *all* of the earlier viewpoints. However, in the current implementation the pairings are limited to readings from two consecutive viewpoints for the following reasons:

- Consecutive viewpoints are frequently close together and it is therefore likely that the same features will be observed from both viewpoints.

- If *all* earlier viewpoints were tested, map-building would take longer as ARNE visited more viewpoints. This loss of performance would be unacceptable for long explorations.

- The odometry error between consecutive viewpoints is less than between viewpoints more widely separated in time. Consecutive viewpoints therefore form a more trustworthy baseline for the triangulation process by which new features are detected.

The first step of feature detection has been named the 'Circle Test' (Leonard & Durrant-Whyte 1992, page 99). For each location, a circle is drawn, centred on the location, with radius set to the value of the sonar reading.

If the returns were from a point, the reflection will be diffuse and the hypothesised point will be at an intersection point of the two circles (Points P1 and P2 in Figure 7.2).

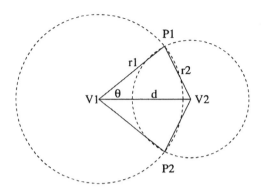

Figure 7.2: Circle Test for Elementary Point Features

The robot has taken range readings from viewpoints V1 and V2. The circles centred on each position have radius equal to the measured range. If both readings are caused by the same point feature, it must be at position P1 or P2, at a point of intersection of the circles.

The direction, θ, to the point can then be determined by the cosine rule:

$$r_2{}^2 = r_1{}^2 + d^2 - 2r_1 d\cos(\theta)$$

or

$$\cos(\theta) = \frac{r_1{}^2 + d^2 - r_2{}^2}{2r_1 d} \qquad (7.1)$$

Equation 7.1 gives two solutions for θ; one with the point above the line of travel and the other below.

Note that there are some cases in which no solution is possible. If $d = 0$ (ARNE hasn't moved between sensor scans), then there is no baseline for the triangulation. If $d > r_1 + r_2$ or $|r_1 - r_2| > d$ then the circles do not intersect.

The direction to the point from v_2 can be derived in a similar way (or by using the sine rule once θ is known).

If the returns were from a line, the reflections will have been normal to the surface and the hypothesised line will be tangential to both circles (lines L1 and L2 in Figure 7.3).

In this case θ is given by:

$$\cos(\theta) = \frac{r_1 - r_2}{d} \qquad (7.2)$$

Again there are solutions for θ above and below the direction of travel and there are circumstances under which no line exists. If $d = 0$ there is again no baseline and if $|r_1 - r_2| > d$ there is no line tangential to both circles.

It was shown in Section 6.4 that the visibility angle of any line feature is much greater than the $18°$ step size of the sonar scan. Therefore, if the robot has an unoccluded view of a

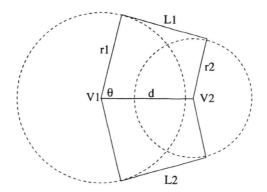

Figure 7.3: Circle Test For Elementary Line Features

The robot has taken range readings from viewpoints V1 and V2. The circles centred on each position have radius equal to the measured range. If both readings are caused by the same line, it must be at position L1 or L2, tangential to both circles.

line feature, the line will be detected by more than one adjacent return (i.e. there will be a reading with a return count, c_{read}, greater than one). These readings are guaranteed not to be affected by the problem of inaccurate range values caused by weak returns (see page 60). To improve the accuracy of the map-building, a restriction was implemented to the effect that a reading was considered to have been caused by a line feature only if $c_{read} \geq 2$.

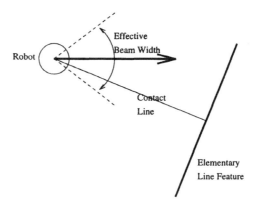

Figure 7.4: The Contact Line Falls Within the Effective Beam of the Reading

The Circle Test generates zero, two or four alternative explanations for the two sensor readings. The number of hypotheses can be decreased by considering the sensor orientation when the readings were taken (the 'Sensor Orientation Test'). For each possible interpretation, *contact points* are defined on the hypothesised object (one for a point, two for a line).

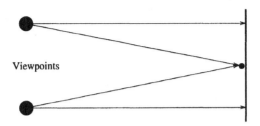

Figure 7.5: Is it a Line or a Point?

The robot takes range readings from the two viewpoints on the left of the diagram. Two contact lines from each viewpoint are possible, one if the readings were caused by a line, the other if the readings were caused by a point. If both contact lines from a viewpoint run in approximately the same direction, the Sensor Orientation Test is unlikely to be able to resolve the ambiguity. The longer the range readings, the more likely such an ambiguity is to arise.

By connecting these points to the sensor positions, two *contact lines* are created. For each hypothesised object, a check is made that both contact lines fall within the effective beam width of the reading (see Figure 7.4). The beam width is calculated by equation 6.1. Note that the effective beam width is different for line and point features.

If both contact lines are accepted, the hypothesised object is accepted provisionally, awaiting support from later sensor data. This test reduces the number of possible objects, often to only one. It is, however, common for an ambiguity to exist between a line and a point, especially when the range readings are long (see Figure 7.5).

If the candidate features lie approximately in ARNE's direction of travel, the Sensor Orientation Test may be unable to distinguish between the above- and below-the-line interpretations. In this situation, neither interpretation is accepted.

If the Circle Test and the Sensor Orientation Test suggest the existence of a line segment, it is necessary to check the length of that segment. Situations could arise in which the two sensor readings do not in fact come from a single line segment but from a broken line such as a doorway or an alcove (see Figure 7.6).

Modelling such an environment as an unbroken line would suggest that the robot can not pass through the doorway or into the alcove. This problem is eliminated by imposing a maximum length restriction on the line segment. A maximum length of 600 mm was used, the width of the narrowest gap through which ARNE could safely pass.

7.2   Clustering Potential Features

The process described in Section 7.1 generates possible interpretations of pairs of sonar readings. However it is still possible that these interpretations are false. There could be alternative explanations for the same pair of readings. Or both readings could have been caused by multiple specular reflections, suggesting the existence of a 'ghost' feature. Further support is needed before multiple sensor readings can be trusted to correspond to the same object in the world. This support is obtained by gathering the hypothetical features into

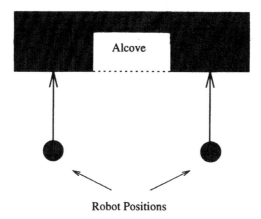

Figure 7.6: The Risk of 'Closing' an Alcove

The two sensor readings do not come from the same line segment but from separate lines on either side of the alcove. A maximum line length is imposed to prevent misinterpretation of the readings.

mutually supportive clusters.

All of the elementary features within a cluster are of the same type. There are therefore 'point' clusters and 'line' clusters. An elementary feature is added to a cluster if it shares a reading with a feature which is already in the cluster.

A cluster remains 'tentative' until enough features have been included in the cluster to justify its promotion to a status of 'confirmed'. The meaning of 'enough features' was determined experimentally by performing a set of wall-following explorations and measuring the map quality that resulted from the use of a number of different thresholds. (The experiments will be described in Section 13.4 after the quality metric, wall-following, and localisation have all been introduced.) These experiments showed that a cluster should be promoted to 'confirmed' when it includes two features (equivalent to three consistent readings). This choice of threshold is the same as that used by Leonard and Durrant-Whyte (1992).

At the confirmation stage a contact point is defined for each reading in the cluster. Since a reading could be linked with more than one elementary feature, the x and y co-ordinates of the contact point are calculated by averaging the points of contact between the reading and its associated elementary features.

The properties stored for a confirmed line and point are documented in Tables A.9 and A.10 in Appendix A. The slope of the line (a_{cl}) is calculated by finding the best-fit line through the contact points by orthogonal regression (see Appendix C). The end-points ($x_{cl}[],y_{cl}[]$) are found by a normal projection of the contact points onto the infinite line at angle a_{cl}.

The co-ordinates of the confirmed point (x_{cp},y_{cp}) are simply the averages of the co-ordinates of the contact points.

For both types of confirmed feature, a number of 'sum' values are held which speed up the later changes to the feature.

7.3   Updating Existing Features

Consider the stage at which the robot's map includes several confirmed features. One of the robot's objectives then is to use its range readings to improve its knowledge about those confirmed features. Before it can do this it is faced with the correspondence problem: *Which readings correspond to which features?*.

The problem can be solved by examining each confirmed feature in turn to decide whether that feature could explain any of the range readings. The decision is based on the following factors:

- Is the object observable from the robot's current location? It may be, for example, that the object is occluded; the contact line from the robot to the object would pass through another confirmed object. For line objects, a check is also made that the line is being observed from the correct side.

- Is the observed object within the effective beam width of the reading?

- Does the predicted range to the object approximately match the measured range? A 'validation gate' is used to check this. This is discussed further in Section 9.3.

- The 'Alcove Test' (page 76) is applied to line features. If the contact point with a line feature would be too far beyond the endpoint of the line, then the correspondence is rejected, to prevent open regions being falsely mapped as closed. This helps to overcome one of the criticisms often levelled at sonar (Zelinsky 1991b) that it fails to detect doorways.

The result of this matching process is that each sonar reading has been associated with zero or more confirmed objects. If the reading matches exactly one object, it is used to update the properties of the object. If no matching objects have been found, the reading is used as input to the 'new object' processing described in Section 7.1. If more than one matching object is found, no further processing is applied to the reading.

The properties of the matched features are updated as follows:

Lines A contact point is obtained by taking a point at the measured distance from the robot in a direction normal to the line. This contact point is added to the list of contact points associated with the line ($cp_{cl}[]$). The 'sum' properties ($sigx_{cl}$, $sigy_{cl}$, $sigx2_{cl}$, $sigy2_{cl}$, $sigxy_{cl}$) are then updated with the co-ordinates of the contact point and the 'geometric' properties ($a_{cl}, x_{cl}[], y_{cl}[]$) are updated by orthogonal regression (see Appendix C).

Points A contact point is obtained by taking a point at the measured distance from the robot in a direction towards the confirmed point. This contact point is added to the list of contact points associated with the confirmed point (cp_{cp}). The 'sum' properties ($sigx_{cp}$, $sigy_{cp}$) are then updated with the co-ordinates of the contact point and the 'geometric' properties (x_{cp}, y_{cp}) are updated by simple averaging.

7.4   Free Space

Section 3.2 explained the need for a grid-based free-space map. This section describes the derivation of this map from the feature-based map of Sections 7.1 and 7.3.

The size of a grid square was chosen to be 100 mm by 100 mm. This satisfied the resolution requirements of the proposed application while giving a reasonably compact data structure.

In subsequent discussion the word 'cell' will be used to describe a square on the free-space map. It will be used interchangeably to denote either an element in the map data-structure or a small region of the robot's environment which is being represented by that element.

Each cell has one of four possible states:

Unknown   Nothing is known about the contents of this cell.

Occupied   This cell contains at least one confirmed feature. A point could be completely contained in the cell, whereas a line would be more likely to pass through the cell.

Free   This cell has been determined to be free of obstacles.

Dangerous   This cell is free of obstacles *but* is close enough to an obstacle that the robot would be risking a collision (or at least an emergency stop) if it were to enter this cell.

The following sections discuss some of the issues arising from each of these classifications and describe the construction of the map in more detail.

7.4.1   Unknown Cells

'Unknown' is the default status of a cell. Whenever a new map is created, all cells are set to 'Unknown'.

It would have been possible to avoid the use of the 'Unknown' status by making a strong default assumption such as that all cells are free until a feature is discovered (the 'Innocent until proven guilty' approach). The acceptability of such an assumption is tightly linked to the navigation techniques which the robot will use; if the robot treats unknown and free space identically when planning paths, then there is no need for the map to distinguish between them.

The objective of the work described in this thesis is to examine a number of alternative exploration strategies; some may need to distinguish between free and unknown space; some may not. The inclusion of the 'Unknown' status allows this flexibility.

7.4.2   Occupied Cells

If any part of a confirmed feature falls within a cell, that cell is labelled 'Occupied'. A peril of the loss of resolution at this stage is that the map will over-represent the fraction of the environment which is occupied. This could be significant if, for example, the grid squares were large and a point feature was in the extreme corner of the square. Gaps between features might appear to be closed. This effect has not created any problems in this research since the grid size is small compared to the size of the robot and its environment.

7.4.3   Free Cells

A cell is labelled as 'Free' if the robot has passed through the cell or the robot has determined that the cell is free while it was detecting a confirmed feature. These alternatives are discussed in more detail in the following sections.

The Robot's Path

Each movement that the robot makes determines that a band of the environment is free of obstacles. The width of the band is 600 mm (the width of the smallest gap through which ARNE can move). Theoretically, the free region should have round ends. For ease of implementation it has been implemented as a rectangular area extending 300 mm beyond the start-point and end-point of the movement.

The Region Seen to be Free

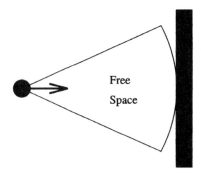

Figure 7.7: A Simple Sector of Free Space

A naïve approach to determining which parts of the environment are free of obstacles would be to assume that each sonar reading defines a sector of free space, centred on the robot, with radius equal to the measured range, direction equal to the direction of the reading, and base angle equal to the effective width of the reading (see Figure 7.7).

The most significant difficulties with this approach arise because of multiple reflections. See, for example, Figure 7.8. In this instance there is actually no feature at the range indicated by the sonar; the range reading is entirely due to multiple reflections. To declare a large sector of the environment to be free would hugely over-estimate the amount of free space. This problem is overcome by selecting which readings to use as a basis for determining free space. Only those readings which have been matched to a confirmed feature are used in this process.

Unfortunately this does not completely solve the problem of multiple reflections. Consider Figure 7.9.

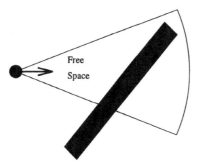

Figure 7.8: Free-Space Sector is Too Long Due to Multiple Reflections

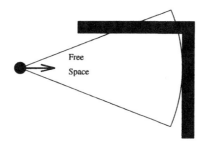

Figure 7.9: Free-Space Sector is Too Wide

In this case the sonar reading *is* caused by a feature in the environment, but it would still be wrong to decide that the entire sector is free space. In particular, the sector extends into and beyond the wall at the top. A strict solution of this problem might be to abandon the idea of a *sector* of free space and to accept that only a *line* is known to be free; the line between the robot and the contact point with the confirmed feature. This does, however, seem to be unnecessarily strict and leads to a very slow growth in knowledge of free space. A compromise solution, and that adopted in this thesis, is to continue to use a sector of free space *but not to extend the sector beyond any other confirmed features* (see Figure 7.10).

This has the effect that some regions will initially be falsely described as free but the number and extent of these errors will decrease as the number of confirmed features increases.

How wide should the sector be? The answer depends on c_{read}, the number of raw sonar returns which have been combined to give the reading. In Section 7.1, c_{read} was used to restrict the angle from which a potential elementary feature could be detected; the lower the value of c_{read}, the greater the angle. In this case c_{read} is used to derive the angular width of the sector. The larger the value of c_{read}, the wider the sector in which no other features have been detected.

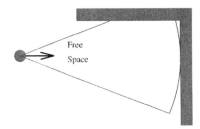

Figure 7.10: Free-Space Sector is Constrained by Other Features

The sector width $w(s, c_{read})$ is given by:

$$w(s, c_{read}) = (c_{read} - 1)s + m \qquad (7.3)$$

where s is the angle between adjacent returns, $18°$ in this implementation, and m is the minimum visibility angle of point and line features. (The minimum width is used to ensure that the sector is free of *all* features.)

7.4.4 Dangerous Cells

The principal use of the free-space map is path-planning. The path-planning algorithm to be employed (described in Chapter 8) treats the robot as a point feature. In order to avoid generating paths which would cause collisions with obstacles (or emergency stops), the features are 'expanded' by an amount equal to the minimum clearance required between the centre of the robot and the obstacles. A minimum clearance of 300 mm was found to be necessary.

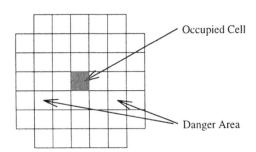

Figure 7.11: The Danger Area Around an Occupied Cell

Each square represents a cell of the free-space map. The pattern of cells shown here approximates a circle around the occupied cell.

Each 'Occupied' cell is examined in turn and all 'Free' cells in a surrounding region are labelled as 'Dangerous'. This region should ideally be circular, but the limited resolution of the grid makes it necessary to approximate a circle with a pattern such as that shown in Figure 7.11.

7.5 Map Construction in Practice

Sections 7.1 to 7.4 have described the map construction techniques used in this thesis. Figure 7.12 shows the graphical user interface that was designed and implemented to show the maps. For many purposes, the most important part of this interface is the confirmed feature map. Figure 7.13 describes this region in more detail.

7.6 Conclusion

This chapter has shown how the sonar readings obtained by ARNE are translated into an environment model. The sonar model from Chapter 6 is used as the starting point for the construction of a feature-based map.

The feature-based map is then in turn translated into a grid-based free-space map which will be used for the path planning in Chapter 8 and the map quality measures in Chapter 10.

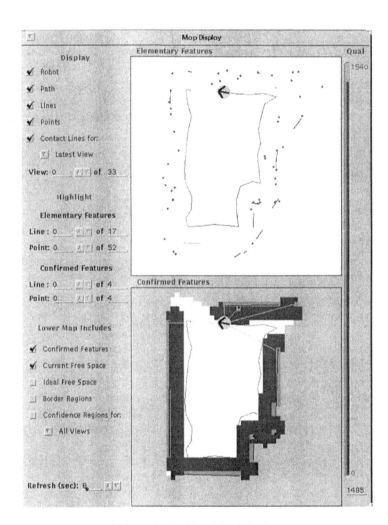

Figure 7.12: The Map Display

An example of a map created by ARNE. The large square windows show the hypothesised elementary features (at the top) and the confirmed features (at the bottom). The buttons and text fields on the left of the display are used to select the contents of the windows and to highlight individual features or viewpoints. The 'thermometer' on the right indicates the quality of the map (as explained in Chapter 10).

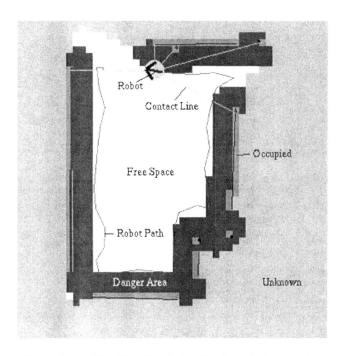

Figure 7.13: The Details of the Confirmed Feature Map
The annotations explain the symbols that are used in this image.

Chapter 8

Path Planning

ARNE's application requires it to follow efficient paths to user-specified delivery points. This chapter describes how these paths are planned.

Path planning serves two purposes in this thesis. First, it is obviously necessary to move during exploration and, although some of these movements (e.g. during wall-following) may be completely reactive and not use the map, others will require ARNE to go to a specified viewpoint while avoiding known obstacles. These movements will need to be planned.

Another, less obvious, need for path planning is in the measurement of map quality. As will be seen in Chapter 10, map quality is measured by predicting how successful ARNE would be at a number of test tasks, given the latest map. Path planning is needed to make this evaluation.

Section 7.4 described the construction of a free-space map from the list of confirmed features. Path planning is based totally on this map.

The planning technique used in this thesis was first presented by Jarvis and Byrne and is described by McKerrow (1991). A 'distance transform' is calculated which indicates, for any given cell in the free-space map, which of the neighbouring cells is closest to the goal. This information can be used repeatedly to generate a list of cells through which the robot can reach the goal.

Section 8.1 gives a brief overview of the technique and Section 8.2 gives the implementation details.

The paths derived from the distance transform are often unnecessarily jerky, giving a zigzag path to the goal. Section 8.3 describes a simple algorithm which was devised to smooth the path by converting it into a smaller number of longer, straight, sections.

8.1   The Basic Idea

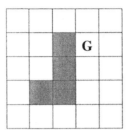

Figure 8.1: An Environment for Path Planning

'G' marks the goal cell. The shaded cells represent an obstacle.

Figure 8.1 gives a simple example of a situation in which path planning is needed. The room contains a single obstacle and the goal position is marked 'G'. (The starting position for the movement is not important when calculating the distance transform. The transform can be used to find a path from *any* starting cell to the goal cell.)

∞	∞	∞	∞	∞
∞	∞		0	∞
∞	∞		∞	∞
∞			∞	∞
∞	∞	∞	∞	∞

Figure 8.2: Initial values for the Distance Transform

Figure 8.2 shows the first stage of the algorithm. All the free cells are assigned a high value (marked '∞') except the cell containing the goal. The goal cell is given a value of zero.

The distance transform assigns each free cell a number which represents the shortest distance from that cell to the goal cell. Consider first the free cells immediately surrounding the goal cell. Some of these are horizontal or vertical neighbours and some are diagonal. To keep the distance values integral, take the distance between horizontal and vertical neighbours to be 10 units and the distance between diagonal neighbours to be 14 (roughly $10\sqrt{2}$). The transform values can then be assigned to the neighbours as shown in Figure 8.3.

One could then continue to assign distance values to the neighbours of the neighbours and so on. The only complication is that the distance transform is required to be the *smallest* distance from a cell to the goal. For example, consider the cell marked with the thick outline in Figure 8.3. What distance value should it be given? It is a distance of 10 units from the cell above it (giving a total distance to the goal of 20 units) and a distance of 14 units

∞	∞	14	10	14
∞	∞		0	10
∞	∞		10	14
∞			∞	∞
∞	∞	∞	∞	∞

Figure 8.3: An intermediate stage in the Distance Transform

Values have been assigned to all cells which border the goal, indicating the distance to the goal. See the text for discussion of the value to be given to the outlined cell.

from the cell diagonally above it (giving a total distance to the goal of 28 units). The cell is assigned the smaller total distance, 20 units. The general rule is that each cell should be assigned a value by calculating, for each of its free neighbours, the sum of the neighbour's transform value and the distance to the neighbour. The smallest such sum is then chosen as the transform value for the cell. Figure 8.4 shows the distance transform calculated by this method for the whole map.

34	24	14	10	14
38	28		0	10
42	38		10	14
52			20	24
54	44	34	30	34

Figure 8.4: The Complete Distance Transform

All cells have been assigned a value which represents the shortest distance to the goal from that cell.

Once the transform is complete, the task of planning a path is simple. Starting at the cell which contains the robot, one simply chooses the neighbouring cell which has the smallest transform value and extends the path into that cell. This process can be repeated from the new cell until the path reaches the goal cell. (Cells from which there is no path to the goal can be easily detected because they keep the high value assigned to them at the start of the algorithm.) Figure 8.5 shows such a path superimposed on the calculated grid. The next section considers the implementation of this algorithm in more detail.

34	24	14	10	14
38	28		0	10
42	38		10	14
52			20	24
54	44	34	30	34

Figure 8.5: Using the Distance Transform to Plan a Path
From each cell, the path goes to the neighbouring cell with the smallest distance value.

8.2 Implementation

The overview of distance transforms presented in Section 8.1 skips over some of the details of the process, the most significant being the need for an iterative calculation procedure. The difficulty arises because of the interdependencies among the transform values; each value can depend upon the values of any of its 8 neighbours. For example, in the transform shown in Figure 8.4, it was impossible to settle on a value for the cells in the bottom left of the room (particularly the value '52') until the transform had spread both clockwise around the bottom of the obstacle and anticlockwise around the top.

The algorithm presented by McKerrow deals with the interdependencies by a form of 'relaxation'; repeated sweeps of the room are made, adjusting incorrect transform values until the entire network of values stabilises and no further changes are needed.

The transform grid is scanned in two different ways. In a 'forward scan', cells are processed in order of increasing column number within increasing row number and changes are determined by examining only those neighbouring cells to the bottom and left (see Figure 8.6). In a 'backward scan', cells are processed in order of decreasing column number within decreasing row number and only cells to the top and right are considered (see Figure 8.7). Forward and backward scans are alternated until no further changes are made.

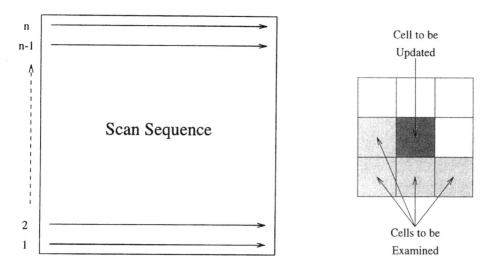

Figure 8.6: A Forward Scan Through the Distance Transform Grid

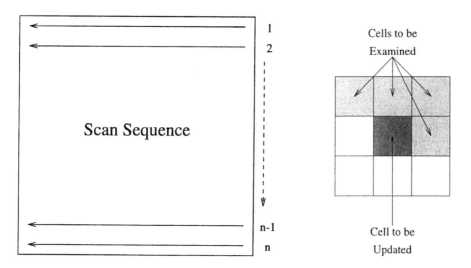

Figure 8.7: A Backward Scan Through the Distance Transform Grid

The full algorithm for generating the transform (McKerrow 1991, page 467) is presented in Figure 8.8.

```
{
 The algorithm acts on two two-dimensional arrays: free-space[][] and
 transform[][]. The subscripts on both run from 0 to x-max and from
 0 to y-max. The elements of free-space[][] are set to 'free' if the
 corresponding map cell is free, blank otherwise. All of the elements
 of transform[][] are set to a large number (x-max * y-max) except the
 goal cell, which is set to 0.
}

REPEAT
  changes = 0;

  {Forward Scan}
  FOR y=0 TO max-y STEP 1 DO
    FOR x=0 TO max-x STEP 1 DO
      IF (free-space[x][y] = 'free')
        FOR {3 neighbours below and 1 to the left} DO
          IF ({neighbour free})
            temp = neighbour value + distance; {distance = 10 or 14}
            IF (temp < transform[x][y])
              transform[x][y] = temp;
              changes = changes + 1;
            END-IF
          END-IF
        END-FOR
      END-IF
    END-FOR
  END-FOR

  {Backward Scan}
  FOR y=max-y TO 0 STEP -1 DO
    FOR x=max-x TO 0 STEP -1 DO
      IF (free-space[x][y] = 'free')
        FOR {3 neighbours above and 1 to the right} DO
          IF ({neighbour free})
            temp = neighbour value + distance; {distance = 10 or 14}
            IF (temp < transform[x][y])
              transform[x][y] = temp;
              changes = changes + 1;
            END-IF
          END-IF
        END-FOR
      END-IF
    END-FOR
  END-FOR
UNTIL (changes = 0)
```

Figure 8.8: The Distance Transform Algorithm

It should perhaps be emphasised at this point that distance transform values are assigned to *free* cells only. This stops a path being planned through any of the dangerous cells described in Section 7.4.4. Since the planned path is actually a trajectory for the *centre* of the robot, this prevents collisions or panic stops.

Once the transform has been calculated for all free cells in the map, the path can be generated as described, with path segments running between centres of cells. The only exceptions occur at the beginning and end of the path. The first path segment starts at the robot's actual position; the last path segment ends at the goal position.

The final complication to be examined is path smoothing. It can be seen from Figure 8.5 that the path resulting from the transform can be unnecessarily jerky. (Why not move directly from 52 to 28?) Path smoothing is the topic of the next section.

8.3   Path Smoothing

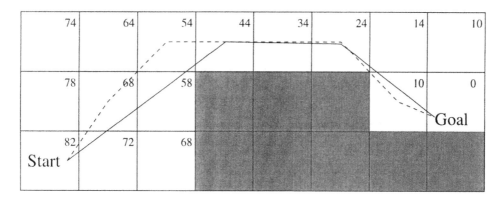

Figure 8.9: Smoothing the Path

The original path (dotted line) is converted to a smoother path with fewer turns (solid line). The number of turns is reduced from four to two.

The paths generated from distance transforms typically consist of a large number of small steps between neighbouring free cells. This section describes an algorithm which was devised to generate a smoother path by grouping these small steps into a smaller number of longer, straight, segments.

In summary, the technique starts at the first cell on the path and examines subsequent cells in turn to see whether that cell can be reached directly from the start cell in a straight movement which stays within free space. A smoothed path segment is then created from the start cell to the furthermost cell which can be reached directly from it. This process is repeated until the target cell is reached. Figure 8.9 gives an example of a jerky path and the resulting smoothed version. The cells are labelled with their distance transform values. In this simple example the number of turns is cut from four to two.

A smoothed path segment may end for one of three reasons:

- The end of the path can be reached directly from the start of the smoothed segment. The path has been completely smoothed.

- The end of the path can be reached directly from the position currently being examined. This segment can then be ended and a new segment created from the current position to the goal, completing the smoothed path. For example, in Figure 8.9, the second smoothed segment is ended (and the third segment created) when the goal comes into view at cell 24.

- The *next* position to be examined can not be reached from the start of the smoothed segment. The current position is the last position which can be reached directly from the start of the smoothed segment. A new segment must be started. For example, cell 34 can not be reached directly from the start of the first segment, making it necessary to end the first segment at cell 44.

To describe the smoothing algorithm precisely, some definitions are needed:

- The original path is represented as an array of locations, path[], with the array subscript running from 0 to max-p.

- The smoothed path is also represented as an array of locations smoothed-path[], with the subscript again running from zero. The maximum subscript value is one of the products of the algorithm. The variable smooth-sub holds the index of the element of smoothed-path which is currently being determined.

- A boolean function, direct-line(), determines whether one location can be reached directly from another while staying in free space throughout.

- The variable seg-start indicates which element of path[] corresponds to the start of the smoothed segment under construction.

- The variable seg-index is added to seg-start to indicate which element of path[] is being considered for inclusion in the current smoothed segment.

- The boolean flag seg-complete indicates whether a reason has yet been found to complete the current smoothed-segment.

With these preliminaries in hand, the smoothing algorithm is presented in Figure 8.10.

8.4   Conclusion

The path planning and smoothing algorithms that have been described in this chapter are used in two distinct ways in this research. The first, and most obvious, use occurs during exploration. Some of the exploration strategies that are implemented and tested in Part III of this thesis use the free-space map to plan paths to interesting areas of the environment. The second use of these algorithms is as part of the map quality metric to be introduced in Chapter 10.

```
smooth-sub = 0;
seg-start = 0;

smoothed-path[smooth-sub] = path[seg-start];

WHILE (smoothed-path[smooth-sub] NOT = path[max-p])
  IF (direct-line(path[seg-start],
      path[max-p])
      )
     smooth-sub = smooth-sub + 1;
     smoothed-path[smooth-sub] = path[max-p]
  ELSE
     seg-complete = FALSE;
     seg-index    = 1;
     WHILE (NOT seg-complete)
       IF (direct-line(path[seg-start + seg-index],
                       path[max-p])
          )
          smooth-sub = smooth-sub + 1;
          smoothed-path[smooth-sub] = path[seg-start + seg-index];
          smooth-sub = smooth-sub + 1;
          smoothed-path[smooth-sub] = path[max-p];
          seg-complete = TRUE;
       ELSE
          IF (NOT direct-line(path[seg-start],
                              path[seg-start + seg-index + 1])
             )
             smooth-sub = smooth-sub + 1;
             smoothed-path[smooth-sub] = path[seg-start + seg-index];
             seg-complete = TRUE;
             seg-start = seg-start + seg-index;
          END-IF
       ELSE
          seg-index = seg-index + 1;
       END-IF
     END-WHILE
  END-IF
END-WHILE
```

Figure 8.10: The Path Smoothing Algorithm

Chapter 9

Localisation

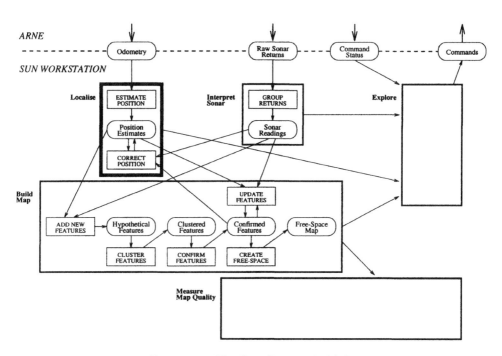

Figure 9.1: The Localisation Module

This chapter describes the design and implementation of a localisation scheme for ARNE. Without such a technique ARNE's estimated position, based only on odometry, would gradually diverge from its true position.

The essence of localisation is to match recent sensory information against prior knowledge of the environment. Some researchers build a 'local' map from the latest sensor readings and then look for the best match between the local map and a global map. The correspondence can then determine the robot's position in the global co-ordinate system. Elfes (1989) does this by seeking the best correlation between local and global probabilistic grids. Crowley

(1989) and Drumheller (1987) both extract line segments from the sensor data and compare the position, orientation and length of the each line with lines in the global model.

The experiments in Chapter 6 showed that it is impossible to determine either the type or position of environmental features from a *single* scan of ARNE's sensor. It is therefore not possible to construct a local map from each viewpoint. Instead, the technique adopted in this thesis is to find immediate correspondences between sensor readings and known features, and to use the range readings to known objects to estimate ARNE's position. Published examples of this approach include Curran (1993), Leonard and Durrant-Whyte (1992), Rencken (1993) and Kleeman (1989). The process of matching ARNE's sensor readings to known objects has already been described in Section 7.3.

The revised estimate of ARNE's position is derived from odometry and multiple range readings to known objects. A Kalman filter has been implemented to generate a position estimate by weighing and combining all of these uncertain pieces of information. (Maybeck (1990) provides a clear and concise introduction to benefits and use of the Kalman filter.) Kalman filters have been widely used for localisation in mobile robotics. (See, for example, Ayache (1990), Cox (1991), Crowley (1989), Hallam (1989), Leonard and Durrant-Whyte (1992), and Kriegman (1990).)

Section 9.1 gives an opening description of the component parts of the localisation system. Each of these components is then described in detail in Sections 9.2 to 9.4.

The presentation of results is delayed until Chapter 13, when the benefits of localisation can be seen in the context of a simple exploration strategy.

9.1   An Outline of the Process

The Kalman filter uses two *models* to characterise the behaviour of the robot. The *plant model* describes the changes in the robot's position in response to the movement commands it receives. It also tracks the uncertainty associated with each position estimate. The plant model is described in Section 9.2.

The *measurement model* uses knowledge of the robot's position and the position of the confirmed environmental features to predict the range readings from the robot's sensors. It also calculates the uncertainty which should be associated with each range reading. The measurement model is described in Section 9.3.

The challenge of localisation is to weigh these two types of uncertainty to get a best estimate of the robot's position. The Extended Kalman Filter is a probabilistic tool which is specifically designed to extract a best estimate from multiple sources of information which are corrupted by Gaussian noise..

The key contribution of the Extended Kalman Filter lies in the way in which the plant and measurement models are combined to derive a best estimate of the robot's actual position. The steps in this process are documented in Section 9.4.

9.2 The Plant Model

ARNE's trajectory is represented as a sequence of *viewpoints*. The *plant model* represents the way in which the properties of one viewpoint are derived from the previous viewpoint and the movements made by the robot.

First, some notation and terminology. The robot's position[1] at viewpoint k is expressed as a *state vector* $\mathbf{x}(k) = [x(k), y(k), \theta(k)]^T$ with respect to a global co-ordinate frame. (The orientation, θ, is measured in the standard mathematical sense with $0°$ being parallel to the positive x-axis, and values increasing anti-clockwise.) Each state vector $\mathbf{x}(k)$ has a degree of uncertainty which is represented as a 3 by 3 covariance matrix $\mathbf{P}(k)$. A more detailed notation, $\mathbf{P}(k+1|k)$ is used to represent the covariance of state vector $\mathbf{x}(k+1)$ given all the sensory information up to and including viewpoint k. (The objective of localisation is then to decrease the uncertainty about $\mathbf{x}(k+1)$ by taking into account the sensory information gathered at viewpoint $k+1$.)

The *control input*, $\mathbf{u}(k)$, represents the movement commands which are acted upon by the robot to take it from viewpoint k to viewpoint $k+1$. In this implementation $\mathbf{u}(k) = [T(k), \Delta\theta(k)]^T$ represents an anti-clockwise rotation through angle $\Delta\theta(k)$ followed by a translation through distance $T(k)$. The *state transition function*, $\mathbf{f}(\mathbf{x}(k), \mathbf{u}(k))$, uses the state vector and control input at one viewpoint to determine the state vector at the next viewpoint.

Using these pieces of notation, the plant model can be expressed as:

$$\mathbf{x}(k+1|k) = \mathbf{f}(\mathbf{x}(k|k), \mathbf{u}(k)) + \mathbf{v}(k) \tag{9.1}$$

The additive term $\mathbf{v}(k)$ represents unpredictable noise. (If this were not present, there would be no need for localisation.) The noise is assumed to be Gaussian with zero mean and covariance $\mathbf{Q}(k)$.

The plant model can be used to determine how the position, and the associated uncertainty, change between viewpoints. The first step is to specify the state transition function. Elementary trigonometry gives:

$$\mathbf{f}(\mathbf{x}(k), \mathbf{u}(k)) = \begin{bmatrix} x(k) + T(k)\cos(\theta(k) + \Delta\theta(k)) \\ y(k) + T(k)\sin(\theta(k) + \Delta\theta(k)) \\ \theta(k) + \Delta\theta(k) \end{bmatrix} \tag{9.2}$$

The noise covariance, $Q(k)$, was modelled on the assumption that there are two independent sources of error, angular and translational. Experience when configuring ARNE showed that the angular error was proportional to the angle turned and that the translational error was independent of the distance travelled. The error variances were modelled on this basis.

Equations 9.1 and 9.2 show how $\mathbf{x}(k+1|k)$ depends upon $\mathbf{x}(k|k)$, $\Delta\theta(k)$ and $T(k)$. Partial differentials of Equation 9.2 with respect to $\Delta\theta(k)$ and $T(k)$ yield the Jacobian, $\nabla\mathbf{f}$, which can be used to translate the uncertainty in $\Delta\theta(k)$ and $T(k)$ into uncertainty in $\mathbf{x}(k+1|k)$.

$$\nabla\mathbf{f}(k) = \begin{bmatrix} -T(k)\sin(\theta(k) + \Delta\theta(k)) & \cos(\theta(k) + \Delta\theta(k)) \\ T(k)\cos(\theta(k) + \Delta\theta(k)) & \sin(\theta(k) + \Delta\theta(k)) \\ 1 & 0 \end{bmatrix} \tag{9.3}$$

---

[1]In this context 'position' is taken to refer to an (x, y) co-ordinate *and* an orientation.

The complete expression for $\mathbf{Q}(k)$ is then:

$$\mathbf{Q}(k) = \nabla \mathbf{f}(k) \begin{bmatrix} \Delta\theta(k)^2 \sigma_{\Delta\theta}^2 & 0 \\ 0 & \sigma_T^2 \end{bmatrix} \nabla \mathbf{f}(k)^T \qquad (9.4)$$

where $\sigma_{\Delta\theta}^2$ and σ_T^2 are system constants to be determined experimentally (see Chapter 13).

$\mathbf{Q}(k)$ measures the uncertainty in $\mathbf{x}(k+1|k)$ due to errors in $T(k)$ and $\Delta\theta(k)$. There is, however, another source of uncertainty. The uncertainty in the position and orientation of viewpoint k, $\mathbf{P}(k|k)$, is carried forward to viewpoint $k+1$. Another Jacobian is needed to determine how the uncertainty is transferred between the viewpoints. The starting point is again Equation 9.2 but this time the partial differentials are with respect to $x(k)$, $y(k)$, and $\theta(k)$. The resulting Jacobian, $\nabla \mathbf{f}'(k)$, is given by:

$$\nabla \mathbf{f}'(k) = \begin{bmatrix} 1 & 0 & -T(k)\sin(\theta(k)+\Delta\theta(k)) \\ 0 & 1 & T(k)\cos(\theta(k)+\Delta\theta(k)) \\ 0 & 0 & 1 \end{bmatrix} \qquad (9.5)$$

Combining the results from Equations 9.4 and 9.5 gives the (pre-localisation) covariance matrix for $\mathbf{x}(k+1|k)$:

$$\mathbf{P}(k+1|k) = \nabla \mathbf{f}'(k)\,\mathbf{P}(k|k)\,\nabla \mathbf{f}'(k)^T + \mathbf{Q}(k) \qquad (9.6)$$

This result shows how the positional uncertainty grows if no localisation system is introduced. (Figure 13.1 gives a graphical illustration of this process.) The next section examines the extent to which ARNE's range sensors can limit the growth of uncertainty.

9.3   The Measurement Model

Section 7.3 described the process which establishes correspondences between sensor readings and map features, taking into account the effective beam width of the readings and the possibilities of occlusion. It also stated that the measured range must 'approximately match' the predicted range. The measurement model makes this criterion explicit by predicting both the measured range and the uncertainty associated with the measurement. The acceptable difference between the predicted and measured ranges is then directly proportional to the measurement uncertainty.

From each viewpoint ARNE can therefore establish correspondences with, and measure the distance to, a number of confirmed features. This information can be used to estimate ARNE's position on the map.

ARNE makes a full sensor scan at each viewpoint. As described in Section 6.3, the raw returns are grouped into *readings*. For the remainder of this section, imagine that ARNE is at viewpoint $k+1$ and attempting to update its estimate of the location of that viewpoint. The readings can be denoted as set $Z(k+1)$ where:

$$Z(k+1) = \{z_j(k+1)|1 \leq j \leq n(k+1)\} \qquad (9.7)$$

Each confirmed feature on the map can be described by a parameter vector p_i. The exact form of p_i differs for point and line features. For points $p_i = (x_{cp}, y_{cp})$ (See Table A.10) and for lines $p_i = (a_{cl}, x_{cl}[1], y_{cl}[1])$ (See Table A.9). The map can then be denoted as set **M** where:

$$\mathbf{M} = \{p_i | 1 \leq i \leq m\} \tag{9.8}$$

For the ith feature there is *measurement function*, $h_i(x(k+1|k), p_i)$, which takes ARNE's position and the position of the feature and predicts the measured range to the feature. For points, the form of the function is:

$$h_i(x(k+1|k), p_i) = \sqrt{(x_{cp} - x(k+1|k))^2 + (y_{cp} - y(k+1|k))^2} \tag{9.9}$$

and for lines:

$$h_i(x(k+1|k), p_i) = \left| (y(k+1|k) - y_{cl}[1]) \cos a_{cl} - (x(k+1|k) - x_{cl}[1]) \sin a_{cl} \right| \tag{9.10}$$

The measurement model then uses these functions to relate a range reading to the geometry of the feature that caused it:

$$z_j(k) = h_i(x(k+1|k), p_i) + w_j(k) \tag{9.11}$$

The term $w_j(k)$ represents measurement noise. It is assumed to be Gaussian with zero mean and variance $r_j(k)$.

The term $w_j(k)$ represents noise in the sensing process which could cause the actual range reading to differ from the prediction. There is another possible source of error: the robot may not be in the exact position indicated on the map. Equation 9.6 expresses the uncertainty in the robot's position. This uncertainty can be translated into measurement uncertainty by the measurement Jacobian $\nabla\mathbf{h}_i$. The Jacobians are derived from Equations 9.9 and 9.10 by partial differentiation with respect to $x(k+1|k)$, $y(k+1|k)$ and $\theta(k+1|k)$. For points:

$$\nabla\mathbf{h}_i = \frac{1}{\sqrt{(x_{cp} - x(k+1|k))^2 + (y_{cp} - y(k+1|k))^2}} \begin{bmatrix} x(k+1|k) - x_{cp} \\ y(k+1|k) - y_{cp} \\ 0 \end{bmatrix} \tag{9.12}$$

For lines the Jacobian is given by:

$$\nabla\mathbf{h}_i = d \begin{bmatrix} -\sin a_{cl} \\ \cos a_{cl} \\ 0 \end{bmatrix} \tag{9.13}$$

where d takes the value of ± 1, depending upon which side of the line the viewpoint lies. To determine d, a vertical is constructed from point $(x(k+1), y(k+1))$, meeting the line at (x_{int}, y_{int}). Then d is selected so that $d \cos a_{cl}$ has the same sign as $(y(k+1) - y_{int})$.

It is now possible to compute the variance in range that would result if the jth reading were due to the ith confirmed feature. The variance, $s_{ij}(k+1)$, includes the uncertainty due to the measurement process *and* the robot's position.

$$s_{ij}(k+1) = \nabla\mathbf{h}_i \mathbf{P}(k+1|k)\nabla\mathbf{h}_i^T + r_j(k+1) \tag{9.14}$$

To decide whether feature i is likely to have caused reading j, the first step is to compute the difference between the predicted range reading to the feature and the actual measured range. This difference is known as the *innovation*, $\nu_{ij}(k+1)$. (For this reason $s_{ij}(k+1)$ is, in general, known as the *innovation covariance*.)

$$\nu_{ij}(k+1) = z_j(k+1) - h_i(\mathbf{x}(k+1|k), \mathbf{p}_i) \tag{9.15}$$

The feature is then accepted as a cause of the reading if:

$$\frac{\nu_{ij}(k+1)^2}{s_{ij}(k+1)} \leq g^2 \tag{9.16}$$

where g indicates the acceptable difference between the measurement and the prediction, expressed as 'a number of standard deviations'. Test 9.16 is known as a *validation gate*. A correspondence is accepted if there is *one and only one* feature to explain a particular reading.

If correspondences are found with two or more confirmed features, the algorithm proceeds to compute a new location estimate. This is the subject of Section 9.4.

9.4   Applying the Extended Kalman Filter

The validation gate test generates a set of readings (from viewpoint $k+1$) which correspond to confirmed features. The localisation process uses all of the matched readings in parallel. The first step is therefore to create composite vectors and matrices which include the properties of all of the matched readings.

The range measurements, $z_j(k+1)$, are simply stacked vertically into a single measurement vector $\mathbf{z}(k+1)$. Similarly the innovation and the measurement Jacobians are stacked to give $\nu(k+1)$ and $\nabla\mathbf{h}$.

The composite measurement noise matrix $\mathbf{R}(k+1)$ is a diagonal matrix with the $r_j(k+1)$ values on the diagonal. The composite innovation covariance matrix, $\mathbf{S}(k+1)$, can then be computed in the same way as Equation 9.14:

$$\mathbf{S}(k+1) = \nabla\mathbf{h}\,\mathbf{P}(k+1|k)\nabla\mathbf{h}^T + \mathbf{R}(k+1) \tag{9.17}$$

The form of the Extended Kalman Filter is:

$$\mathbf{x}(k+1|k+1) = \mathbf{x}(k+1|k) + \mathbf{W}(k+1)\nu(k+1) \tag{9.18}$$

In other words the new position estimate, taking the latest range readings into account, is the position estimate without the range readings *plus* a multiple of the innovation. The term $\mathbf{W}(k+1)$ is known as the *Kalman gain* and can be calculated as follows (Gelb 1974, page 188) :

$$\mathbf{W}(k+1) = \mathbf{P}(k+1|k)\nabla\mathbf{h}^T\mathbf{S}^{-1}(k+1) \tag{9.19}$$

The final step in the localisation process is to determine the variance of the new position estimate. The Kalman gain is used again to give (Gelb 1974, page 188):

$$\mathbf{P}(k+1|k+1) = \mathbf{P}(k+1|k) - \mathbf{W}(k+1)\mathbf{S}(k+1)\mathbf{W}^T(k+1) \tag{9.20}$$

9.5 Conclusion

This chapter has presented the localisation technique which was implemented on ARNE. The Extended Kalman Filter balances the information from the odometry and range sensors to generate an optimal position estimate.

The results of this process, and the setting of the error variances, are discussed in Chapter 13.

Chapter 10

Map Quality Metrics

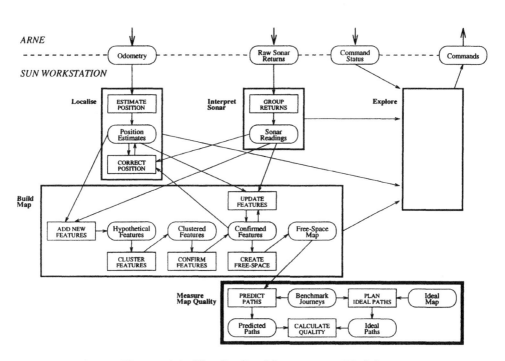

Figure 10.1: The Quality Measurement Module

This research places great emphasis on practical experimentation and quantitative evaluation of the results. To do this it is essential to have a precise measure of map quality. It is then possible to tune the map-building algorithms or to evaluate an exploration strategy by monitoring the quality of the map as exploration progresses. This chapter examines the issue of measuring the quality of a robot's map.

As an introduction, Section 10.1 examines some of the properties which one would expect to find in a useful quality metric, illustrating with examples of quality measures used by other researchers. The properties are that:

1. The metric must be clearly defined.

2. The metric must be multi-valued.

3. The metric must reflect the purpose of the map.

4. The metric must balance coverage and detail.

5. The metric must be applicable *during* the construction of the map.

Section 10.2 discusses the need for an 'omniscient' observer. Is it possible for the robot to determine the quality of its map independently or can quality only be judged by comparison with a perfect map held by an external observer? It concludes that some quality measures can indeed by created by the robot independently but that measures derived from an ideal map are the most useful for the current purpose.

Section 10.3 surveys previous research in map-building, documenting the types of metrics which have been used. No ready-made metric was found which could be used in the current research. It was therefore necessary to construct a novel quality metric. Section 10.4 describes this metric. The idea is to generate a set of tasks which the robot will have to perform and to use the map to *predict* the robot's effectiveness if it were to use its map when executing the task.

Once the metric has been defined, Section 10.5 checks whether the metric fulfills the requirements in Section 10.1.

Section 10.6 summarises the results of this chapter.

10.1   Requirements of a Metric

10.1.1   The Metric Must Be Clearly-Defined

A clearly-defined metric is essential if we are to make objective statements about the quality of maps. This may seem obvious but it is common for published work to use no quality metric whatsoever (Ayache & Faugeras 1990; Crowley 1989; Moravec 1988; Thrun 1993). Images of maps are often presented, leaving the reader to judge their quality by visual inspection. Such an approach is highly subjective since different readers will react differently to the same map. The lack of a quantitative measure also presents problems. Even if all readers agreed about the quality of a particular map, they would only be putting it into a qualitative category ('useless','adequate','wonderful' . . .). It would then be extremely difficult to determine the exact moment at which the map changed from 'useless' to 'adequate'. Without a clear link between exploration events and changes in map quality it will be impossible to evaluate exploration strategies.

10.1.2   The Metric Must Be Multi-Valued

Some researchers have implicitly used metrics with a small number of discrete values. For example, in the the mathematical approach to terrain acquisition (Lumelsky, Mukhopadhyay, & Sun 1991), interest is focused on the computational effort needed to obtain a *perfect* map. In this work the metric is binary: perfect or not. Dudek *et al.* (1991) used a similar all-or-nothing measure for their topological maps.

Alternative exploration strategies will increase the map quality at different rates at different stages of the exploration. With this in mind, we need a multi-valued metric which reflects the gradually increasing quality of the map. When metrics are described in published work, they are usually of this form (e.g. (Cho 1990; Engelson & McDermott 1992)).

10.1.3   The Metric Must Reflect the Purpose of the Map

It is important to be clear about the potential uses of the map; a high-quality map for one purpose may be useless for another purpose.

Leonard and Durrant-Whyte (1992) warn against judging by appearances:

> We feel that the ultimate test of a map is not 'does it look good?' but 'how accurately, adequately, or quickly can X be performed with it?' (X in our case stands for localization, ...).

Elfes (1991) makes a similar point:

> To guide the perceptual activities of a robot, we need metrics to evaluate the robot's world knowledge. The specific metric used depends on the robot task and the particular kind of information required for successful execution of the task.

When these authors talk about 'what' the map will be used for, they are usually mean 'which robotic task' (path planning, obstacle avoidance, ...). To design a meaningful metric, we may also have to consider the eventual application envisaged for the robot (domestic cleaning, security patrol, mail delivery, ...). The research described in this thesis focuses on the production of a map for *path-planning* in a *delivery* application. (The impact of this choice of application was discussed in Section 3.1.)

10.1.4   The Metric Must be Applicable *During* Exploration

One way to evaluate the quality of the map would be to allow the robot to use the map and measure the quality of the robot's performance. This approach would be easy to apply once exploration was complete, but is less useful as a way to measure map quality during exploration. The quality metric is thus required to be a *predictor* of the performance quality which will be obtained by using the map.

10.1.5   The Metric Must Balance Coverage and Detail

Imagine two people who explore a house. The first person moves quickly around the house, checking all the doors in all the rooms. He is soon confident that he has visited all the rooms in the house, that he knows how the rooms are interconnected and that he knows the purpose of each room. Meanwhile the second person is still in the first room. She has examined the room in detail. She knows precisely what furniture is in the room, what colour the carpet and walls are and what books are on the bookshelf.

This example is intended to highlight the difference between *coverage* and *detail*. The first map is 'complete' in the sense that it covers the entire environment but it lacks the detail of the second map. Given that both aspects seem to be important, how should we decide how much weight to attach to each factor in our quality metric?

The extent to which detail is useful in a map is directly linked to the precision with which the robot is required to execute its task. At one extreme one could imagine a robot whose objective is to go to a specified room in a building, without caring precisely where in the room it is. The other extreme could be a robot to perform intricate assembly tasks. Clearly the second task requires a much more detailed world model than the first. A metric should reflect the fact that, beyond the appropriate level for the task in hand, excessive detail becomes worthless.

To be effective, the robot must have a map which covers all of its operational environment. This could vary from a tiny workspace, through a room or building, to a country or even a planet. Once the environment size has been decided, the metric should indicate the fraction of the environment that has been mapped.

In some of the published work on map construction, attention is focused on the accuracy with which the map represents individual features and not on the coverage of the map. Leonard and Durrant-Whyte (1992), for example, list the location errors in points and line segments but do not combine these to give an overall map quality.

10.2   Do We Need an Omniscient Observer?

The quality of a map can be judged in two different ways. In the first approach, an observer examines the robot's map and decides how good a representation it is of the true world. It is assumed that the observer has complete knowledge of the world. In the second approach, the robot has to judge the quality of its own map without the benefit of knowledge about the true state of the world.

The first approach can answer the question 'what fraction of the environment has been covered?'. (With the second approach, the robot can not know how much of the environment remains to be explored until it has explored it all.) The degree of coverage is important when evaluating an exploration strategy. An omniscient observer is therefore essential.

There is, however, useful information which the robot can glean without knowing the true state of the world (Am I still adding to my knowledge of this room? Do I have any ambiguities in my map? Is there sensor information that I've not yet used? ...). For example, a useful measure of the rate at which new information is being added to the map could be obtained by comparing the map at the present moment with the map from an earlier stage. Sharp

(1991, pages 107–108) uses a pixel-by-pixel correlation to compare earlier and later versions of her 'place cell' maps. Another map property which can be measured without reference to an ideal map is 'closure'. When the robot has completely explored its environment, the free space will be a closed region bounded by obstacles (or dangerous areas caused by obstacles). In the earlier stages of exploration, there will be points at which the free space comes into contact with unknown regions. Closure could possibly be used as a criterion for stopping the exploration. (See, for example, Chapter 17.)

A practical use of these two types of information would be for the robot to use its own knowledge to direct its exploration strategies and for an observer to use knowledge of the true state of the world to judge the success of those strategies.

10.3 Quality Metrics used In Previous Research

Section 10.1 gave a number of examples of published work in which the requirements of a quality metric had, or had not, been satisfied. This section provides a more systematic review of published work in map-building, reporting the types of quality metric which have been used and the extent to which each quality metric satisfies the criteria.

Table 10.1 lists a number of representative publications on map-building, indicating whether an explicit quality metric was used and, if so, whether it satisfies each of the criteria.

The most striking observation is that less than half of the publications (10 out of 22) use *any* explicit, objective measure of quality. The judgement of quality is usually left to visual inspection.

Of the 10 publications that *did* specify an explicit metric, only 5 were multi-valued measures which could be applied *during* the construction of the map. The others were either binary-valued or needed a completed map.

The only metrics which were found to satisfy all of the criteria were those proposed by Lim (1992), Cho (1990) and Elfes (1991), all of which used a probabilistic grid representation. Unfortunately these metrics are dependent on the probabilistic approach and are not applicable to the free-space map that was described in Section 7.4. They also suffer from the limitation, which will be described further in Section 10.5.2, that they fail to take into account the geometry of the environment.

In summary, no metric was found which satisfied all of the criteria and was applicable to the type of grid-based free-space map to be used in the current research. It was therefore decided to design and implement a new quality measure. This measure is described in the following section.

Reference	Map Type Metric Type	Explicit[1] Multi[2]	During[3]	Cover[4]
(Ayache & Faugeras 1990)	3D Metric Feature -	No -	-	-
(Borenstein 1991)	Vector Field Histogram Average Run Speed	Yes Yes	No	No
(Bozma & Kuc 1992)	Metric Feature -	No -	-	-
(Cho 1990)	Probability Grid Mean Square Error	Yes Yes	Yes	Yes
(Chung, Choi, & Lee 1992)	Probability Grid -	No -	-	-
(Cox & Leonard 1991)	Multiple Metric Feature -	No -	-	-
(Crowley 1989)	Metric Feature -	No -	-	-
(Dudek *et al.* 1991)	Topological All Nodes and Paths Found	Yes No	No	Yes
(Elfes 1991)	Probability Grid Average Entropy	Yes Yes	Yes	Yes
(Engelson & McDermott 1992)	Metric Topological Rate of Map Correction	Yes Yes	Yes	No
(Iijima, Asaka, & Yuta 1989)	Feature *and* Grid -	No -	-	-
(Leonard & Durrant-Whyte 1992)	Metric Feature Individual Feature Positions	Yes Yes	Yes	No
(Lim & Cho 1992)	Probability Grid Weighted Probability Match	Yes Yes	Yes	Yes
(Moravec 1988)	Probability Grid -	No -	-	-
(Moutarlier & Chatila 1991)	Metric Feature -	No -	-	-
(Nagashima & Yuta 1992)	Metric Feature -	No -	-	-
(Nehmzow, Smithers, & Hallam 1991)	Topological Landmark Recognition	Yes Yes	No	No
(Sankaranarayanan & Masuda 1992)	Full Metric All Obstacles Detected	Yes No	No	Yes
(Sharp 1991)	Neural Net -	No -	-	-
(Shieh & Calvert 1992)	Full Metric All Obstacles Detected	Yes No	No	Yes
(Thrun 1993)	Neural Network Grid -	No -	-	-
(Zelinsky 1992)	Free-space Grid -	No -	-	-

Table 10.1: Quality Metrics in Previous Research

---

[1]Is any explicit quality metric defined?

[2]Is the metric multi-valued?

[3]Is the metric applicable *during* map construction?

[4]Does the metric balance coverage and detail?

10.4   The Measure to Be Used in This Work

The metric implemented in this research is designed to predict the robot's effectiveness if it were to use its map to perform a set of test tasks. In summary, the main steps in deriving the metric are:

1. Using an ideal map of the test environment, generate a set of test journeys for the robot.

2. For each journey, use the robot's map to plan a route between the start and end point of the journey.

3. Examine each route planned by the robot and, using the ideal map, determine how successful the robot would be if it were to execute the plan.

4. Summarise the above results across all the test journeys to give a number of quality metrics for the whole map.

Sections 10.4.1 to 10.4.3 describe these steps in detail and discuss the reasons for design decisions which have been made.

10.4.1   How Are The Test Journeys Selected?

If one knew in advance the exact application for which the robot and map were destined, it would be possible to select a set of test journeys which gave a representative sample of the robot's intended workload. The current research is seeking general results and has therefore not restricted the test application to a predefined set of paths in a single environment. The exploration strategies will be tested in a variety of environments and it is necessary to find a way to generate a set of test routes which provide good coverage of *any* environment.

Each journey is defined by selecting a start and an end point. The chosen method was to superimpose a square grid over the ideal map and to view each grid point as a candidate start or end point. The set of test journeys is then generated by selecting all pairs of grid points such that a journey between those points is possible (according to the ideal map). Note that each journey is made in one direction only. The maximum number of journeys between n points is therefore $n(n-1)/2$.

How should the superimposed grid be determined? Since the free-space map already uses a grid, it was decided to build the test grid on top of the free-space cells. If one could place a test grid point in the middle of each 100 mm map cell, it would be possible to test *all* journeys, using the same granularity as the free-space map. Unfortunately the time necessary to evaluate all of these paths was impractical. Table 10.2 shows the time to determine the quality of a typical map, with a range of grid sizes. A 100 mm grid would require more than 3 minutes for each quality calculation (or nearly 6 hours to plot the quality of an exploration with 100 viewpoints). A grid size of 3 map cells (300 mm) was selected to give a large number of test journeys while keeping the calculation time less than 12 seconds, the time needed for a typical 300 mm movement and sonar scan. With a 300 mm grid, the most complex test

Grid Size (mm)	Calculation Time (sec)
100	206.0
200	13.5
300	4.0
400	2.1
500	0.9

Table 10.2: Quality Calculation Times for Differing Sizes of Path Grid

environment, 'Walls' (see page 214), still includes over 400 test journeys. This was found to be enough to give a fine-grained quality metric.

The ideal map is used to plan a path between each pair of grid points. (See Chapter 8 for details of the path planner.) If both points are in free space and a path between them is possible, then the pair of points are used as a test journey. The time required for the journey is calculated and stored for later comparison with the predicted journey time, according to ARNE's map.

10.4.2   How Are The Paths Evaluated?

Each journey in the test set is specified as a pair of locations. The next step is then, for each journey, to use ARNE's free-space map to plan a path between the locations. But before this can be done, ARNE's map and the ideal map have to be aligned.

Each of ARNE's explorations starts from a predefined position in the room. ARNE is placed by hand at the required position and orientation and a command is sent to the *Mapmaker* to initialise the map with ARNE at that position. The actual physical position is, however, only accurate to within about 5 cm and 5 degrees. Before the test journeys can be planned on ARNE's map, it is necessary to make sure that ARNE's map and the ideal map are using the same co-ordinate system. To do this, the operator examines ARNE's map and establishes correspondences between lines on ARNE's map and lines on the ideal map. Each correspondence is expressed as a pair of numbers (the line number in ARNE's map and the corresponding line number on the ideal map). The *Mapmaker* uses the information about two non-parallel corresponding lines to calculate the translation and rotation that would be necessary to bring ARNE's map into alignment with the ideal map. The translation and rotation are expressed as a starting point for ARNE in the co-ordinate system of the ideal map. Before the quality can be calculated, the Trace file is edited to include the new starting position and orientation.

Once ARNE's map has been aligned correctly with the ideal map, paths can be planned on ARNE's map for each of the test journeys. For each journey, one and only one of the following conditions is true:

- At least one of the end points of the journey is in a cell which is marked as occupied, dangerous, or unknown *or* both end points are free but there is no path between them. The journey is categorised as *impossible*.

- The map indicates that there is a safe path between the two points but, by superimposing the path onto the ideal map it can be shown that the path would actually result in a collision or an emergency stop. If any segment of the smoothed path passes through a cell on the ideal map which is occupied, dangerous, or unknown, the journey is categorised as a *collision*.

- The map indicates that there is a safe path between the two points and the ideal map confirms that it is indeed safe. The journey is then categorised as *safe*.

Counts are kept of the number of journeys which fall into each of the categories.

Totals are also kept of the total time required for all of the safe journeys, according to both the ideal map and ARNE's map. Comparison of these totals gives an indication of the 'efficiency' of the safe paths. If, for example, the safe journeys took substantially longer according to ARNE's map than the ideal map, it would be likely that ARNE's paths included unnecessary diversions to avoid non-existent obstacles.

10.4.3   How Are The Results Summarised And Used?

Which of the measurements described in the previous section should be used to measure map quality? The most obvious interpretation is that the quality of a map corresponds to the number of safe paths which can be planned using that map. This is in fact the measure which is used in the remainder of this thesis. Unless otherwise stated the expression 'map quality' is equivalent to 'percentage of the test journeys which are safe'.

In some contexts, however, other measures may be useful. Again one has to consider the details of the robot's intended application. If the robot is to operate alone, making *all* of the required deliveries, them it is clearly important that it can plan paths for as many journeys as possible. The percentage of safe journeys would then be a key measure.

On the other hand, imagine that the robot is to work in tandem with a human. The human could then make the deliveries that the robot had found to be impossible. In this situation it would make sense to pay attention to the total journey time for the safe journeys. This would indicate whether the robot was finding efficient paths for the deliveries it *was* making.

Similarly, consider an application in which the robot's payload was fragile. (An intelligent wheelchair would fit into this category.) It would then be important that the robot did not have any collisions or sudden stops. It could be preferable for the robot to refuse to try a journey (classing it as *impossible*) instead of trying it and having a collision. In this situation, a high-quality map would be one which led to a small number of collisions.

It seems that the majority of delivery applications would require the robot to operate alone and that occasional panic stops would not be a significant problem. For these reasons the measure of 'percentage of safe journeys' was chosen.

10.5   How Good Is This Metric?

The measure of map quality defined in the previous sections appears to be intuitively reasonable in that a higher quality value means that the robot can do a greater number of useful things with its map. But how well does this metric satisfy the criteria for a quality metric that were listed in Section 10.1? Section 10.5.1 examines the 'safe journeys' metric in the light of these requirements.

The following criticisms can be levelled at the proposed metric:

- Surely this measure is unnecessarily complicated. Since an accurate representation of free-space is essential for a delivery application, why not simply measure the amount of free space that the robot has successfully detected?

- This measure does not deal correctly with false positives; there is no penalty associated with incorrectly believing that a region of space is free. Surely a high quality score would be given to a map which showed all of the environment to be free?

These comments are discussed in Sections 10.5.2 and 10.5.3.

10.5.1   Does This Metric Satisfy Our Criteria?

Section 10.1 listed five requirements of a map quality metric. How well does the 'safe journeys' metric satisfy these requirements?

Firstly, this chapter has described a clearly-defined, precise algorithm by which the map quality can be calculated. The measure is quantitative and objective.

The metric is multi-valued, with the number of test journeys in each test environment varying from 406 to 1540, depending upon the amount of free space. This was found to be enough journeys to measure the gradual increase in map quality during exploration.

The map is intended to be used for path planning in a delivery application. The metric measures the number of such deliveries that the robot would be able to perform successfully if it were to use its map. The metric therefore reflects the purpose of the map precisely.

The metric was explicitly designed to be *predictive*. It predicts the results of using the map to execute a number of journeys. It can therefore be used at any time during the exploration process.

The number of safe journeys detected is always considered as a fraction of the *total* number of safe journeys in the environment. This means that the metric directly measures the coverage of the map. The degree of detail is inversely related to the grid size of the map and the spacing of the test points. The metric is therefore adaptable to any required level of detail.

10.5.2   Why Not Just Measure Free Space?

This appears to be an attractive argument. Why not just count the number of cells which have been correctly identified as free? This would surely give an indication of map quality.

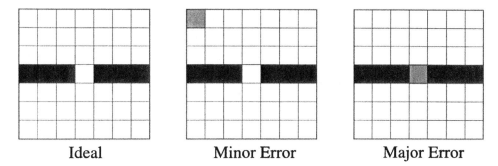

Figure 10.2: The Significance of the Location of a Mapping Error

The figure on the left represents an ideal map of an environment (white cells are free space, black cells are occupied). In the other two figures the map-maker has made a single error, marking a free cell as occupied (grey cell). The error is much more damaging in the map on the right.

Such an approach fails to recognise one fact: *not all cells are equally important.*

For example, consider Figure 10.2 which shows an ideal map of a simple room and two alternative maps of the same room. Both maps have correctly identified 42 out of 43 free cells. The important difference is in the location of the erroneous cell. In the first map the error is in the corner. This error would only be significant if the robot were required to start or finish a journey in that cell. In the second map, the error closes the doorway between the two halves of the room. A robot using this map would be unable to plan any journeys between different halves of the room. This is a much more significant error. The quality metric proposed in this thesis would recognise the difference in quality between the two maps; a simple count of free space would not.

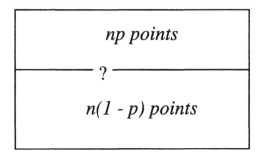

Figure 10.3: The Impact on Quality of Environmental Geometry

This figure represents an environment in which there are, in total, n points from which a test journey could start or end. These points are split between two halves of the room, as shown. What would be the loss of map quality if the doorway (marked '?') were erroneously closed? The result is derived in the text.

To expand upon the previous example, consider Figure 10.3. It shows a room divided into two regions with a doorway between them. The room includes a total of n end-points for test journeys. Of these points, np are in the top region and $n(1-p)$ are in the bottom region ($0 < p < 1$). Consider the loss of map quality that would be caused by the doorway between the regions being incorrectly mapped as closed.

The total number of journeys in the whole room is $n(n-1)/2$, of which $np(n(1-p))$ go *between* the two regions. If the doorway were incorrectly mapped as closed, the loss of quality would therefore be:

$$\frac{2np(n(1-p))}{n(n-1)}$$

For large n, this expression is approximately $2p(1-p)$. The quality loss is therefore at a maximum of 50% when $p = 0.5$. The metric nicely captures the intuition that a closed door would be most significant if it divided the room into equal portions. Again, a simple count of free space would not show this.

The quality metric proposed in this thesis reflects the fact that the importance of a map-making error depends both on the location of the error and the configuration of the environment.

10.5.3   What About False Positives?

The first point to note about false positives is that the 'safe journeys' metric is deliberately designed to take false positives into account *if the error is significant for one or more of the test journeys*. This is exactly the motivation behind taking a path out of the 'safe' category and classing it as a 'collision'. Collisions occur when a cell is falsely classified as free space.

On the other hand, it is true that the 'safe journeys' metric does not take into account false positives which do not affect the planned path for any of the test journeys. If, for example, ARNE had mistakenly 'seen through' a wall and had mapped an unknown area behind the wall as free space, this would not decrease the measured map quality. This can best be explained by again considering the target application. One of the application assumptions made in Section 3.1 was that the robot's target location for any movement will be user-specified and expressed in a co-ordinate frame independent of the robot's position. The user is only going to specify journeys *which the user knows to be possible*. The fact that the robot erroneously believes that some unknown space is free is not going to tempt the user to request a movement into that region.

To clarify this point, consider the opposite extreme. Imagine that the robot were building a map to be used by an autonomous vacuum cleaner. The cleaner's objective would be to move systematically over all free floor space in the environment. It would effectively be choosing its own journeys. In such a situation an area of space which was erroneously thought to be free would be a significant problem. One could imagine the cleaner trying repeatedly to enter the 'free' region, encountering an obstruction every time. This would greatly reduce its operational efficiency. The 'safe journeys' metric would not be applicable in such an application.

One observation made when this question was being outlined in Section 10.5 was 'Surely a high quality score would be given to a map which showed all of the environment to be free?'.

This is an interesting point. In fact, in some environments a completely free map is indeed a high-quality map. If the free space were a solid area with a convex boundary (an empty rectangular room, for example), then the robot's best path to any specified point is to go directly to it. In such a case, a completely free map would be perfect. The more the room deviates from this simple ideal (adding a non-convex boundary, internal obstructions,...) the more value can be derived from a map which marks the obstructions that the robot will encounter. The robot can then avoid collisions.

10.6 Conclusion

This chapter began by considering the properties that one would expect to find in a measure of map quality and examined a range of published work in search of a metric that could be used in this research. Since no suitable metric was found, a novel measure was defined, based on the idea of using the map to *predict* the robot's effectiveness at a set of test tasks. This metric was shown to satisfy the requirements of this research and to correspond closely to an intuitive sense of 'quality'.

The principal use of the metric will be to monitor the quality of maps during the exploration experiments that will be reported in Part III of this thesis. Chapter 13 will show that the metric can also be used to tune the control parameters of the map-making and localisation algorithms.

Part III

Experiments

Chapter 11

Experimental Evaluation

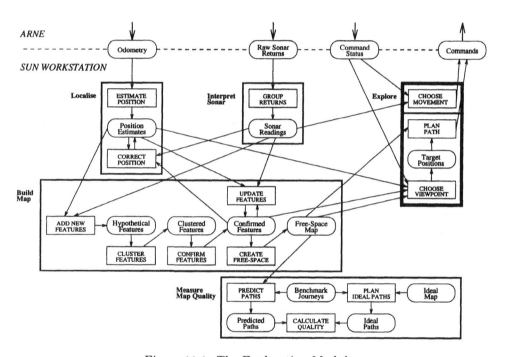

Figure 11.1: The Exploration Modules

Chapters 12 to 17 will examine individual exploration strategies and compare their results. This chapter introduces this part of the thesis by examining some general issues which are important whichever strategy is being tested.

Figure 11.1 shows the possible links between exploration algorithms and the rest of the system software. Two extreme types of exploration are represented on the diagram. The top portion of the 'Explore' box depicts reactive exploration in which the movement commands are based solely on the most recent sonar readings and the result of the previous command. In contrast, the lower portion depicts exploration which is totally map-driven. The experiments described in this part of the thesis investigate the potential benefits of striking a balance between these two extremes.

What would it mean to say that one exploration strategy is better than another? A reasonable interpretation would be that the first strategy produced a higher quality map than the second, for the same cost of exploration. One then has to decide how to measure the 'cost of exploration'. Section 11.1 considers some alternatives and selects 'the total time taken by the robot's movement and sensing actions'.

To make a fair comparison, the strategies must be tested in a variety of circumstances. The effectiveness of a strategy can depend on the environment being explored and on the starting position of the robot within that environment. Each of ARNE's strategies is therefore tested in at least 3 different environments and from 10 starting positions spread throughout each environment. The test environments are described in Appendix B.

Section 11.2 describes the tests of statistical significance which were used to decide whether one strategy was indeed better than another. The tests determine whether, at a specific stage of exploration, the mean quality value from one strategy is significantly higher than the mean quality value from another. Two different types of t-test are used, depending on whether or not the experiments can be put into pairs in which both started from the same position.

The experimental results can best be presented graphically. A graph enables the reader to see how the strategies compare at different stages of exploration. Graphs are used in later chapters to show the variation of quality *and* the significance of the quality differences over time.

11.1   The Choice of Exploration Cost Measure

One exploration strategy can be argued to be better than another if it produces higher quality maps for the same cost (or equal quality maps for less cost). The meaning of 'quality' has been discussed in Chapter 10. This section considers the interpretation of 'cost'.

Three possible meanings of 'cost' can be found in the literature:

- The total distance travelled during exploration.

- The energy expended on movement and sensing actions during exploration.

- The time spent on exploration.

When watching a robot explore, one's attention is focussed on the movements the robot makes. The most obvious signs of inefficient exploration are wasted movements. It is therefore very attractive to compare exploration strategies in terms of the distance that the robot travels. For example, Lumelsky (1989; 1991) devises exploration strategies which minimise the distance that an idealised robot would have to travel to detect all the obstacles in its environment. But the robot has to do more than just move around its environment; it also has to use its sensors. The cost of sensing must therefore be included in an exploration cost measure.

If movements and sensing actions are both to be included in the cost of exploration, it is essential to be able to describe the cost of each type of action in the same way. It would, in general, be of little use to state that one strategy achieved a certain map quality after travelling m metres and making n sensing actions whereas the other strategy required a journey of p metres and q sensing actions. A common currency is needed.

One idea for a common currency is supported by work in the field of animal behaviour. Research into foraging strategies (McFarland 1992) suggests close parallels with robot exploration. In this work, the energy expending during foraging is offset against the energy gained from any food that is found. It would be straightforward to measure the electrical energy consumed as the robot makes a sensing action or moves a given distance. The total energy consumption would then provide a useful cost measure, especially in situations where battery life was the primary constraint on the operating period of the robot.

Energy is not the only cost of foraging considered by biologists. Time can also be critical. Animals may have a limited time period during which conditions are right for foraging (when the risk of attack by predators is low, for example). Similarly, time may be a more important constraint than energy for an exploring robot. Whether or not it is the primary constraint depends on implementation details such as the robot's power supply. If the robot were likely to spend a lot of time recharging batteries, it would make sense to conserve power. If, on the other hand, the robot had a ready source of power (e.g. a supply of pre-charged batteries), then time becomes the key constraint. Time also appears to be a reasonable measure of exploration cost because one would expect that the user of a robot would want to gain benefits from it in its operational environment as soon as possible.

In general there seems to be little to choose between time and energy as exploration cost measures. Both include the cost of movements *and* sensing actions; both are likely to be linear functions of the distance travelled or the angle turned. The choice depends in practice upon implementation details. Time was selected for use in this thesis.

In this thesis, the 'exploration time' includes the time taken by movement and sensing actions only, and explicitly excludes the time taken by the computations to interpret the sensor results and to build the map. The reasons for this exclusion are twofold:

- The computations often proceed in parallel with movement and sensing actions.

- Computation speeds have increased, and will continue to increase, dramatically with advances in computer technology. Computation times are therefore unpredictable. In contrast, the time taken by a ultrasonic rangefinder is limited by physical constants such as the speed of sound.

Experiments derived the following expressions for the time taken by each type of movement.

The time $t_t(\theta)$, in seconds, for a turn of θ degrees is:

$$t_t(\theta) = 1.56 + 0.017\theta$$

The time $t_m(d)$, in seconds, for a straight movement of d millimetres is:

$$t_m(d) = 6.10 + 0.010d$$

Each 360° sonar scan takes 3.1 seconds.

These functions are used to maintain a cumulative exploration cost which is recorded with the map quality at each viewpoint.

11.2   Tests for Statistical Significance

This section describes the statistical tests which are used in this thesis to decide whether one exploration strategy is significantly better than another in a given test environment.

For each strategy, explorations are usually performed from the same set of starting points in each room. The effectiveness of an individual exploration could therefore depend on the the exploration strategy *and* the starting point. (One could easily imagine a particular starting location, maybe tucked away in a cluttered corner of a large environment, which would cause problems for *any* strategy.) These experiments are described statistically as 'paired data' (Ryan, Joiner, & Ryan 1985, page 101), requiring a slightly different statistical treatment from unpaired data.

There are therefore two distinct cases to consider:

Paired Readings Each of the two strategies is tested from the same set of starting points. The results can therefore be taken in pairs, where the members of the pair come from explorations which started at the same place, but with different strategies.

Unpaired Readings Alternatively, it may be that there is no reasonable way to pair the readings. This could occur, for example, if *all* of the explorations began from the same location or if a different set of starting positions were used for each strategy.

The majority of the experiments reported in this thesis fall into the 'Paired Readings' category. 'Unpaired Readings' have arisen occasionally when testing which strategy performs best *from a given starting point*. In this case *all* of the experiments have the same starting point and there is no reason to assume, for example, that the effectiveness of the first exploration with one strategy would be correlated with the first exploration with the other strategy.

In each of these cases, one needs to test whether, at a number of times during the exploration, the mean quality generated by one strategy is significantly higher than the mean quality generated by the other strategy. The statistical technique used in both cases is Student's t-test, although the exact calculations vary between the cases. The details are given in Sections 11.2.1 and 11.2.2.

There is, however, some preliminary processing which is needed before the t-tests can be applied. During each exploration, the quality measurements are taken each time the robot stops and performs a sensor scan. The times at which the measurements are taken therefore differ for each exploration. But the t-tests are designed to compare the mean qualities of the two strategies at the same time during exploration. The results are therefore pre-processed to give the quality values for *all* explorations whenever *any* quality value changes.

11.2.1   Paired Readings

At a given time during exploration[1], the results to be evaluated consist of 2 sets of n quality percentages, $(q_{11}, q_{12}, \ldots, q_{1n})$ and $(q_{21}, q_{22}, \ldots, q_{2n})$, one set for each strategy. For each of the n starting points, q_{1i} and q_{2i} are paired readings.

---

[1]Sections 11.2.1 and 11.2.2 describe the test of significance at a single moment. This test is repeated every time one of the raw quality measurements changes.

The question to be asked is:

> How significant are the differences between the paired values? Specifically, is the mean of the first set of values significantly greater than the mean of the second set?

Following the procedure for paired data described in (Ryan, Joiner, & Ryan 1985, pages 181–184), the Student's t distribution is used to derive a confidence interval for the mean of the difference between the two sets of results.

First calculate the sample differences $(d_1, d_2, d_3, \ldots, d_n)$ where $d_i = (q_{1i} - q_{2i})$ for $i = 1, \ldots, n$.

The sample mean, $\bar{d}$, and variance, s^2, are then:

$$\bar{d} = \sum_{i=1}^{i=n} d_i / n$$

$$s^2 = \frac{\sum_{i=1}^{i=n} (d_i - \bar{d})^2}{n-1}$$

The confidence interval for the difference between the means then runs from $\bar{d} - h$ to $\bar{d} + h$ where:

$$h = t_{\alpha/2}(n-1)\sqrt{s^2/n}$$

where $t_{\alpha/2}(n-1)$ is the t-test statistic with $n-1$ degrees of freedom and the confidence level is $1 - \alpha$.

If the entire confidence interval falls above zero, it can be stated with confidence $1 - \alpha$ that, at the time under test, strategy one is outperforming strategy two. The converse can be stated if the entire interval falls below zero. If zero falls within the confidence interval, no conclusion can be reached at the required level of confidence.

11.2.2 Unpaired Readings

When the results are unpaired, the t-test is again used to derive a confidence interval for the difference between the means, but the variance and degrees of freedom are calculated differently (Ryan, Joiner, & Ryan 1985, pages 185–190).

The starting point is again 2 sets of n quality percentages, $(q_{11}, q_{12}, \ldots, q_{1n})$ and $(q_{21}, q_{22}, \ldots, q_{2n})$, one set for each strategy.

A sample mean, $\bar{q}_i$, and variance, $s_i{}^2$, are calculated for each set of results:

$$\bar{q}_i = \sum_{j=1}^{j=n} q_{ij} / n$$

$$s_i{}^2 = \frac{\displaystyle\sum_{j=1}^{j=n}(q_{ij} - \bar{q}_i)^2}{n - 1}$$

The confidence interval for the difference between the means then runs from $(\bar{q}_1 - \bar{q}_2) - h$ to $(\bar{q}_1 - \bar{q}_2) + h$ where:

$$h = t_{\alpha/2}(d)(\sqrt{s_1{}^2 + s_2{}^2}/\sqrt{n})$$

The degrees of freedom, d, is approximated by the following:

$$d = (n - 1)\frac{(s_1{}^2 + s_2{}^2)^2}{s_1{}^4 + s_2{}^4}$$

As in Section 11.2.1, conclusions can be drawn depending upon whether the confidence interval lies above. lies below. or includes zero.

Chapter 12

Wall-Following

Section 4.1 described the attraction of wall-following as an exploration strategy and gave examples of its use in a number of research projects. It was argued in Section 4.3 that wall-following should be the first strategy to be implemented and tested because it will give an indication of what can be achieved when ARNE acts only on the basis of immediately-available information and does not use the map to guide its exploration. This chapter describes the way in which wall-following was implemented on ARNE and presents the results of some explorations using this strategy.

12.1 Implementation

Wall-following has been implemented in two stages. First, ARNE approaches the nearest object that it can detect and positions itself ready for wall-following proper to start. The bulk of the exploration is then a repetitive process of 'scan,turn,move' actions in which ARNE moves so as to maintain an ideal distance from the nearest detected object. The remainder of this section describes the implementation of these two stages.

The first stage is quite simple. ARNE performs a complete sensor scan and groups the raw returns into readings, as described in Section 6.3. ARNE then selects the smallest range reading and moves so as to be at a standard distance, *IDEAL-WALL-CLEARANCE*, from the object. If the minimum range is greater than *IDEAL-WALL-CLEARANCE*, this means turning in the direction of the minimum reading. Otherwise ARNE turns directly away from the shortest reading. ARNE then moves forward a distance equal to the absolute difference between *IDEAL-WALL-CLEARANCE* and the minimum range. A value of 400 mm was used for *IDEAL-WALL-CLEARANCE* to keep ARNE close to the wall, while exceeding the minimum side clearance (300 mm) by a reasonable safety margin. Once the starting position has been reached, ARNE turns through 90° to place the detected object at the side of the robot. Whether this turn is to the left or right depends upon the rotational sense of the exploration. In the experiments described in this thesis, ARNE moved to the left of the object that was being followed. The 90° turn was therefore to the left if ARNE was initially too far from the detected object, and to the right otherwise.

There is, of course, no guarantee that a single range reading actually corresponds to an environmental object. A false, long, range reading could be caused by multiple reflections

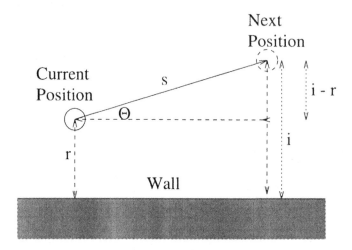

Figure 12.1: The Direction of a Wall-Following Step

The direction of movement, θ, is given by $\theta = \arcsin \frac{i-r}{s}$ where r is the minimum range, i is *IDEAL-WALL-CLEARANCE*, and s is the length of the step.

of the sonar signal. However, selecting the *shortest* range reading decreases the risk that ARNE will move in the direction of a multiple reflection. In all of the experimental tests, ARNE started by approaching a real object.

Once ARNE is positioned correctly, wall-following proper can start. This consists of multiple steps, each of which is designed to move ARNE forward while maintaining an ideal distance from the object that it is following.

At each step ARNE makes a full sonar scan, groups the returns, and selects the shortest range reading. This reading is assumed to correspond to a wall. ARNE then chooses the direction for its next step so that it will end the step at distance *IDEAL-WALL-CLEARANCE* from the wall. Figure 12.1 shows how the direction of movement is calculated.

The step size was set to ARNE's diameter. This choice was motivated by the need to strike a balance between map detail and coverage. A small step could outline objects in detail, but at the expense of exploration time. Conversely, a large step could map the environment rapidly but would miss details. The 'Alcove Test' (page 76) also gives an upper bound on the step size; if the steps were longer than the maximum line segment length, then a wall would not be detected as ARNE moved parallel to it. Equating the step size and the robot diameter is a good compromise.

Elfes (1991, page 86) has suggested that the robot could modify its step size according to the complexity of its environment. He proposes the application of a Fast Fourier Transform to a region of the occupancy grid to determine the complexity of the environment. Such ideas can not be applied to simple wall-following, since the map is explicitly excluded from the navigation decisions. The step size therefore stays constant. (A later strategy (see Chapter 14) includes the possibility of changing the step size.)

In the absence of obstacles, ARNE's step size is always the same. However, situations do arise in which a full-sized step is not possible (when ARNE has followed a wall into a corner, for example). After turning, and before moving forward, ARNE examines the most recent sonar scan to determine the range reading *in the direction in which it is now facing*. ARNE uses this range reading to decide whether a standard-sized step would bring it too close to the object in front of it. If the range reading minus the standard step size is greater than a specified minimum clearance, *MIN-WALL-FOLLOWING-RANGE*, then ARNE can safely make a full-sized step. Otherwise, the step size is decreased so that ARNE ends up at the minimum clearance from the object in front.

It might at first appear more sensible to approach the object in front to the *ideal* distance instead of the *minimum*. If, however, the robot were following a wall into a corner and approached the wall in front to the ideal distance, it would then find itself at approximately the same distance from both walls. It might then become 'stuck', trying to follow the same wall but unable to move forward. Moving a little closer to the wall in front makes that wall the nearest object so that the robot begins to follow that wall and negotiates the corner successfully.

The value of the minimum clearance (350 mm) was the same as the value used by ARNE's collision-avoidance software for obstacles in the direction of travel. This was, in turn, set by experiments to determine a safe clearance, given ARNE's speed of movement and rate of sensing.

The preceding discussion has emphasised the power of this wall-following to negotiate straight walls and concave corners. The strategy also copes well with 'point' features, such as convex edges and small free-standing objects. The effect of the calculation in Figure 12.1 is that ARNE's steps form an approximate arc, centred on the point. Examples of this behaviour will be seen in the results presented in the next section.

The experiments described in this chapter did not use any localisation scheme; ARNE's position estimate was based solely on odometry. (The localisation method described in Chapter 9 is in place for all the experiments described in later chapters.) The validation gate described on page 102 could therefore not be used in these experiments to determine whether a range reading corresponded to a confirmed feature. Instead, a simple threshold was used. The match was accepted if the measured and predicted ranges differed by no more than the 4 cm error associated with a weak sonar return (see Section 6.3).

The wall-following algorithm is summarised in Figure 12.2. The procedure 'make-best-turn' performs the calculation from Figure 12.1 and then executes the turn. Procedure 'make-step' limits the step size if the latest sensor reading indicates that a full step would bring ARNE too close to an obstacle.

```
{
        Wall-Following
}
approach-nearest-object();

step-size = WALL-FOLLOWING-STEP;

sensor-scan();
find-minimum-range();
make-best-turn();

WHILE (NOT {exploration complete})

  make-step(step-size);

  sensor-scan();
  find-minimum-range();
  make-best-turn();

END-WHILE
```

Figure 12.2: The Wall-Following Algorithm

12.2   Experiments

Figure 12.3 shows the confirmed features detected when the wall-following strategy was used in the 'Empty' environment. ARNE moved to a total of 100 viewpoints in the room, making nearly 3 circuits of the room.

The strategy has worked well, guiding ARNE successfully along straight walls and around convex and concave corners.

Given that the navigation is driven by the environment and not by an internal representation, multiple circuits of the room follow approximately the same path in the real world. But the traced path in Figure 12.3 diverges from the first track on subsequent circuits. As the odometry errors accumulate, the estimate of ARNE's position becomes increasingly inaccurate. When the error becomes large enough, range readings no longer appear to match the confirmed objects that caused them. The *Mapmaker* then decides that the readings must have been caused by objects which are not yet on the map. It therefore creates new objects to explain the readings. This effect is clearly visible on Figure 12.3; multiple confirmed lines appear, all of which correspond to a single wall in the real world.

To quantify the performance of wall-following, ARNE was set to explore the 'Empty' environment from the set of 10 starting positions marked on Figure B.1 in Appendix B. Map quality was measured during all 10 explorations. Figure 12.4 shows the mean quality

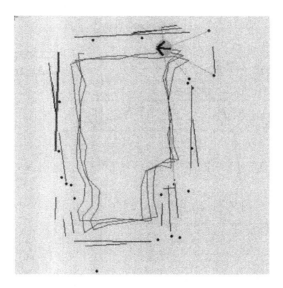

Figure 12.3: Features Detected by Wall-Following (Without Localisation)

Note the apparent variation in the trajectory of repeated circuits and the duplication of walls. These are both caused by inaccurate position estimates.

during these explorations.

The map quality can be seen to change in three distinct phases:

The First Movements For a short period at the start of the exploration (until about 50 seconds), the quality stays close to zero. During this period, ARNE is awaiting confirmation of the first features that it has detected.

Rapid Growth Once features begin to be confirmed, there is a period (from 50 to 600 seconds) of rapid growth in quality. The quality peaks at a value of about 93%.

Deterioration After the map quality has peaked, the effect of odometry errors begins to dominate. From 600 seconds until the end of the exploration period, the quality decreases, ending at about 82%.

Figure 12.4 also shows the standard error of the mean quality. This reaches its peak after about 240 seconds, reflecting differences in exactly when the period of rapid growth occurred. Table 12.1 lists the quality values after 240 seconds of exploration from all 10 starting points. It confirms that there is a wide variation in quality at that time. The explanation can be found by considering the path followed by ARNE during those first 240 seconds. In all cases, the distance travelled is about 4 m. The most rapid quality increase occurs when ARNE is moving along either the left or the right wall and is able to map both side walls simultaneously, thereby discovering large areas of free space. (This does not happen with the top and bottom walls because they are further apart than the maximum sonar range.)

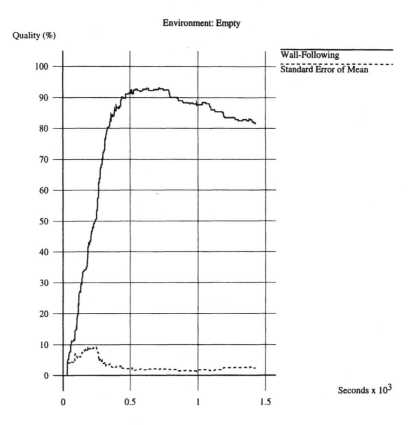

Figure 12.4: Map Quality During Wall-Following (Without Localisation)

Note the decrease in map quality after about 700 seconds as odometry errors accumulate.

Consider, for example, starting point '0'. This achieves a high quality after 240 seconds because ARNE's first movements are down the left wall. In contrast, a low quality is achieved from starting point '2' because the 4 m path keeps ARNE within the narrow region at the bottom of the room. The other results can be explained in a similar way. This confirms the importance of the starting position of an exploration and supports the analysis of the exploration results as 'Paired' data. (See page 124.)

After the peak at 240 seconds, the standard error drops and stays low for the rest of the exploration period, showing that the loss of quality occurs consistently across all of the explorations.

Starting Point	Quality (%)
0	89.5
1	36.4
2	5.0
3	72.3
4	16.4
5	89.5
6	26.4
7	73.2
8	76.4
9	46.3

Table 12.1: The Impact of Starting Position on Quality Values After 240 Seconds of Exploration of the 'Empty' Environment

12.3 Conclusions

These experiments confirmed that wall-following is a simple, reliable, navigation strategy. ARNE tracked the edges of the room well, coping with convex and concave corners. No collisions or panic stops occurred during the 10 explorations.

High-quality maps can be produced reasonably quickly by wall-following. For a fixed step size, the longest line segment can be found if the robot moves parallel to the wall. Wall-following is therefore well-suited to the chosen method of map construction.

These advantages are, however, somewhat masked by the quality degradation due to odometry errors. For this reason, no further experiments were performed without a localisation algorithm. Chapter 13 demonstrates the benefits of localisation and then shows the results of wall-following in other environments.

Chapter 13

The Results of Localisation

Chapter 12 showed the loss of map quality which arises as odometry errors accumulate and ARNE's position estimate becomes increasingly inaccurate. Chapter 9 presented a method by which ARNE can improve its position estimate by measuring the distance to known objects in its environment. The following sections describe the implementation of this localisation method and show the results of experiments to test its effectiveness.

A key component of the localisation method, the plant model, models the growth in positional uncertainty as ARNE moves. The plant model requires parameter values which are specific to the individual robot. Section 13.1 describes experiments to check that the parameters were approximately right for ARNE.

Section 13.2 then repeats the experiments from Chapter 12, but this time with the localisation system in place, and compares the results. The loss of quality in the later stages of exploration is eliminated.

After the benefits of localisation have been demonstrated, Section 13.3 presents the results of wall-following *with* localisation in two other, more complicated, environments. The quality is shown to increase more slowly and to reach a lower maximum value in more cluttered environments. The reasons for this loss of quality are discussed.

The results of wall-following are then used to determine the best value for one of the central parameters of the map construction process, the confirmation threshold. Section 13.4 describes the experimental basis on which this choice is made.

Section 13.5 summarises the results of the chapter.

13.1   Setting the Uncertainty Parameters

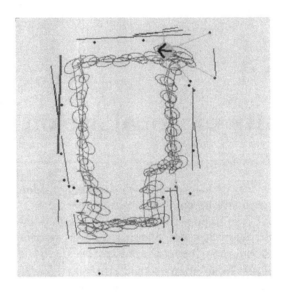

Figure 13.1: Growth of Positional Uncertainty During Wall-Following

Single-σ error ellipses at each viewpoint represent the positional uncertainty, which can be seen to grow on repeated circuits of the room.

The localisation process is controlled by a number of parameters which are specific to the robot implementation. This section describes the values which were chosen as being reasonable for ARNE. The selections were based on intuition and informal experimentation; time constraints have not permitted a thorough experimental search for the ideal values. The selected values do, however, work well and produce the practical results presented in Section 13.2.

Section 9.2 defined a plant model to represent the way in which ARNE's position and orientation change in response to movement commands. An important feature of the plant model is the covariance matrix, $\mathbf{P}(k|k)$, which represents the uncertainty associated with the position and orientation estimates at viewpoint k.

The derivation of $\mathbf{P}(k|k)$ is built on the assumption that each movement introduces additional uncertainty into the position and orientation estimates. In Equation 9.4 this additional uncertainty is defined in terms of two system constants, σ_T^2 and $\sigma_{\Delta\theta}^2$.

The first of these parameters, σ_T^2, represents the variance in the translational component of the movement. Experience while configuring ARNE showed that this error was small and independent of the total distance travelled. It was assigned a standard deviation of 1 mm.

The second parameter, $\sigma_{\Delta\theta}^2$, represents the variance in the rotational component of the movement. This error appeared to be larger for larger turns. The standard deviation of the error was therefore taken to be proportional to the turn angle. A standard deviation of 3° per 360° turn was used in the experiments described below.

These two parameters can be shown to be reasonable by re-examining the exploration presented in Section 12.2. It was observed there that the actual path followed by ARNE on repeated circuits of the room was approximately the same and that the apparent path variation was due totally to odometry error. It would therefore seem reasonable that the uncertainty associated with viewpoints on later circuits should include the possibility that ARNE is actually in the position shown on the first circuit.

Figure 13.1 shows the same results as Figure 12.3 but with single-σ error ellipses superimposed to show the positional uncertainty at each viewpoint. One would expect ARNE's true position to lie within the ellipse approximately 68.3% of the time. It can be seen that the position from the first circuit lies within the error ellipse of most of the later viewpoints. This supports the choice of error parameters.

Two parameters remain to be set. The first, $r(k)$, represents the variance in the sonar range readings. The experimental results in Section 6.3 showed that a weak return could lead to an error of up to 4 cm. (Grouping of adjacent returns eliminates many of the errors caused by weak returns, but errors may still arise with single returns.) The standard deviation was therefore set to 4 cm.

The final parameter is g, the number of standard deviations accepted in the validation gate (Equation 9.16). A appropriate value for this parameter was determined experimentally, using the results of wall-following and localisation in the cluttered environment 'Walls' (to be presented in full in Section 13.3). The sensory data from these explorations was replayed with a range of values of g to determine which value produced the highest map quality. (The most cluttered environment was chosen so that the localisation algorithm would have to use a wide variety of confirmed features.) The results are summarised in Table 13.1. (The reasons for the general low quality values in this environment will be discussed in Section 13.3.1.) The results show very little variation for different values of g, indicating that the choice is not crucial. However, the highest mean quality value occurs when g is 3. This is the value that was used in this research.

g	Mean Quality (%)	Standard Error of Mean (%)
1	48.6	6.5
2	51.6	7.7
3	56.1	7.1
4	47.7	5.0
5	51.9	5.3
6	47.7	4.2
7	50.7	5.9
8	43.0	5.2

Table 13.1: Mean Quality After Exploring the 'Walls' Environment with a Range of Values for the Validation Gate Parameter g

13.2   Experimental Results

To test the localisation algorithm, Trace/Replay mechanism (as described in Section 1.3) was used to re-analyse the exploration results from Chapter 12 with the algorithm in operation. Figure 13.2 shows the result. Comparison with Figure 12.3 shows a much closer agreement about ARNE's position during the repeated circuits. Each wall is now represented as a *single* line segment, with none of the duplication seen in Figure 12.3. The positional uncertainty has also been decreased. The uncertainty ellipses are much smaller and their size remains approximately constant throughout the exploration.

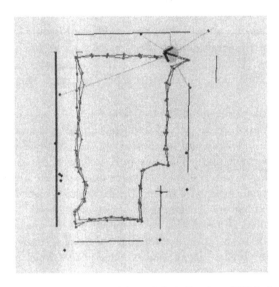

Figure 13.2: Features Detected by Wall-Following (With Localisation)

With the localisation system in operation, repeated circuits are correctly shown to follow similar paths. Comparison with Figure 12.3 shows that the duplication of walls has been eliminated. The positional uncertainty is much less, and shows no sign of growing during multiple circuits of the room.

A quantitative comparison of map quality was obtained by replaying all 10 explorations from Chapter 12. Figure 13.3 compares the quality with and without localisation. The following points should be noted:

1. Little difference can be observed until about 500 seconds. During this period the map quality is growing quickly enough to mask any localisation problems.

2. After about 500 seconds, the rate of quality growth decreases and the benefits of localisation become apparent. The quality reaches a higher peak value (about 95%) with localisation and does not decrease as exploration continues.

3. The 95% confidence interval shows when the difference between the two quality graphs is statistically significant. Until about 800 seconds the confidence interval includes

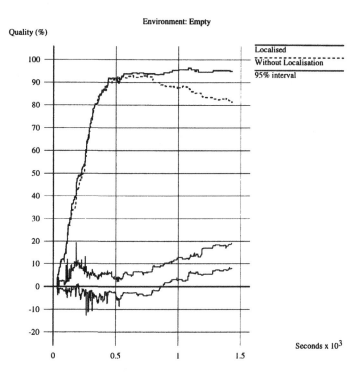

Figure 13.3: The Impact of Localisation on Map Quality

The mean quality for 10 wall-following explorations of the 'Empty' environment, with and without localisation. The characteristic loss of quality due to accumulated odometry errors has been eliminated by the localisation algorithm. The quality is significantly higher from about 800 seconds onwards.

zero (apart from one *very* brief period at about 200 seconds). This means that it is impossible to argue with confidence that either result is better than the other during that period. However, from 800 seconds onwards, the entire confidence interval lies above zero. One can therefore state, with at least 95% confidence, that the localisation results are better.

These results clearly show the value of the localisation technique. The Extended Kalman Filter performs well, despite the fact that its normality requirements may not fit perfectly in this application. For example, the path shown in Figure 13.1 suggests that there is probably a systematic odometry error during turn movements; the path shows a gradual anticlockwise 'twist'. The sonar range measurements are also more likely to be overestimates (due to isolated weak returns) than underestimates. However, despite these deviations from the assumptions of the Kalman Filter model, the localisation method still provides substantial quality improvements in the later stages of exploration.

It is interesting to note how the Extended Kalman Filter handles orientation errors. Orientation errors are a particularly destructive type of odometry error because they can add significant positional errors to subsequent movements. It is therefore important that the localisation method can correct orientation errors. It might seem that the method implemented here is incapable of doing this because the sensor orientation is not used directly in the Kalman Filter. The sensor orientation is used to restrict the matches between readings and confirmed objects but thereafter the filter uses only range information to estimate ARNE's position. However, the orientation can be corrected indirectly because there is a correlation between ARNE's position and its orientation; certain position errors can only have occurred with corresponding orientation errors. A position correction therefore implies an orientation correction.

Since the localisation algorithm has proved to be successful, it will be used in all experiments reported in the remainder of this thesis. The next section completes the set of wall-following explorations by showing the results in more complex environments.

13.3   Wall-Following in More Cluttered Environments

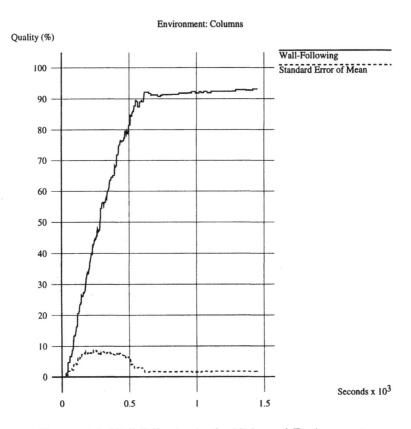

Figure 13.4: Wall-Following in the 'Columns' Environment

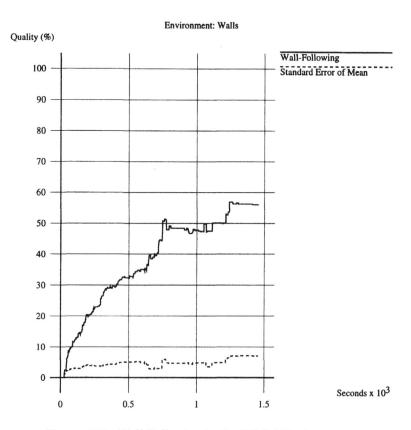

Figure 13.5: Wall-Following in the 'Walls' Environment

Figures 13.4 and 13.5 show the results of wall-following (with localisation) in two other environments, 'Columns' and 'Walls' (see Appendix B for plans of these environments). Each figure shows the mean quality across explorations from 10 different starting positions. In each case, ARNE visited 100 viewpoints.

'Columns' is a slightly more complex environment than 'Empty' in that free-standing objects have been added to the central region of the room. Comparison with the results for 'Empty' (Figure 13.3) shows that:

- The quality grows more slowly. In 'Empty' the quality has reached about 92% after 500 seconds whereas, after the same time, the exploration of 'Columns' has reached a quality of only 80%. Exploration takes longer because of occlusion by the free-standing objects.

- The quality reaches a slightly lower peak value (93% versus 95%).

'Walls' is a much more complex environment than 'Columns' (partitioning walls have been added as well as more free-standing objects). The explorations of 'Walls' demonstrate the above results more strikingly. After 500 seconds the quality has reached only 32% and the peak value is about 56%.

In both 'Empty' and 'Columns' the quality shows very little increase beyond about 750 seconds (50 viewpoints). It was therefore decided to limit subsequent explorations of these environments to 50 viewpoints. In 'Walls' 100 viewpoints were still used.

13.3.1   Map Quality and Environmental Complexity

The results of wall-following in the 'Columns' and 'Walls' environments showed that the map quality peaked at a lower value in more complex environments. This section considers the reasons for this.

Figures 13.6 and 13.7 show typical maps of the 'Empty' and 'Walls' environments. Visually, both maps show a reasonable correspondence to the ideal maps (see Appendix B). However, the metric reveals significant differences in map quality; the 'Empty' environment scores 96% whereas 'Walls' scores only 48%. Similar differences were observed across multiple explorations of these environments; the maps of the more complex 'Walls' environment were typically of lower quality than the maps of the 'Empty' room.

Classification	Empty (%)	Walls (%)
Safe	94.9	56.1
Impossible	4.9	24.0
Collisions	0.2	19.9

Table 13.2: Route Classifications in the 'Empty' and 'Walls' Environment

Table 13.2 shows the classifications of the test routes, averaged across 10 maps of each environment. The fraction of 'Impossible' paths has increased from 4.9% to 24.0% and the fraction of 'Collisions' has increased even more dramatically from 0.2% to 19.9%. As an example of the 'Collision' classification, Figure 13.8 shows all 194 of the collisions which were detected while measuring the quality of the map in Figure 13.7. The grid pattern shows the free space cells, according to the ideal map. Each dotted line is a line segment from a smoothed path which, according to ARNE's map, is an efficient implementation of the test journey. Each line segment shown has strayed into a region which, according to the ideal map, is occupied, dangerous, or unknown, thereby causing ARNE's proposed path to be classified as a 'Collision'.

There are clearly 'hotspots' in which many collisions would occur, the main one being at the top of the vertical wall in the centre of the room. Small errors in the mapped position of such an obstacle can lead to a large number of collisions. The more complex the environment, the more likely such points are to exist, limiting the map quality. The sensitivity of the quality metric to small errors in the mapped position of these hotspots causes a higher variance in map quality in more complex environments.

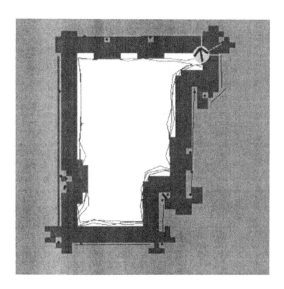

Figure 13.6: An Example Map of the 'Empty' Environment
See Figure 7.13 on page 85 for an annotated example of this type of map.

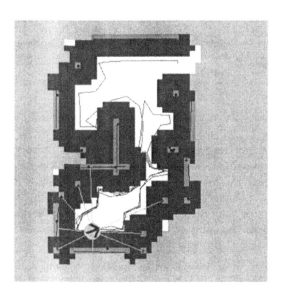

Figure 13.7: An Example Map of the 'Walls' Environment
See Figure 7.13 on page 85 for an annotated example of this type of map.

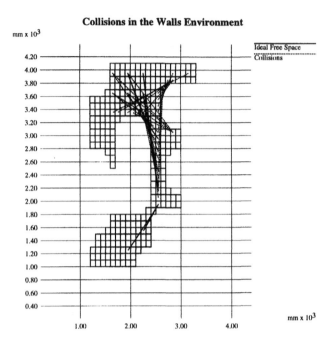

Figure 13.8: Collisions in the 'Walls' Environment

The rectangular grid represents the cells which are free, according to the ideal map. Each dotted line is a path segment which was planned using ARNE's map and which has been classified as a 'Collision' because it goes outside the free space on the ideal map. There are a number of 'hotspots' at which many collisions would occur, most noticeably near the top of the vertical wall in the centre of the room (at about x=2200 mm, y=3300 mm).

The existence of hotspots also explains the sudden increase in map quality that can be seen in Figure 13.5 after about 1200 seconds. By this point, most of the strategies had already reached their peak value, generating the plateau from about 750 seconds onwards. However, two of the explorations, starting from viewpoints 2 and 6, had been making repeated circuits of limited regions of the environment (in the top left and bottom of the environment respectively). Both explorations chanced to escape from these circuits after about 1200 seconds, enabling ARNE to examine the central vertical wall from new viewpoints. These examinations led to a more accurate mapping of the hotspots at the top and bottom of the wall and to a significant increase in quality. v

Section 2.1.2 described the recent growing interest in hybrid architectures which mix reactive and planned behaviours. The examples presented here give support to such an approach. Many of the path segments illustrated in Figure 13.8 could be implemented by, for example, taking the direct route until an obstacle is encountered, then switching to reactive wall-following for a period before continuing along the direct route. Such a hybrid architecture is beyond the scope of the research reported here, but is an interesting topic for further investigation.

13.4 Tuning the Confirmation Threshold

Section 7.2 described the technique of building clusters of observed elementary features. These clusters are promoted to a status of 'confirmed' when they include enough elementary features. It was stated there that the meaning of 'enough' would be determined experimentally once the localisation algorithm had been implemented. This section describes experiments to decide which value to use for this threshold.

The range readings that were obtained by wall-following in the 'Walls' environment were replayed with a number of alternative values for the confirmation threshold. This made it possible to see which threshold gave the highest mean quality at the end of the exploration. The results are presented in Table 13.3.

Confirmation Threshold	Mean Quality (%)	Standard Error of Mean (%)
1	19.5	2.6
2	56.1	7.1
3	44.2	4.4
4	40.7	4.1

Table 13.3: The Variation of Map Quality with Confirmation Threshold

Paired t-tests (as described in Section 11.2.1) were performed between the results for consecutive values of the threshold. These showed firstly that the quality improvement when the threshold changes from 1 to 2 was significant at a confidence level of 99.8%. This gives very strong support to the idea of clustering the elementary features instead of accepting them immediately.

The second t-test showed that the drop in quality when the threshold was increased from 2 to 3 was significant at a confidence level of 94%. Finally, the quality dropped again as the threshold was increased to 4 (although the drop was only significant at a 60% confidence level).

These results indicate that the quality peaks at a threshold value of 2 and decreases as the threshold value is increased. A value of 2 was therefore used in this research.

13.5 Conclusion

The experiments reported in this chapter have clearly shown that higher-quality maps can be produced by using a Kalman filter to improve ARNE's position estimate. This localisation method will be used during all of the exploration experiments to be reported in the remainder of this thesis.

This chapter has also reported the results of using wall-following to explore three test environments. These results will form a 'base case' against which alternative exploration strategies will be compared. The map quality was found to be lower in more complex environments because small mapping errors can lead to significant increases in the number of collisions.

The results of wall-following in a more complex environment were then used to determine the best value for the confirmation threshold.

The next chapter considers some of the limitations of wall-following as an exploration strategy and examines ways in which they can be overcome.

Chapter 14

Supervised Wall-Following

Chapters 12 and 13 showed the results of exploring by wall-following. How, if at all, can that performance be bettered? This chapter begins by describing, in Section 14.1, some circumstances in which wall-following appears to be inefficient and then, in Section 14.2, proposes a new strategy, Supervised Wall-Following, to eliminate these inefficiencies.

Section 14.3 presents the results of experimental tests of Supervised Wall-Following. Its value is shown to be higher in more complex environments.

Section 14.4 summarises the results and suggests some directions in which the algorithm could be developed.

14.1   Shortcomings of Wall-Following

In the wall-following experiments described in the previous two chapters, ARNE was specifically denied access to the map while making navigational decisions. A consequence of this was that a human observer watching the exploration (and looking at the map) would become frustrated by ARNE's inflexibility. In certain circumstances ARNE would make movements which, to the human observer, would simply appear to be 'stupid'. Three of the most obvious circumstances are: falling into traps, re-examining known objects, and repeating fruitless examinations. The remainder of this section considers each of these problems in turn, illustrating with examples.

Figure 14.1 shows a simple example of a wall-following trap. ARNE began at position 6 in room 'Columns', close to one of the free-standing cylinders. It began to circulate around the cylinder and continued to do so for the entire exploration period. This obviously restricted its view of the environment and limited the quality of the map.

In this example ARNE did not escape from the trap. In other cases, the exploration path went around the cylinder several times before small variations in position chanced to bring ARNE nearer to one of the walls than to the cylinder. ARNE then escaped. This symmetry-breaking is a good example of the type of behaviour that can occur with a real-world robot but which might not occur in a simulation.

This is, of course, a very simple example of a trap in that it only involves a single object. A slightly more complicated example can be seen in Figure 14.2. The robot starts by following the lower wall and finds itself caught in an endless alternation between the two walls.

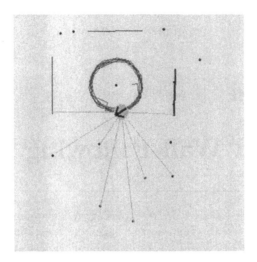

Figure 14.1: A Simple Trap for a Wall-Following Robot

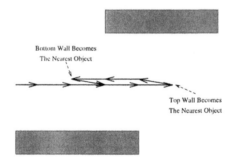

Figure 14.2: A Two-Object Trap for a Wall-Following Robot

As an example of the second type of problem, consider the situation in Figure 14.3. ARNE is part-way through the first circuit of the 'Empty' environment and has detected the long wall on the left and the shorter wall on the far right. ARNE is about to continue the exploration by following the wall on the far right. This sequence of movements is unlikely to extract much new information. It would surely be more effective to focus attention on the regions in which no objects have yet been found.

The third problem is illustrated by Figure 14.4. ARNE is part-way through its second circuit of the room and is about to repeat a sequence of movements which previously failed to gather any information. On the first circuit of the room, no details were obtained about the region in the top right corner of the room. ARNE is about to duplicate those movements and is therefore unlikely to learn anything new.

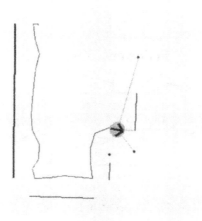

Figure 14.3: ARNE About to Re-Examine a Known Wall

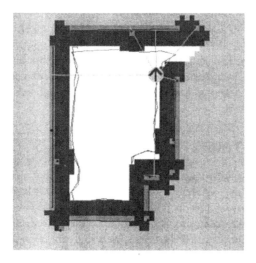

Figure 14.4: ARNE About to Repeat a Fruitless Examination

14.2   Implementation

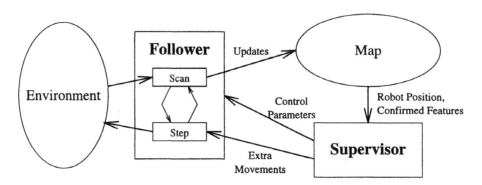

Figure 14.5: The Concept of Supervised Wall-Following

The inefficiency of the above behaviours is apparent to a human observer precisely because he or she has access to the developing map. This suggests the possibility of allowing ARNE to continue to follow the boundaries of objects, but to add a supervisory process which, by examining the map, can detect situations in which wall-following is inefficient. The *Supervisor* can then interrupt the wall-following to make corrective movements or change the parameters which control the wall-following (e.g. step size). This forms the basis of Supervised Wall-Following, as represented in Figure 14.5.

The *Supervisor* described in this thesis is designed to detect and mitigate the problems discussed in Section 14.1. Sections 14.2.1 to 14.2.3 consider each problem in turn, examining how the situation can be detected and what corrective actions can be taken. Section 14.2.4 then summarises the algorithm.

14.2.1   Avoiding Traps

The traps described above are examples of the difficulties that arise when an agent enters a temporal cycle of actions. A recent paper by Mali and Mukerjee (1994) gave a formal characterisation of temporal cycles in purely reactive systems. The paper illustrates with a problem from Connell's can-collecting robot (1990) which attempted to re-collect cans that it had just deposited in the destination area. Mali and Mukerjee discuss the prevalence of such temporal cycles and consider ways in which they can be eliminated. One method, which they call 'stimulus specialisation', requires addition of memory so that the robot can check whether it has recently performed a particular task. A similar approach is adopted in the implementation described in this chapter, in that the map can be used to check for cycles of movements.

Since the map includes a record of ARNE's movements, the exploration path can be divided into 'circuits'. A circuit can be considered to be complete when a movement brings ARNE close to the position from which the circuit started. (In this implementation, a movement was considered to have come 'close' to the starting position if, at any point during the movement, the circle of the robot physically passed over the starting position.) The first circuit was taken to have started after ARNE had made the initial approach to the nearest object.

When a circuit is completed, it might be that ARNE has just circumnavigated a free-standing obstacle and therefore needs to escape from a trap. On the other hand, the circuit might have been around the perimeter of the room, in which case a different action would be appropriate. To distinguish between these two cases, circuits are classified as 'Interior Circuits' or 'Perimeter Circuits'. The algorithm classifies a circuit by monitoring the total angle turned by ARNE during the circuit. If the wall-following is trying to keep the nearest object to ARNE's right (the default case), then a positive (anticlockwise) total turn angle characterises a perimeter circuit and a negative (clockwise) angle characterises an interior circuit.

If an interior circuit is detected, ARNE is in a trap and the *Supervisor* should interrupt with an escape action. The action selected in this implementation was to move ARNE to the nearest end of an unvisited wall, positioned at distance *IDEAL-WALL-CLEARANCE* from the wall. Wall-following can then continue, starting a new circuit. In a large environment with several free-standing obstacles, this strategy would generate a very similar trajectory to Lumelsky's 'Sightseer' strategy (page 43); ARNE would circumnavigate each obstacle in turn, moving on to the nearest unvisited obstacle after completing each circumnavigation.

14.2.2 Skipping Past Known Objects

The matching process described in Section 7.3 attempts to associate a confirmed map feature with each sonar reading. These matches can be used during wall-following to determine whether a confirmed feature is being followed at any moment. It may, of course, be that the feature has just been added during ARNE's current visit. In this case there is no problem and the *Supervisor* does nothing. On the other hand, ARNE may just have begun to follow a feature that was added to the map at an earlier stage of the exploration. In this case the *Supervisor* can intervene to prevent a wasteful duplication of effort. This decision has to be made whenever ARNE begins to follow a new wall.

If ARNE is following a previously confirmed line, then the *Supervisor* can initiate a movement which takes ARNE to the far end of the line and positions it at distance *IDEAL-WALL-CLEARANCE* from the wall. In this implementation, no action is taken if the confirmed object is a point; it is not clear where ARNE should go in such a situation to avoid re-examining the point.

14.2.3 Avoiding Fruitless Examinations

This situation arises when ARNE has already completed one circuit of the environment and is coming back for a second look. In the terminology of Section 14.2.1, the first circuit would be a 'Perimeter Circuit'. If the *Supervisor* detects that one perimeter circuit has been completed and that ARNE is about to embark upon another, it alters the wall-following process by decreasing the step size. This, combined with the process of skipping past known

```
{
        Supervised Wall-Following
}
approach-nearest-object();

circuits = 0;
store-circuit-start-position();
total-turn-angle = 0;

clear-visited-flags();
step-size = WALL-FOLLOWING-STEP;

sensor-scan();
find-minimum-range();
make-best-turn();

WHILE (NOT {exploration complete})
  IF ({latest movement came close to start of circuit}) {Circuit Complete}
    IF (circuits = 0 AND total-turn-angle > 0)
        circuits = circuits + 1;                      {}
        step-size = DETAIL-WALL-FOLLOWING-STEP;        {}
        IF ({visiting confirmed line})                 {First}
           leap-to-line-end();                         {Perimeter}
        ELSE                                           {Circuit}
           make-step(step-size);                       {}
        END-IF                                         {}
    ELSE
        circuits = 0;                                  {Interior Circuit}
        step-size = WALL-FOLLOWING-STEP;               {or Second}
        go-to-nearest-unvisited-line();                {Perimeter Circuit}
    END-IF
    store-circuit-start-position();                    {Start New Circuit}
    total-turn-angle = 0;                              {}
  ELSE-IF (visiting confirmed line)
    leap-to-line-end();                                {Skip Confirmed Line}
  ELSE
    make-step(step-size);                              {Normal Step}
  END-IF

  update-visited-flag();                               {Flag Current Object}
  update-total-turn-angle();

  sensor-scan();                                       {}
  find-minimum-range();                                {Prepare Next Move}
  make-best-turn();                                    {}

END-WHILE
```

Figure 14.6: The Supervised Wall-Following Algorithm

objects, ensures that ARNE will focus attention on the unknown regions of the perimeter on the next circuit.

An outcome of the processes of feature extraction and clustering (as described in Chapter 7) is that a feature must be detected at least three times before it can become confirmed. With this in mind, the step size for the detailed examination was taken to be one third of the original value.

Once ARNE has completed a second perimeter circuit, the *Supervisor* adds a movement to the nearest end of an unvisited line (as in Section 14.2.1). This is useful when ARNE has failed to pass through a small gap and has passed twice around the perimeter of *part* of the environment. (This situation arises in the 'Walls' environment.) Exploration terminates if there are no unvisited lines left.

14.2.4 The Algorithm

The Supervised Wall-Following algorithm is summarised in Figure 14.6. For ease of implementation, the algorithm is implemented as a single physical process instead of the two suggested by Figure 14.5. Comparison with Figure 12.2 shows that the essential loop structure of the wall-following algorithm has not changed. Instead, a collection of supervisory tests have been inserted before each movement, giving the *Supervisor* the opportunity to execute a corrective action before wall-following continues.

14.3 Experiments

This section reports the results of Supervised Wall-Following in different test environments.

The first experiments were performed in the 'Empty' room. Figure 14.7 shows the results. As usual, explorations were initiated from 10 starting positions and the average map quality was plotted over time. The quality values alone would suggest that Supervised Wall-Following performs slightly better than simple wall-following. However, the 95% interval includes zero throughout the entire exploration period, making it impossible to argue with confidence that either strategy is better.

The results from the 'Columns' environment (Figure 14.8) were very similar. The quality graphs show a preference for Supervised Wall-Following throughout most of the exploration period, but the difference is not enough to be significant.

The results from the 'Walls' environment (Figure 14.9) present a much stronger case for Supervised Wall-Following. The mean quality values are comparable for the first 200 seconds but thereafter they diverge widely for the remainder of the exploration. The confidence interval shows that Supervised Wall-Following is significantly better than simple wall-following from about 250 seconds to 1200 seconds. The increase in the variance among the wall-following results at about 1200 seconds (as described on page 144) makes it impossible to be confident about comparisons in the last seconds of the exploration.

Supervised Wall-Following clearly performed better in the 'Walls' environment than in 'Empty' or 'Columns'. It is interesting to consider why this might be.

One might at first have expected that the 'trap-avoidance' feature would have shown benefits in 'Columns'. However, two factors have decreased its impact. First, notice that

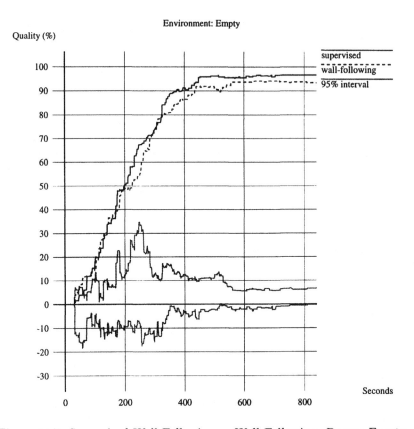

Figure 14.7: Supervised Wall-Following vs Wall-Following. Room: Empty.

only 4 of the 10 starting points (3,4,6 and 7) are likely to trap ARNE. Second, experience showed that ARNE often escaped when started from the two lower positions because the steps around the obstacle sometimes brought ARNE close enough to one of the walls. The impact of the traps was therefore greatly diluted by the other explorations which avoided traps.

'Empty' and 'Columns' are both very open environments with very little occlusion. The walls and obstacles are easy to see and so the map quality grows quickly. One consequence of this is that ARNE can see most of the environment even when caught in a trap. Another is that the quality has already reached a high value before the *Supervisor* begins to take effect. Very little benefit can then be derived from the *Supervisor*.

In contrast, 'Walls' is a much less open environment with considerable occlusion. The quality grows more slowly, leaving time for the *Supervisor* to make an impact. Although there are no free-standing traps in the environment, ARNE did sometimes fail to detect the gaps during wall-following, with the result that it would be caught in the type of 'Perimeter Trap' introduced in Section 14.2.3. The *Supervisor* can escape from these traps.

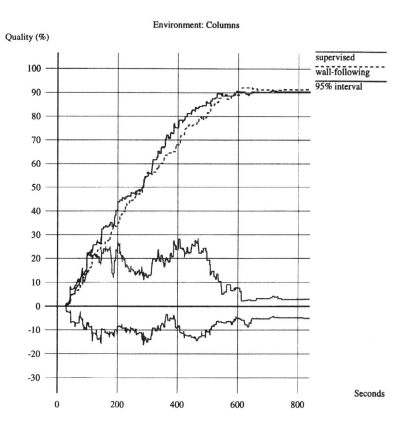

Figure 14.8: Supervised Wall-Following vs Wall-Following. Room: Columns.

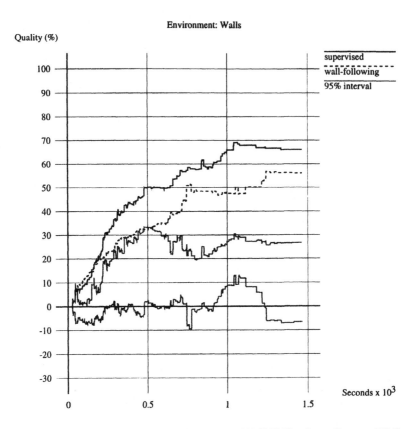

Figure 14.9: Supervised Wall-Following vs Wall-Following. Room: Walls.

Figure 14.10: Supervised Wall-Following vs Wall-Following. Room: Trap.

The significance of traps is clearly related to the size of the environments. The environments used in this thesis were constrained to be fairly small and the damage caused by traps was consequently limited. At the other extreme one could imagine a robot getting trapped by a waste bin when it was supposed to be exploring an entire floor of an office building. The effect of falling into such a trap would be huge.

The 'Trap' environment was specifically designed to illustrate a more significant trap than the ones in 'Columns'; the obstacle and the wall were deliberately positioned so that a trapped robot would have a more restricted view. All 10 explorations began from the same location so that they would all fall into the trap. The results are presented in Figure 14.10[1]. There is no significant difference in mean quality until about 200 seconds, but thereafter the mean quality by wall-following increases only slowly whereas the mean quality from Supervised Wall-Following increases very significantly faster. After 200 seconds the supervised ARNE has escaped from the trap.

---

[1]Note that this is a situation in which an 'unpaired' comparison is more appropriate (see page 125).

14.4 Conclusions

Supervised Wall-Following has been shown to be a significant improvement over simple wall-following in an environment which contains traps or in which there is considerable occlusion.

The algorithm described above has been designed to overcome some of the more obvious inefficiences of wall-following. Further experimental analysis of wall-following may reveal additional undesirable behaviours which can be recognised and eliminated within the framework of Supervised Wall-Following.

A shortcoming of the current implementation was observed during experimentation. Although the trap-detection algorithm described above successfully detects 'simple' traps, such as that illustrated in Figure 14.1, it does not reliably detect more complex traps which occasionally arise mid-way through a circuit. A later version could perhaps remove this restriction with a more thorough 'loop detection' algorithm.

The experiments in this chapter showed that Supervised Wall-Following was not significantly better than basic wall-following in the simple environment 'Empty'. This raised the question of whether these two sets of results are approximately the best that can be achieved in that environment or whether there is still room for improvement. The next chapter describes experiments with human-guided exploration which attempt to answer this question.

Chapter 15

Can a Human Do Any Better?

15.1 Motivation

This chapter describes a brief digression from autonomous exploration into human-guided exploration. The results in Chapter 14 showed Supervised Wall-Following to be an effective exploration strategy in environments with occlusion and traps. It was not, however, significantly better than simple wall-following in the 'Empty' environment. This raised the question:

> Is it possible to improve the exploration performance in the 'Empty' environment or is Supervised Wall-Following generating the best possible results, given the physical robot and its sensors?

To answer this question, experiments were performed to see whether a human operator, guided only by the developing map, could direct ARNE's movements so as to produce better results than Supervised Wall-Following. Similar experiments were performed in the more complicated 'Walls' environment.

15.2 Procedure

The exploration software includes an X-Windows interface which enables an operator to send commands ('move forward', 'turn left', 'turn right', and 'scan') directly to ARNE. This interface was used in the experiments described in this section. The interface also has the facility for the user to indicate, using the mouse, a position on the map to which ARNE should move. The system then plans and executes such a path. This facility was used for the longer movements between regions of interest.

Consideration was given to the choice of operator for these experiments. It was felt that a volunteer would have no experience of the way in which ARNE senses the world and builds the map and would therefore be unable to explore efficiently. Since the object of the experiments was to get an approximate idea of the best performance that could be expected, it was important that the operator fully understand the operation of the robot. The author therefore took the job.

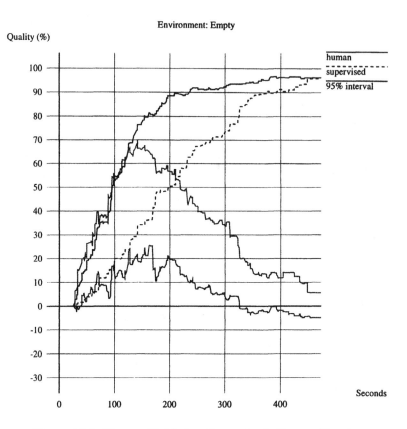

Figure 15.1: Human-Guided vs Supervised. Room: Empty.

As with previous experiments, 10 starting points were used in each environment. Each exploration consisted of at most 50 viewpoints. After each movement and sensor scan the operator examined the current map to choose the next viewpoint.

15.3 Experiments

Figure 15.1 compares the mean results of human-guided exploration and Supervised Wall-Following in the 'Empty' environment. Two observations can be made:

- The human-guided exploration performs significantly better than Supervised Wall-Following for about the first 300 seconds. There is clearly scope to improve the effectiveness of the early stages of autonomous exploration.

- The human-guided exploration reaches a peak quality of 96% after about 380 seconds. Supervised Wall-Following catches up with this quality value at about 450 seconds. The two strategies achieve the same maximum quality.

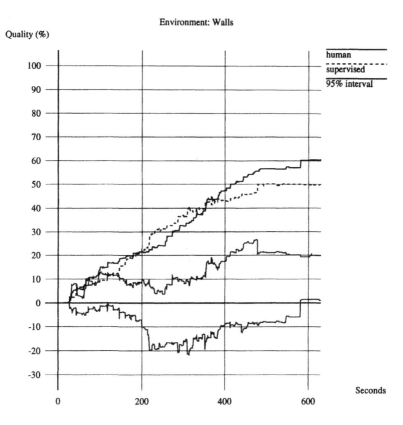

Figure 15.2: Human-Guided vs Supervised. Room: Walls.

Figure 15.2 shows the same comparison, but in the 'Walls' environment. No significant difference between the strategies appears until before 600 seconds. Supervised Wall-Following appears to be a difficult strategy to beat in the early stages of the exploration of a cluttered environment.

It is not possible to tell from these results whether human-guided exploration might have peaked at a higher quality than Supervised Wall-Following. In this environment, Supervised Wall-Following reaches a maximum quality of nearly 70% after about 1100 seconds (Figure 14.9). The human-guided experiments, being labour-intensive, were limited to 50 viewpoints (about 600 seconds), by which point the mean quality had not exceeded 60%.

15.4   Conclusions

These experiments show that it is possible to obtain better exploration results than those generated by Supervised Wall-Following. Supervised Wall-Following has clearly not reached the limit of ARNE's information-gathering rate. It is unlikely, however, that ARNE will be able to achieve results as good as those of a human operator. First, a human can use visual skills to extrapolate from the information on the map to the likely geometry of the environment, a difficult task for a computer. Second, the human operator is not in practice working exclusively from the map; his decisions are influenced to some extent by knowledge of the true shape of the environment[1].

Even if one does not expect an autonomous exploration strategy to match the performance of the human operator, it is still useful to see whether any lessons can be learned from the human-guided exploration. Examination of the exploration paths reveals the following:

- A useful technique is to direct ARNE through the middle of regions which are likely to be free space. In particular, if the map suggests two normal walls which meet at a corner, a path away from the corner, diagonal to both walls is a good idea. Such a path enables ARNE to 'triangulate' effectively on both of the walls.

- Standard, ARNE-diameter, steps are generally effective when gathering information about unknown regions. Longer steps can be used when passing though a known region to get to the next region of interest.

- The interesting regions of the map are those in which the free space 'leaks' into the unknown region. A complete map would contain a contiguous region of free space, bordered only by the dangerous regions around obstacles. If free space is bordering on the unknown area, this ideal has not yet been achieved and the border region should therefore be investigated.

These insights have been used as the basis for the strategies to be described in Chapters 16 and 17.

---

[1]This is a point in favour of using a number of inexperienced volunteers, who could perform the explorations remotely, without having seen the test environment. This advantage was, however, outweighed by the need to understand ARNE's operation.

Chapter 16

Longest Lines of Sight

16.1 Motivation

Experience with human control of the exploration process suggested that map quality could be increased rapidly in the early stages of exploration by heading into open regions of space instead of staying close to one of the walls (Section 15.4). The 'Longest Lines' strategy described in this chapter was motivated by this observation. The essential idea is to perform a full sensor scan and head in the direction of the longest reading. As many steps as possible are then taken in that direction until an obstacle is encountered. The algorithm then continues by heading in the direction of the longest reading from this new position.

This strategy shares with wall-following the fact that it is totally reactive. Navigational decisions are made solely on the basis of the latest sensor readings.

Section 16.2 gives the details of the implementation and Section 16.3 compares the results to those of Wall-Following and Supervised Wall-Following. Section 16.4 summarises the experimental results and considers the strengths and weaknesses of the strategy.

16.2 Implementation

The strategy, as described in the previous section, is straightforward. The only slight complication is the problem of multiple reflections. Wall-following used the shortest range readings from each viewpoint; multiple reflections were not a problem because they typically cause long range readings. On the other hand, the 'Longest Lines' strategy is particularly interested in the long readings. It is therefore necessary to acknowledge the likelihood of multiple reflections and to compensate for them.

The approach adopted here is to try each range reading in turn, working down from the longest, until a direction is found in which ARNE can safely move. ARNE's on-board controller will not allow a movement to begin if objects are detected which are too close either in front or to the side. If objects are preventing the movement, a status code is returned to indicate this. The strategy is therefore to turn in the direction of the longest reading and to attempt to move forward. If the 'blocked' status is received and ARNE has been unable to move at all, the next longest reading is tried and so on until a safe direction is found.

```
{
        Following the longest lines
}
step-size = WALL-FOLLOWING-STEP;

sensor-scan();

WHILE (NOT {exploration complete})

  DO
    turn-to-face({longest untried reading});
    flag-direction-as-tried();
    move-status = move-forward(step-size);
    sensor-scan();
  WHILE (move-status NOT = 'successful' AND
         current-position = previous-position)
  END-DO

  WHILE (move-status = 'successful' AND
         NOT {object too close in front}
        )
      move-status = move-forward(step-size);
      sensor-scan();
  END-WHILE

END-WHILE
```

Figure 16.1: The 'Longest Lines' Algorithm

ARNE moves in the safe direction in standard steps equal to ARNE's diameter (300 mm) until an emergency stop occurs or *one more step* would bring ARNE within a diameter of the object in front. A full 360° sensor scan is performed after each step.

The algorithm is summarised in Figure 16.1.

16.3   Experiments

The strategy was tested in the 'Empty', 'Columns' and 'Walls' environments from 10 starting positions in each room. The explorations were limited to 50 viewpoints in the first two environments and 100 viewpoints in the last environment.

The first comparisons to be made are between this strategy and its reactive partner, Wall-Following. The comparisons are made in Figures 16.2, 16.3 and 16.4. In the 'Empty' environment the new strategy performs significantly better than Wall-Following in the early part of the exploration, between about 80 and 250 seconds. Thereafter 'Longest Lines' loses its advantage and the final map qualities are practically identical.

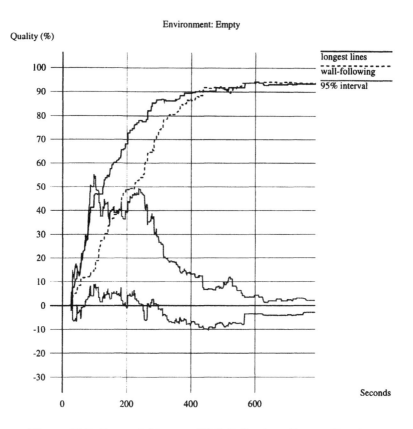

Figure 16.2: Longest Lines vs Wall-Following. Room: Empty.

In the 'Columns' environment the new strategy starts well again, outperforming Wall-Following between about 150 and 350 seconds. After this, Wall-Following comes back into its own and the exploration ends with the quality due to Wall-Following steadily higher than that from 'Longest Lines' (although the final difference is not quite enough for 95% confidence).

The 'Walls' environment shows a similar result to 'Columns', although the differences are not enough for 95% confidence.

The other comparison which should be made here is between the 'Longest Lines' strategy and Supervised Wall-Following. The results of this comparison are shown in Figures 16.5, 16.6 and 16.7.

The same general shape can be seen in all three environments. 'Longest Lines' starts by producing higher quality maps than Supervised Wall-Following, but the situation is reversed in the later stages. The benefit of Supervised Wall-Following is most noticeable in the 'Walls' environment.

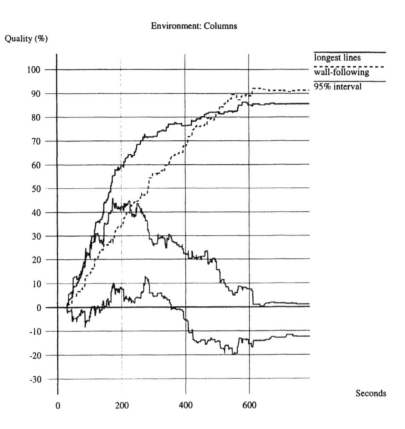

Figure 16.3: Longest Lines vs Wall-Following. Room: Columns.

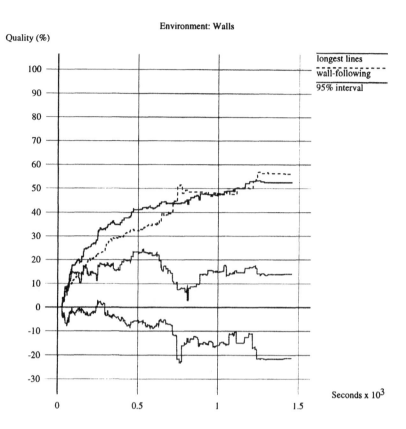

Figure 16.4: Longest Lines vs Wall-Following. Room: Walls.

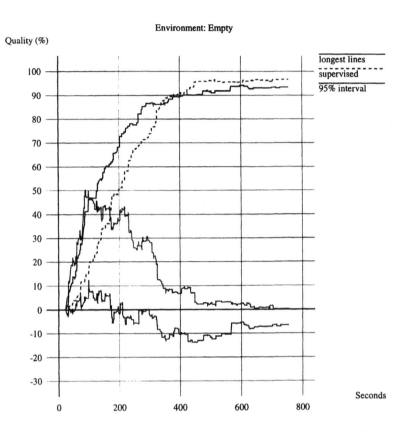

Figure 16.5: Longest Lines vs Supervised Wall-Following. Room: Empty.

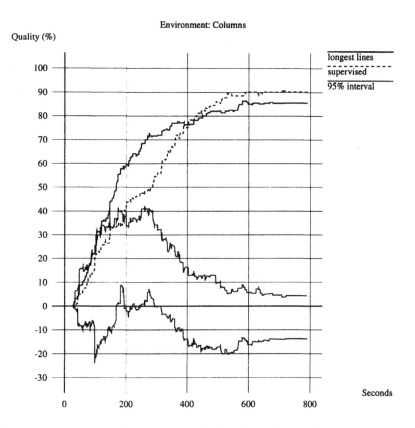

Figure 16.6: Longest Lines vs Supervised Wall-Following. Room: Columns.

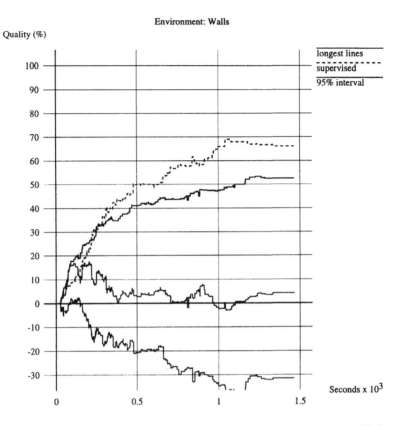

Figure 16.7: Longest Lines vs Supervised Wall-Following. Room: Walls.

16.4 Conclusions

The intuition gained in Chapter 15 does indeed seem to be valid; 'Longest Lines' is an effective strategy in the early stages of exploration.

It is perhaps not surprising that 'Longest Lines' becomes less effective as the exploration goes on. Supervised Wall-Following is designed to move ARNE systematically throughout the whole environment. (This is usually also true for Wall-Following although there is the danger of traps.) In contrast, 'Longest Lines' does not explicitly direct ARNE to all regions of the environment. In several of the test explorations, ARNE repeated a sequence of movements back and forth between the same viewpoints, effectively trapped in a small part of the environment.

The more cluttered the environment, the greater the danger of the 'Longest Lines' strategy becoming trapped and examining only a fraction of the environment. In the experiments reported here, 'Longest Lines' was at its most effective in the 'Empty' room and at its least effective in 'Walls'. One could easily contrive situations in which 'Longest Lines' would be extremely ineffective. Consider the task of exploring an office area with many rooms. If the robot were to start in a large, empty room with a doorway leading into a narrow corridor, the longest readings would always be within the room. The robot would never leave the first room. This is another example of a reactive strategy being trapped into an ineffective cycle of actions because of its lack of persistent state.

The next chapter examines whether better results can be obtained by applying the other insight from Chapter 15 and focusing on the open boundaries of free space.

Chapter 17

Free Space Boundaries

17.1   Motivation

The exploration strategies presented so far in Part III of this thesis have differed in the extent to which the map has been used to control the navigational choices. Wall-Following (Chapter 12) and Longest Lines (Chapter 16) were both totally reactive, not using the map at all. Supervised Wall-Following (Chapter 14) used the map to detect circumstances in which wall-following was becoming ineffective. Chapter 15 showed the results that could be obtained when a human operator used the map to guide the exploration. This chapter will present an exploration strategy in which ARNE's decisions are driven primarily by the information present in the partially-formed map.

The implementation described in Section 17.2 builds on the ideas presented in Section 4.2; ARNE approaches the interesting regions of the environment. The central issue is, of course, the definition of 'interesting'. The definition adopted here focuses on the edges of free space, the regions in which free cells are next to unknown cells.

Section 17.3 presents the results of experiments to evaluate this strategy and Section 17.4 summarises the results.

17.2   Implementation

The first step in this implementation was to identify the cells on the free-space map which were to be examined. The decision was made that ARNE should *approach* unknown regions but, to avoid collisions or panic stops, it should not actually *enter* unknown regions. The interesting cells are therefore those on the boundary between free and unknown space.

The *Mapmaker* was modified to add another status, 'boundary', to the free-space map. The boundaries are determined at each viewpoint after the occupied, free and dangerous cells have already been identified. A cell is classed as a 'boundary' if it is a free cell with at least one of its 8 neighbours unknown. Figure 17.1 shows an example of a map with boundary cells.

Given that the boundary cells are interesting candidates for exploration, how should ARNE move between them? A first idea is simply to move repeatedly to the nearest boundary cell. Preliminary experiments suggested two problems with this simple approach:

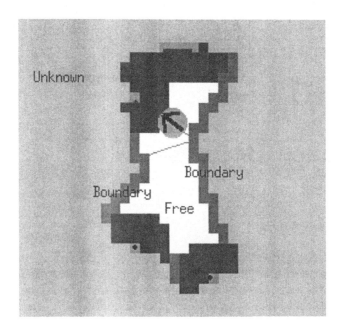

Figure 17.1: Examples of Boundary Regions

Multiple Visits There is a danger that ARNE will visit the same cell repeatedly without
    increasing the map quality. An implicit principle in the 'go where it's interesting'
    school of exploration strategies is that the region will cease to be interesting after the
    robot has visited it. One might hope, for example, that a boundary cell would cease
    to be a boundary cell after ARNE had visited it; new information would be added to
    the map so that the cell was no longer next to an unknown cell. Unfortunately this
    can not be guaranteed with a real-world robot. Circumstances were observed in which
    ARNE moved back and forth amongst a set of boundary cells without changing the
    status of those cells. It was therefore felt to be necessary to add a restriction that
    ARNE should not visit the same cell twice during an exploration.

Step Size Wall-Following used a step size equal to ARNE's diameter. Other strategies
    tested in this thesis have used the same step size to enable direct comparisons to be
    made between strategies. The map-based strategy should therefore have a standard
    step size equal to ARNE's diameter. Moving directly to the nearest boundary cell
    would generate much smaller steps.

The problem of multiple visits is solved simply by associating a 'visited' flag with each
cell in the free-space map. A cell may not be visited again once the flag has been set by an
earlier visit.

The second issue, step size, was addressed in the following way. At each viewpoint, the
free cell containing ARNE is treated as a goal cell and a distance transform is propagated

as described in Section 8.2[1]. The distance transform then indicates how far each cell on the map is from ARNE's current position. (The distance transform values are multiplied by 10 to give distances in millimetres.) The ideal would then be to find an unvisited boundary cell which was exactly ARNE's diameter away from the current cell. This is, of course, not always possible. The selected cell is therefore the unvisited boundary cell which is as far as possible from ARNE *but* no further than ARNE's diameter. ARNE then moves directly to the selected cell. This method of choosing the next cell to visit has the effect of making ARNE explore a cluster of boundary cells. If there are no unvisited boundary cells within the maximum step distance, then ARNE plans and executes a path to the nearest unvisited boundary cell. This moves it on to the nearest cluster of boundary cells.

The map plays a dominant role in the 'Boundaries' algorithm. However, there are two circumstances in which it was decided to make reactive movements; at the start of the exploration and when the incomplete map proposes invalid actions. Each of these circumstances will now be examined in turn.

ARNE starts the exploration with a completely empty map; no *a priori* knowledge is supplied. There are therefore no boundary cells to be used as targets for exploration. An alternative navigation method is needed until enough information has been added to the map for the boundary-seeking behaviour to be effective. The results in Section 16.3 showed that the strategy of following the longest lines of sight is effective in the early stages of exploration. ARNE therefore begins the 'Boundary' exploration by following the longest lines of sight until the map contains one or more confirmed objects.

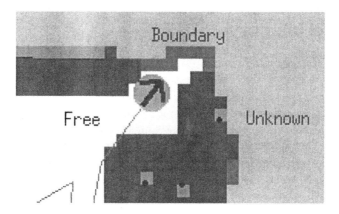

Figure 17.2: ARNE About to Make an Invalid Action

Figure 17.2 shows a circumstance in which total reliance on the map causes ARNE to make an invalid movement. A wall can be seen at the top left of the map. In reality this wall runs all the way to the right beyond ARNE's current position, but the map does not yet show this. If ARNE now moves forward into the boundary region, it will come too close

---

[1]If ARNE was not in a free cell - if, for example, it had strayed into a dangerous area - the goal cell was taken to ⠀ the nearest free cell.

to the wall and will have to make an emergency stop if it is not to collide with the wall.

Emergency stops indicate a disagreement between the map and the world. Although ARNE can recognise that its path is blocked by an obstacle, it is unable to determine the type or exact position of the obstacle from only one viewpoint. ARNE therefore has to move if it is to add the obstacle to the map.

When an emergency stop occurred, early implementations of this algorithm simply switched to the next best target and tried again. This was found to be inefficient because the neighbours of an unreachable cell are usually also unreachable. The technique adopted in the final implementation reported here was to revert to reactive behaviour for a period after an emergency stop. The 'Longest Lines' strategy was used until a new confirmed object was added to the map. This was found to have two benefits:

1. 'Longest Line' movements head away from obstacles, into large regions of free space. During these movements the obstacle was frequently detected and added to the map.

2. At the end of the period of reactive exploration, ARNE was usually closer to a new boundary region. If the uncertainty about the region which contained the obstacle had not been resolved, ARNE would move on to examine a new boundary region, returning to the original region later in the exploration.

The 'Boundaries' algorithm is summarised in Figure 17.3.

17.3   Experiments

The 'Boundaries' strategy was investigated by the same experiments as previous strategies; 10 starting points in each of the 'Empty', 'Columns', and 'Walls' environments.

The performance of the 'Boundaries' strategy is similar to that of 'Longest Lines'. Figure 17.4 compares the performance in the 'Empty' room. The quality graphs are almost identical; the only noticeable difference is the slightly higher finishing quality for the 'Boundaries' strategy, although this difference is not significant at a 95% confidence level.

In the other two test environments, the quality graphs of the two strategies differ more noticeably, although again the differences are not statistically significant (Figures 17.5 and 17.6)[2]. In each environment the final quality values for the two strategies are similar, with the differences arising in the early stages of the exploration. The surprising result was that 'Boundaries' appeared to perform better in 'Walls' but worse in 'Columns'. One would have expected that a map-based strategy would come into its own the more cluttered the environment became and that it would therefore also do better in 'Columns'. Further experiments would be necessary to determine whether this apparent difference is significant.

---

[2]The average duration of the 'Boundaries' explorations of the 'Walls' environment was only 1036 seconds, less than the duration of the other autonomous strategies. The comparative graphs are therefore limited to this period.

```
{
        Investigating the Boundaries of Free Space
}

{Flag all cells as 'unvisited'}

longest-lines();                              {Until a new confirmed feature}

WHILE ({unvisited boundary cells remain})

  {Find nearest free cell to robot's current position}
  {- to use as the goal for a distance transform      }

  distance-transform(nearest-free-cell);

  max-transform = 0;

  FOR ({all cells})
    IF (NOT cell-visited(examined-cell) AND
        boundary-cell(examined-cell) AND
        transform <= threshold AND      {Path length <= ARNE diameter}
        transform > max-transform
        )
        max-transform = transform;
        target-cell   = examined-cell;
    END-IF
  END-FOR

  IF ({nearby point found})
     flag-cell-as-visited(target-cell);
     go-directly-to(target-cell);
     IF ({emergency-stop})
        longest-lines();                    {Until a new confirmed feature}
     END-IF
  ELSE
     {Find nearest boundary cell}
     IF ({boundary cell found})
        IF ({robot not in free cell})
           go-directly-to(nearest-free-cell);
        END-IF
        flag-cell-as-visited(nearest-boundary-cell);
        follow-path-to(nearest-boundary-cell);
        IF ({emergency-stop})
           longest-lines();                 {Until a new confirmed feature}
        END-IF
     END-IF
  END-IF
END-WHILE
```

Figure 17.3: The Boundary Algorithm

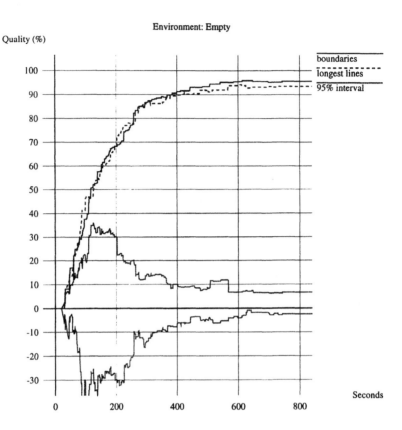

Figure 17.4: Boundaries vs Longest Lines. Room: Empty.

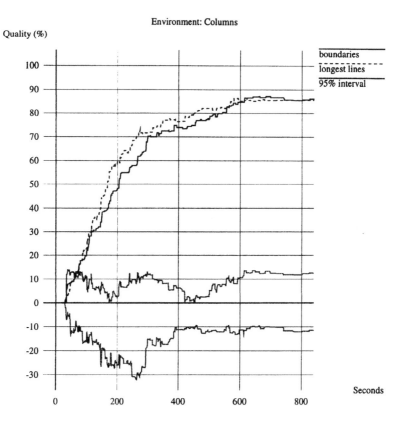

Figure 17.5: Boundaries vs Longest Lines. Room: Columns.

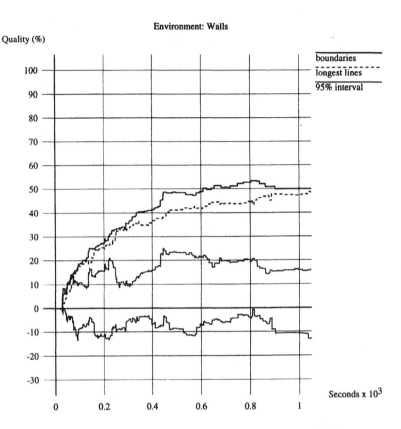

Figure 17.6: Boundaries vs Longest Lines. Room: Walls.

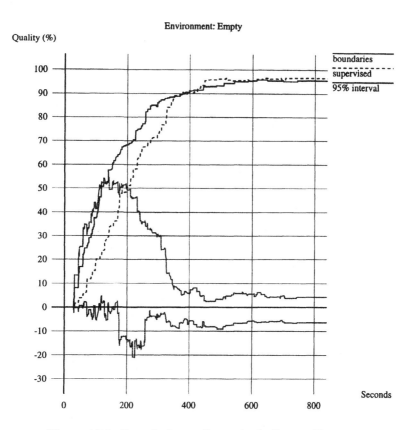

Figure 17.7: Boundaries vs Supervised. Room: Empty.

Supervised Wall-Following is the most promising algorithm from the previous experiments. How does the 'Boundaries' strategy compare to it? In 'Empty' (Figure 17.7) there is a brief early period (until about 150 seconds) during which 'Boundaries' significantly outperforms Supervised Wall-Following. Thereafter the two strategies do not differ significantly.

The differences are also not significant in the 'Columns' environment (Figure 17.8) although the quality graphs do suggest that 'Boundaries' performs better in the early stages of the exploration, but is overtaken by Supervised Wall-Following in the later stages.

In the 'Walls' environment (Figure 17.9), Supervised Wall-Following significantly outperforms the 'Boundaries' strategy from about 900 seconds onwards.

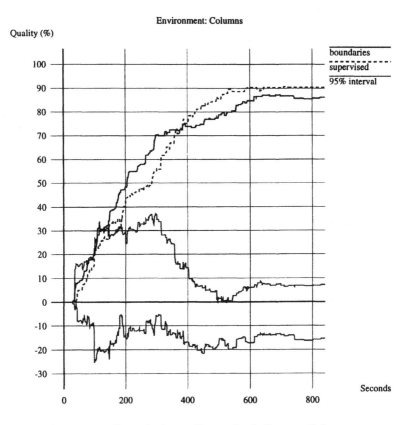

Figure 17.8: Boundaries vs Supervised. Room: Columns.

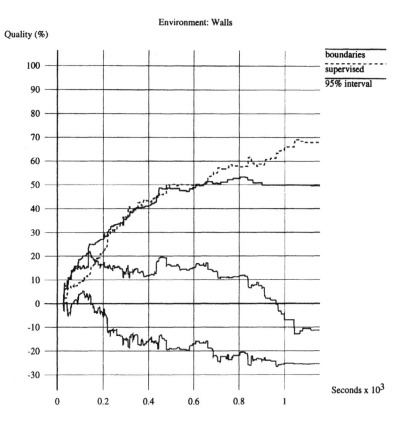

Figure 17.9: Boundaries vs Supervised. Room: Walls.

17.4   Conclusions

The 'Boundaries' strategy was designed to make extensive use of the map to guide the exploration. The experiments were intended to test whether this more map-based strategy could outperform the totally reactive strategy of 'Longest Lines' or the mixed strategy of Supervised Wall-Following.

The experiments have shown no significant difference between 'Boundaries' and 'Longest Lines' in any of the test environments. It would, however, be interesting to continue this series of experiments in larger and more complicated environments in which the 'Longest Lines' strategy is likely to keep the robot trapped in a small part of the environment. It seems likely that 'Boundaries' would be more valuable than 'Longest Lines' in such an environment.

Environment	All Viewpoints		LL Episodes		LL Viewpoints		Viewpoint
	Mean	Std. Err.	Mean	Std. Err.	Mean	Std. Err.	Percentage
Empty	50.7	3.4	5.2	0.7	17.8	3.5	35.1
Columns	72.9	8.0	8.1	1.3	25.5	5.7	35.0
Walls	74.7	5.6	7.4	1.2	23.2	4.3	31.1

Table 17.1: 'Longest Line' Episodes

This table shows how much of the 'Boundaries' explorations was taken up by episodes of 'Longest Line' navigation. For each of the three main environments, it shows the mean and standard error of: the total number of viewpoints, the number of 'Longest Line' episodes, and the number of viewpoints in those episodes. Finally it presents the number of 'Longest Line' viewpoints as a percentage of the total.

Section 17.2 explained that the reactive 'Longest Lines' strategy would be used whenever emergency stops occurred or ARNE was unable to move in the planned direction. The similarity in the results of 'Boundaries' and 'Longest Lines' strategies raises the question of how often these reactive movements happened during the 'Boundaries' experiments. Analysis of the Trace files of these experiments reveals the results shown in Table 17.1. Across the three environments, the average number of 'Longest Line' episodes per exploration varied from 5.2 to 8.1 with the highest number, surprisingly, occurring in the 'Columns' environment. The percentage of viewpoints which were due to 'Longest Line' episodes ranged from 31.1% to 35.1%. The 'Longest Line' movements appear to be more effective than the 'Boundaries' movements; although they make up only about one-third of the total viewpoints, they seem to dominate the strategy, producing results similar to those from 'Longest Lines' alone.

Supervised Wall-Following was shown to outperform 'Boundaries' in the 'Walls' environment, reaching a significantly higher final quality value. Two factors contributed to this better performance:

Systematic Examination of Objects The wall-following step size was chosen to be less than the maximum line segment length (page 128). An effect of this is that ARNE adds length to line features quickly when wall-following. In contrast, the long movements between boundary regions which are made by the 'Boundaries' strategy are not constrained to end at an ideal distance from the end of incomplete line features. These movements do not increase the map quality so efficiently.

Simultaneous Discovery of Related Objects A wall-following robot examines neighbouring objects at approximately the same time. For example, a convex corner (a point object) and the walls which form the corner (line features) will be discovered at approximately the same time. This helps to minimise misinterpretations of the sonar readings. To continue with the example, consider the situation in which the walls have been confirmed but the corner has not yet been confirmed. Sonar readings which actually originate from the corner could be matched with one of the confirmed lines, possibly causing that line to be extended incorrectly beyond the true corner. However, once the corner has been confirmed, ambiguous readings (which could have been caused by the confirmed point or a confirmed line) will be rejected. If the robot makes larger steps around the environment it is more likely that neighbouring objects will be discovered at different times, increasing the likelihood of misinterpretations.

Chapter 18

Summary of Experimental Results

This chapter summarises the results of the experiments that were reported in Part III of this thesis.

Section 18.1 examines the performance of the sensor model by analysing the results of the wall-following explorations that were presented in Chapter 13. Section 18.2 uses the same experimental data to consider the effectiveness of the feature-based map-building algorithm.

Chapters 12 to 17 described a variety of exploration strategies and presented the results of experiments to evaluate those strategies. Section 18.3 collects those experimental results together in order to compare all of the autonomous strategies across the set of test environments.

18.1 The Sensor Model

Environment	Readings (by number of grouped returns)					
	1	2	3	4	5	6
Empty	8836 (79.4%)	1447 (13.0%)	755 (6.8%)	88 (0.8%)	6 (0.1%)	1 (0.0%)
Columns	10287 (78.5%)	2174 (16.6%)	594 (4.5%)	48 (0.4%)	5 (0.0%)	0 (0.0%)
Walls	10984 (80.2%)	2080 (15.2%)	576 (4.2%)	53 (0.4%)	8 (0.1%)	1 (0.0%)

Table 18.1: Distribution of Reading Sizes

Section 6.3 introduced a sensor model in which adjacent sonar returns of similar range were grouped into 'readings' to decrease the uncertainty caused by the width and uneven strength of the sonar beam. Table 18.1 shows the number of readings of each size that were taken during the wall-following explorations of the three main test environments. It can be seen that approximately 20% of the readings contained two or more returns. Expressed in terms of the raw returns instead of the readings, the results show that 37.5% of the returns were included into groups of size two or more. (Maximum-range returns are excluded from the grouping process and from this calculation.) This supports the opportunistic nature of this approach, grouping the returns where possible but using *all* of the available information. An insistence that groups contain at least two returns would have eliminated almost two-thirds of the returns.

The distribution of reading sizes appear to be consistent across the three test environments. One might perhaps have expected a greater proportion of single-return readings in the 'Walls' environment because of the larger number of point features, with their narrower visibility angles.

The experiments in Chapter 6 found that the largest visibility angle, for any object, was 61.2°. This fact, combined with the effective beam width calculation on page 60, implies that a reading could contain at most four returns. More than 99.9% of the readings do indeed include four returns or less. The remainder may be due to incorrect grouping of returns from more than one object.

Environment	Returns		
	Explained	*Unexplained*	*Maximum Range*
Empty	6984 (36.0%)	7399 (38.2%)	4997 (25.8%)
Columns	8480 (43.8%)	8154 (42.1%)	2746 (14.2%)
Walls	8787 (45.3%)	8343 (43.0%)	2250 (11.6%)

Table 18.2: Explained, Unexplained, and Maximum-Range Readings

The sonar returns are used to provide information about environmental features. Table 18.2 shows how many of the returns were 'explained' by being associated with confirmed features on the map. Returns at the maximum range of the sensor are discarded before the remainder are grouped into readings. As one would expect, the greatest proportion of maximum-range returns is found in the open 'Empty' environment and the smallest proportion is found in the cluttered 'Walls' environment. After excluding these returns, roughly half of the remainder have been explained. Many of the unexplained returns are likely to have been false readings caused by multiple reflections.

18.2   The Feature Map

Environment	Lines		Points	
	Mean	Std. Err.	Mean	Std. Err.
Empty	7.7	0.5	19.5	1.1
Columns	7.5	1.0	19.1	1.3
Walls	7.9	0.5	26.9	1.9

Table 18.3: Confirmed Features In Each Environment

Table 18.3 shows the number of confirmed features detected during the wall-following explorations of the three main test environments.

The number of confirmed lines is roughly 8 in all three environments. The floor plan of the empty room (Figure B.1 in Appendix B) shows 12 line segments. Some of these are, however, very short (the edges of the brick pillar) or infrequently seen (the lower wall of the region in the top right corner). The greater number of lines in the 'Walls' environment appears to be offset by the greater likelihood of occlusion.

The floor plan of the empty room shows 12 point features, less than the number of confirmed points. The extra confirmed points were often found to be caused by surface irregularities on the walls. As would be expected, the number of confirmed points is highest in the 'Walls' environment, the floor plan of which shows 22 point features.

18.3 Exploration Strategies

The exploration strategies that were presented in Chapters 12 to 17 differ in the extent to which the map is used during the exploration. They range from Wall-Following and 'Longest Lines' (totally reactive) through Supervised Wall-Following (basically reactive with map-based interventions) to 'Boundaries' (map-based with reactive episodes). In comparing strategies, this section is indirectly examining the issue of how the map information and the immediate sensory data should be balanced to create an efficient exploration strategy.

The section begins with a brief review of the individual strategies and then presents some graphical comparisons.

The first strategy to be tested was wall-following. By reacting to its immediate sensory input, the robot was able to execute collision-free paths which enabled it to examine large regions of its test environments. The strategy was simple to implement and coped well with temporary obstructions.

Simple wall-following was, however, found to have some significant limitations. The most striking was its tendency to become trapped in one part of the environment, repeating a sequence of actions from which very little new information could be obtained. The strategy of Supervised Wall-Following was designed and implemented to overcome such limitations. A supervisory process, with access to the developing map, detects ineffective wall-following actions and intervenes to direct the robot's attention to a more profitable region of the environment. The benefits of Supervised Wall-Following were most apparent in environments in which there was considerable occlusion.

Ideas for additional exploration strategies were generated by a brief digression into human-guided exploration. An operator, looking at the latest map, selected the next viewpoint for the robot. Experiments showed that a human operator could easily outperform Supervised Wall-Following in the open 'Empty' environment, but no significant difference could be detected in the more cluttered 'Walls' environment. The human operator was found to be using two heuristics: 'head for the open spaces' and 'examine the boundaries of unknown areas'. These ideas formed the basis for the last two strategies to be tested.

The 'Longest Lines' strategy, like simple wall-following, is completely reactive, making decisions exclusively from the most recent sensory information. However, in contrast to wall-following, it seeks the *longest* range reading from any position and heads in that direction until it encounters an obstacle. This policy takes it way from walls and through regions of open space. This strategy performed significantly better than wall-following in the early stages of exploration of the 'Empty' and 'Columns' environments. The benefit was less pronounced in the 'Walls' environment. The 'Longest Lines' strategy also outperformed Supervised Wall-Following early in the explorations of 'Empty' and 'Columns', although Supervised Wall-Following came into its own in the later stages. Supervised Wall-Following was much more successful than 'Longest Lines' in the 'Walls' environment, suggesting, as one

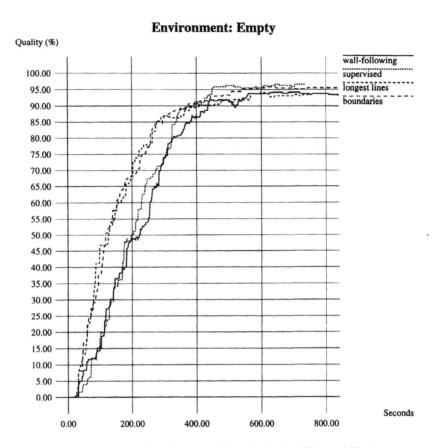

Figure 18.1: Summary of Exploration Results in the 'Empty' Environment

would expect, that the 'Longest Lines' strategy is best suited to more open environments.

The second heuristic from the human-guided exploration gave rise to the 'Boundaries' strategy. The robot, basing its decisions on the partly-formed map, makes small movements along the boundary regions between 'free' and 'unknown' space. This strategy is designed to detect objects in the unexplored area. Total reliance on the map was found to cause difficulties when the robot encountered obstacles which had not yet been mapped, or when the map contained errors. In these circumstances, the robot reverted to the reactive 'Longest Lines' strategy until the map changed. The results of the 'Boundaries' strategy were not significantly different from those of 'Longest Lines' alone, suggesting that it was the 'Longest Line' movements which were the most effective in the test environments.

Figure 18.1 shows the results obtained when exploring the 'Empty' environment, using each of the four autonomous strategies just described. The overall shape of the graph is similar for all strategies; a short period of very low quality followed by a rapid increase to a plateau. The final qualities are very similar with all strategies peaking at about 95%.

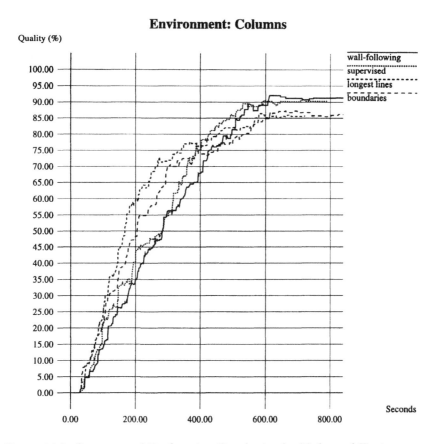

Figure 18.2: Summary of Exploration Results in the 'Columns' Environment

During the early stages the strategies appear to form two distinct pairs. 'Boundaries' and 'Longest Lines' show a more rapid increase in quality than the two strategies based on wall-following.

Figure 18.2 shows the same comparison for the 'Columns' environment. Again the general shapes are similar. 'Boundaries' and 'Longest Lines' again show a faster increase in quality at the start of the exploration (although the pairing is less pronounced than in Figure 18.1). In this environment, however, their final quality is *lower* than that of the wall-following strategies. The final qualities are all lower than in the 'Empty' environment. (See Section 13.3.1 for a discussion of the causes of lower map quality in more complex environments.)

To complete the set, Figure 18.3 shows the comparison for the 'Walls' environment. If one temporarily disregards Supervised Wall-Following, the observations from the previous two environments can also be applied here. 'Longest Lines' and 'Boundaries' outperform Wall-Following in the early stages but Wall-Following ends with a higher quality. But it is Supervised Wall-Following which provides the difference from the other environments.

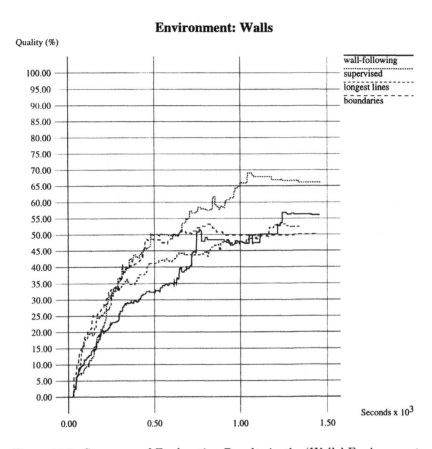

Figure 18.3: Summary of Exploration Results in the 'Walls' Environment

For the first 200 seconds the results are very similar to simple Wall-Following but thereafter Supervised Wall-Following comes into its own. It diverges from Wall-Following and produces similar results to those of 'Boundaries' until about 700 seconds, when 'Boundaries' begins to level out. The quality from Supervised Wall-Following continues to improve, ending much higher than any of the other strategies.

How can these results be quantified and used to select an appropriate strategy? It seems reasonable to ask two questions about an exploration strategy:

1. What quality of map can be expected if this strategy is used?

2. How long will it take to produce the map?

These questions are the motivation behind Figures 18.4, 18.5 and 18.6. There is one graph for each of the three main test environments. On each graph there is a single marker for each

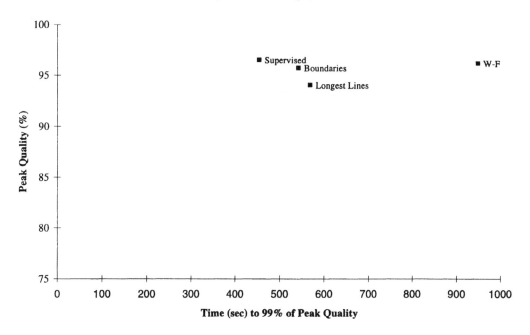

Figure 18.4: Comparison of Exploration Strategies in the 'Empty' Environment

For comparison purposes this figure and the next two figures show the peak mean quality achieved by each exploration strategy in the specified environment, plotted against the time taken to reach 99% of that value.

strategy, indicating the peak average quality achieved by that strategy and the time taken to reach 99% of that maximum value. (A value of 99% was used to eliminate distortions due to very small fluctuations in the quality.) An ideal strategy would, of course, obtain the highest quality *and* do so in the minimum time, placing its marker towards the top left of the graph.

The experimental results did not indicate that a single strategy was superior in *all* of the test environments. It is therefore necessary to consider each environment in turn.

First, consider the 'Empty' environment (Figure 18.4). The first point to note is that there is only a small difference (2.5%) between the greatest and smallest peak quality values. All of the strategies generate roughly the same final quality result. As for timing, simple wall-following (peaking at 950 seconds) is noticeably slower than the other three strategies, all of which reach peak quality at roughly the same time (between 450 and 600 seconds). Supervised Wall-Following comes out slightly ahead, in both quality and timing.

The 'Columns' environment (Figure 18.5) shows a larger spread of peak quality values (6.7%) and again shows simple wall-following taking longer than the other three strategies to reach its peak value. The significant difference here is that simple wall-following generates

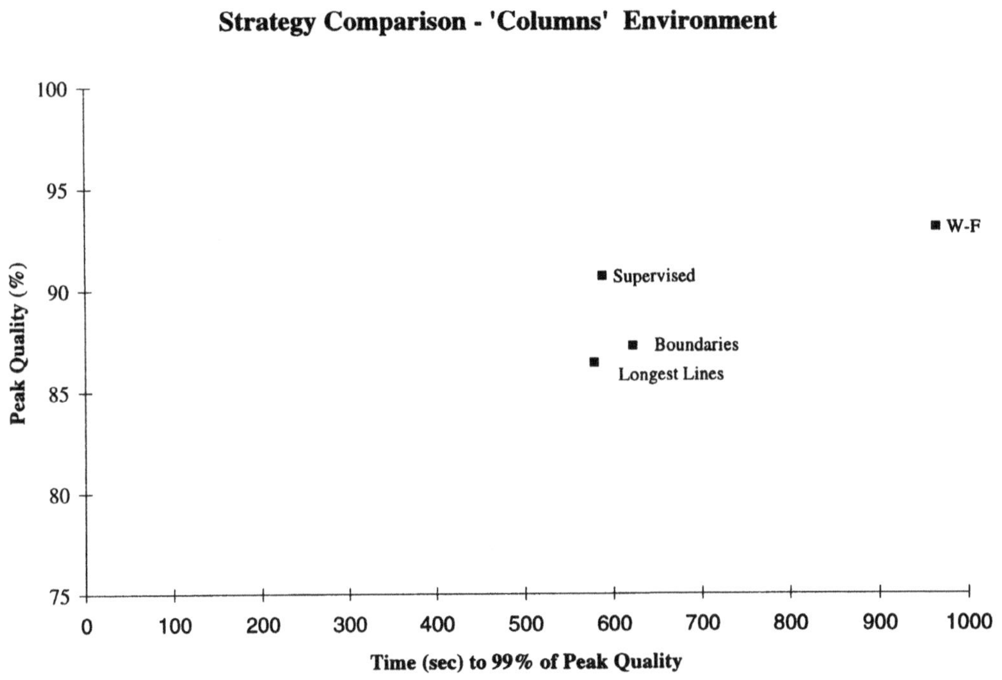

Strategy Comparison - 'Columns' Environment

Figure 18.5: Comparison of Exploration Strategies in the 'Columns' Environment
See Figure 18.4 for an explanation of this graph.

the *highest* peak value. A user choosing a strategy would have to weigh the increased quality value against the extra time needed to obtain that quality. Of the other three strategies, all of which reach peak quality after approximately 600 seconds, Supervised Wall-Following gives the highest quality.

The greatest spread in peak quality readings (15.8%) comes from 'Walls', the most complex environment (Figure 18.6). Supervised Wall-Following reaches a peak quality of 69% while the other three strategies peak at roughly 55%.

The results presented in this section show clearly how difficult it is to choose an exploration strategy. The effectiveness of an individual strategy varies not only between environments but also at different stages of the exploration. Chapters 12 to 17 and the summary at the start of this section do, however, provide some general guidance about the strengths and weaknesses of each strategy.

It is perhaps worth commenting on the promising performance of Supervised Wall-Following. This strategy appears to merit further investigation because:

- It generated the highest peak quality in two of the three test environments.

- It generated a much higher peak quality than the other strategies in the most com-

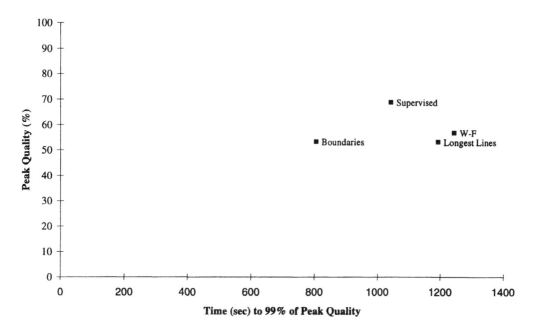

Figure 18.6: Comparison of Exploration Strategies in the 'Walls' Environment
See Figure 18.4 for an explanation of this graph.

plicated environment. The more complicated the environment, the more useful a map will be and therefore the more important it is to have an effective exploration strategy.

- The only strategy to achieve a higher peak quality was simple wall-following (in the 'Columns' environment). Simple wall-following has been seen to be vulnerable to 'traps', which can greatly restrict the map quality (page 157). The potentially lower peak quality from Supervised Wall-Following in some environments could prove to be an acceptable price for trap-avoidance.

- Supervised Wall-Following is a flexible exploration framework which could be extended by the addition of new pairs of triggers and actions.

Given the difficulty of deciding in advance which strategy will be most successful in a particular environment, it is tempting to consider the possibility of allowing the robot to switch between strategies as the exploration progresses. This idea is considered further in Section 20.2.

Chapter 19

Conclusions

This thesis has described an investigation into the complementary problems of map-building and exploration by a mobile robot. This chapter highlights the most significant results of this investigation.

The novel contribution of this research can be summarised as:

- The integration of a physical robot, a sonar model, map construction algorithms, and a localisation algorithm into an effective working system;

- The definition and implementation of a novel quantitative measure of map quality;

- A thorough quantitative and statistical evaluation of the map-building and exploration capabilities of the system, using the quality metric and a variety of exploration strategies.

The system components and the quality metric were described in Part II of this thesis. Sections 19.1 to 19.4 briefly review these topics. The experimental evaluation of exploration strategies formed the bulk of Part III of this thesis. The results of this work have already been summarised in Chapter 18.

Chapter 2 described the continuing debate between the 'traditional' supporters of model-based robotics and the proponents of behaviour-based robotics. An outcome of the current research has been an awareness of the need to balance these two approaches. The value of reactive navigation became more apparent as the research progressed. Section 19.5 reviews the course of the research in the context of the 'models versus behaviours' debate.

19.1 The Ultrasonic Sensor Model

Chapter 6 presented a set of experimental results which showed how the Polaroid ultrasonic rangefinder detected each type of object that would be encountered in the test environments. These results demonstrated the positional uncertainty that arises from the wide beam and uneven signal strength of the transducer. A sonar model was presented in which this uncertainty is decreased by grouping multiple overlapping sensor returns which are likely to have been caused by the same object.

197

The experiments revealed a wide variation in the 'visibility angles' of different objects. Point objects, such as convex edges, could only be detected if they were close to the central axis of the sonar beam. In contrast, flat surfaces, such as smooth walls, could be detected at much greater angles from the centre of the beam. This variation was included in the model.

The performance of this sensor model has been summarised in Section 18.1.

19.2 The Feature-Based and Area-Based Maps

The review of previous map-building research in Chapter 2 categorised metric maps as either *feature-based* or *area-based* (page 22). The research in this thesis used both types of map.

The sonar model from Chapter 6 was used to construct a feature-based map. Elementary objects were hypothesised to explain the sonar readings, these elementary objects were gathered into mutually-supportive clusters, and the clusters were then promoted to confirmed objects when they had been detected enough times.

An area-based map was developed to represent the free space available to the robot. A square grid indicated whether a region was free space, occupied by an object, dangerous (too close to an object), or unknown.

The two types of map were found to be an effective combination. The high precision of the feature-based map was useful for explaining sonar readings and for localisation, whereas the discrete nature of the free-space map enabled efficient path planning and quality judgements.

19.3 Localisation

The robot's estimate of its own position becomes increasingly inaccurate the more movements it makes. A localisation algorithm was necessary to prevent a corresponding loss of map quality.

A key component of the map construction algorithm is the establishment of correspondences between sonar readings and confirmed features. These correspondences make a useful starting point for a localisation scheme. An Extended Kalman Filter was used to derive an estimate of the robot's position from the differences between the expected and the measured distances to confirmed features of the environment.

This localisation technique was shown to be highly effective, significantly increasing map quality in the later stages of exploration.

19.4 The Map Quality Metric

The map-building and exploration research described in this thesis have placed an exceptional emphasis on the need for practical experimentation and quantitative evaluation of the results. An essential component of the research was therefore a measure of map quality.

The central idea of the metric was to predict the robot's behaviour if it were to use its free-space map to plan a number of test journeys. The metric could then indicate how successful this behaviour would be. In this context 'successful' refers to the number of test journeys which would be completed safely, the number which would result in collisions, and the number which would be deemed by the path planner to be impossible.

This measure was shown to satisfy the practical and intuitive requirements of a quality metric. It was put to two main uses:

- The map building and localisation algorithms were tuned by experimentation with a range of control parameters. The parameters which generated the highest map quality were used.

- Map quality was measured repeatedly during experiments to evaluate exploration strategies.

19.5 Model-Based and Sensor-Based Navigation

The research described in this thesis began from the premise that mobile robots need maps. Although the behaviour-based research of Brooks and others had shown that a surprising amount could be achieved without representations, the fact remained that certain tasks would require the robot to plan its actions with reference to a world model. The delivery application which was selected as the target for this research (see Section 3.1) would need a full metric model. It seemed unlikely that reactive navigation would play a significant part in this research.

Once the sensor model and map construction algorithms had been implemented, they were submitted to extensive testing. These tests were initially performed by a human operator specifying the exact movements required from ARNE. It was, however, soon found to be necessary to implement a simple exploration strategy so that large amounts of test data could be gathered quickly. Wall-following was selected for its ease of implementation. At this stage it was viewed as a 'base case' which was likely to be easily outperformed by more 'intelligent' exploration strategies which were driven by the current state of the map.

The more wall-following was used, the more impressive it appeared. A few adjustments to the control parameters were needed at first to prevent ARNE from becoming stuck in corners (see page 129) but once the algorithm was tuned it proved to be reliable, gathering data during many hours of experimentation.

It proved to be surprisingly difficult to achieve the same robustness in a map-based exploration strategy. The 'Boundaries' strategy described in Chapter 17 evolved from several attempts to formalise the type of strategy which would be used by a human operator. Typically such attempts would start with a simple guiding principle (e.g. 'explore the largest boundary region') which would be implemented and tested. Exceptions and difficult circumstances would arise during the tests. For example, the map could change as the result of sensor scans made during the journey to the boundary region, altering the shape of the region. That region might then no longer be the largest region. Should ARNE then continue to explore the region as planned, or go to the region which has become the largest? As another example, consider the situation in which an error in the map causes ARNE to plan a path which proves to be impossible. ARNE may not yet have enough information to add the obstruction to the map, but it is necessary to take the failed path into account when deciding which region to examine next. It is possible to devise strategies to cope with any one of these difficulties, but the exploration algorithm rapidly becomes complex as processing is added to deal with more and more special cases. In the light of this experience, the simplicity of wall-following became increasingly attractive.

It was, however, clear that simple wall-following was too limited to be a general exploration strategy. Chapter 14 described some of the pitfalls of purely reactive behaviour (traps, re-examining known objects, and repeating fruitless actions). The design and implementation of Supervised Wall-Following were motivated by the desire to keep the robustness and simplicity of wall-following whilst eliminating some of its most obvious shortcomings.

The general conclusion of the exploration experiments was that effective exploration requires a combination of map-based and reactive navigation. This thesis therefore supports the recent work (see page 15) which attempts to develop hybrid systems which combine the strengths of both approaches.

It is interesting to consider whether this conclusion is valid only during exploration or whether it can be extended to the day-to-day operation of the robot. Can reactive navigation be abandoned once the robot has a complete map? In response to this question, it is worth reconsidering the idea of the 'predictability continuum' that was proposed in Chapter 2 (page 16). It was argued there that the mix of model-based and reactive navigation should be linked to the degree of predictability of the robot's environment. The results presented in Section 13.3.1 suggest that the idea of 'predictability' should be extended to encompass the possibility of errors in the map; small errors in the map were shown to decrease the effectiveness of the map for path planning. If the robot were equipped with a *perfect* map of an unchanging environment, then it could base all of its decisions on the map. A reactive component would be of value if the environment were likely to change *or* the map were likely to contain errors. In either case, the reactive component is able to cope with disagreements between the internal representation and the external environment.

Chapter 20

Directions for Further Research

The experience gained during the development of this thesis has suggested a number of directions in which the research could be extended. This final chapter examines these ideas under four groupings:

- Mixing planning and reactive navigation.

- Modifying the exploration method as the exploration progresses.

- Testing new sensors and new environments.

- Examining the feature map for inconsistencies.

A section is devoted to each of these areas.

20.1 Mixing Planning and Reactive Navigation

The Supervised Wall-Following strategy has shown that effective exploration can arise from a combination of reactive and model-based decisions. The application of the quality metric to maps of the 'Walls' environment showed that small errors in the map could lead to collisions unless the robot's movements took into account the latest information from the robot's sensors. These results suggest that it would be useful to extend the current research by implementing a navigation strategy which combines planning and reactive components.

There are clear parallels between this idea and the concept of *compliance* in automated assembly (McKerrow 1991, page 293). In both cases the robot uses its stored understanding of the state of the world to plan its actions, but it has to adjust its behaviour if sensory input disagrees with that understanding.

The work of Payton, Rosenblatt, and Keirsey (1991) is attractive in this context. They propose the use of 'internalized plans' which act as information resources to guide the reactive behaviour of the robot. The plan might indicate that a goal can be reached by heading in a certain direction, but the robot's movements could be influenced by a collision-avoidance behaviour which would change the heading. Payton *et al.* argue that such an approach would be robust in the presence both of mapping errors and dynamic obstacles.

The representation proposed by Payton *et al.* for their internalized plans is a grid-based map similar to the free-space map that has been used in this thesis. They also advocate the use of a distance transform algorithm as was described in Chapter 8. Their approach is therefore highly compatible with the work described in this thesis.

An interesting research direction would be to extend ARNE's navigation algorithm in this way and to modify the quality metric to predict the map's effectiveness if it were used as an internalized plan instead of as a source of detailed, unchangeable, paths. The metric would have to predict the robot's path if it used the constructed map as an internalized plan whilst avoiding the objects that were shown on the ideal map. The strategies from this thesis could then be tested in this new context to discover any differences in their relative strengths.

20.2   An Evolving Exploration Strategy

The experimental results in Part III of this thesis showed that different strategies were at their most effective at different stages of the exploration. For example, the results in Chapter 16 showed that the 'Longest Lines' strategy was more effective than Supervised Wall-Following in the early stages of exploration of the 'Empty' and 'Columns' environments, but that the dominance was reversed in the later stages.

This suggests the possibility of implementing and testing strategies which change as the exploration progresses. For example, a strategy which changed from 'Longest Lines' to Supervised Wall-Following at an appropriate stage could perhaps outperform either strategy alone. Testing such a mixed strategy would form an interesting extension to the current research.

The difficulty lies of course in choosing when to switch between strategies. Such a choice would have to be autonomous, made by the robot without the aid of the 'omniscient observer' that was used to make quality judgements.

One could imagine two different types of criteria for changing strategies. The first would be to monitor the rate at which new information was being added to the map. Examples could include the rate at which features or free-space were being detected. A drop in this rate would suggest that the current strategy was becoming ineffective and that a change was due. Alternatively, the robot could examine the map *as a whole* to determine which type of strategy to use. If, for example, the map showed a high degree of clutter, it might be more effective to use Supervised Wall-Following than 'Longest Lines'.

20.3   Different Sensors

The results in this thesis show what can be achieved with a single Polaroid range sensor with off-the-shelf echo detection hardware. It would be interesting to repeat the research either using vision or a more 'intelligent' sonar sensor.

Recent interest in the construction of smarter sonar sensors has taken two distinct forms. Some researchers have focussed on the use of multiple transducers while others have emphasised the value of analysing the complete echo, not just triggering a threshold. Both techniques could have an impact on the current research.

Nagashima and Yuta (1992) provide an example of the former approach. Using a set of one transmitting and two receiving transducers, they measure the position *and* orientation of segments of smooth wall. Such a method could detect elementary line segments from a single position instead of the two positions currently required by ARNE. A limitation of their approach is that it does not attempt to distinguish between specular reflections from walls and diffuse reflections from point or edge sources. Further verification would be necessary to check whether the reading was indeed caused by a smooth wall.

Manyika and Durrant-Whyte (1993) use a pair of Polaroid sensors to localise the robot on a given feature map. The two transducers are mounted on a common baseline and attached to a high-speed servo. One of the transducers transmits and both of them receive. The two time-of-flight readings are used to determine the distance *and direction* to the echo source. The servo is used to rotate the pair of sensors until the difference between the two time-of-flight readings is zero, ensuring that the sensor is facing directly towards the echo source. The detected echo is then guaranteed to be caused by the strong central lobe of the beam, avoiding any problems with weak returns, and the direction to the object can be used as an input to the localisation algorithm. As the robot moves, the sensor continues to face towards a single object, effectively overcoming the correspondence problem. Interestingly, repeated firings of the sensor from the same position did not give the same difference between the time-of-flight readings, making it necessary to use a Kalman filter to estimate the true difference. It would be interesting to extend the research described in this thesis to include this type of sensor. A practical approach might be to equip the robot with a number of rotating sensors, some of which track confirmed objects for localisation, as in Manyika and Durrant-Whyte's work. The remaining sensors could then rotate to focus attention on the unknown regions of the environment.

A prominent source of research in the 'complete echo' camp is the Intelligent Sensors Laboratory at Yale University. Bozma and Kuc (1992) propose the 'ENDURA' method which uses the energy, duration and range information in a dense scan to characterise the roughness and orientation of the reflecting surfaces. The roughness is determined by matching against templates for the energy and duration of the echoes from different surface types. The direction to the surface is taken to be in the centre of the matched template. This method, like Leonard and Durrant-Whyte's work with RCDs, requires a dense scan of the environment (Bozma and Kuc appear to be taking about 300 readings in 360°). It would be interesting to see whether the roughness information could be derived from the sparser scans used in this thesis. If so, the map construction process might be improved by relating the visibility angle of a feature to its roughness.

Bozma and Kuc state that, with their system, it is impossible to distinguish a smooth surface from a smooth corner from a single location. In contrast, Sasaki and Takano (1992) present results which suggest that the type of the reflecting object can be decided by examining the 'acoustic transfer function' of the object. The acoustic transfer function of an object determines how the transmitted waveform is changed to give the echo waveform. Sasaki and Takano's results are presented as graphs of the transfer functions from a variety of objects. Further research would be required to determine whether this method could form the basis of a reliable, automatic, classification system. If so, it could eliminate one of the most troublesome ambiguities in the map construction in this thesis: line objects versus point objects.

20.4   Eliminating Ambiguities and Inconsistencies

An essential property of the sonar model and the map construction algorithms described in this thesis is that sensor data is interpreted in terms of previously-obtained knowledge. A sonar reading is used to update the properties of a matching confirmed object, if such an object has been found; otherwise, it could be used to create a new object. Each reading is explained in the context of earlier readings.

It became clear during the map-building experiments that it would sometimes be useful to re-examine *earlier* readings in the context of *later* ones. For example, it is possible that a 'ghost' feature could be created in the early stages of map building because of multiple reflections from a smooth wall. That smooth wall would later be added to the map, making it obvious to a human observer that the original feature was a ghost. Re-examining the early conclusions in the light of the later findings could eliminate that ghost object. Zelinsky (1991a, page 15) uses a similar idea to identify false reflections when tracking the boundary of an object.

A similar situation was observed when ARNE was mapping a wall which lead to a convex corner. The wall had already been confirmed and ARNE was gradually extending the line towards the corner. If ARNE then steps beyond the corner it could detect the corner for the first time. At this stage there would not be a confirmed point to explain the confirmed reading and the reading might be consistent with an echo from the wall. ARNE would then slightly over-extend the line beyond the corner. Later in the exploration, the corner might be detected and confirmed from elsewhere in the room. Re-examination of the wrongly-interpreted reading would now show that it could have been caused by the corner *or* by the wall. This ambiguity would justify reversing the earlier interpretation and shortening the line.

It would, of course, not be practical to keep old sensor data indefinitely, but a small store could prove useful in cases such as those described above.

Table 18.2 showed that roughly half of the sonar returns that were taken during the wall-following explorations remained unexplained. It is likely that ideas such as these could decrease that fraction.

Appendix A

The Feature-Map Data Structure

Figure A.1 is a simplified entity-relationship diagram which shows the main components of the feature-based map and the relationships between them.

Tables A.1 to A.11 list the data elements owned by each of the entities in Figure A.1. Note that all of the entities are contained, either directly or indirectly, within the "Map" entity. This reflects the fact that the map is implemented as a single shared data structure within 'C'.

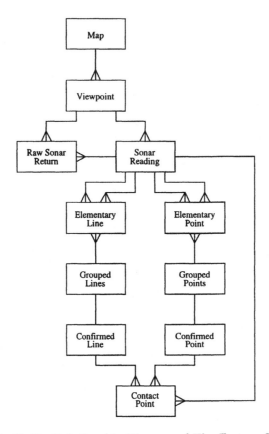

Figure A.1: Entity-Relationship Diagram of The Feature-Based Map

The relationships between the entities within the feature-based map. The "crow's feet" are used on the 'many' end of a one-to-many relationship.

Map	
$vp[]$	Array of viewpoints
$el[]$	Array of elementary lines
$gl[]$	Array of grouped lines
$cl[]$	Array of confirmed lines
$ep[]$	Array of elementary points
$gp[]$	Array of grouped points
$cp[]$	Array of confirmed points

Table A.1: Data Elements of the "Map" Entity

Viewpoint	
x_{vp}	X co-ordinate of robot
y_{vp}	Y co-ordinate of robot
o_{vp}	Orientation of robot
$raw_{vp}[]$	Array of raw sonar returns
$read_{vp}[]$	Array of sonar readings

Table A.2: Data Elements of the "Viewpoint" Entity

Raw Sonar Return	
a_{raw}	Angle of the return (relative to the robot's orientation)
r_{raw}	Range of the return
s_{raw}	Status

Table A.3: Data Elements of the "Raw Sonar Return" Entity

Sonar Reading	
a_{read}	Angle of the reading (relative to the robot's orientation)
r_{read}	Range of the reading
$elptr_{read}[]$	Array of pointers to the elementary lines which explain the reading
$epptr_{read}[]$	Array of pointers to the elementary points which explain the reading
c_{read}	Count of the number of raw sonar returns which have been merged to produce the reading
s_{read}	Status

Table A.4: Data Elements of the "Sonar Reading" Entity

Elementary Line	
$x_{el}[2]$	X co-ordinates of end-points of line
$y_{el}[2]$	Y co-ordinates of end-points of line
$vpptr_{el}[2]$	Pointers to viewpoints from which the line was seen
$rdptr_{el}[2]$	Pointers to readings by which the line was seen
s_{el}	Status

Table A.5: Data Elements of the "Elementary Line" Entity

Elementary Point	
x_{el}	X co-ordinate of the point
y_{el}	Y co-ordinates of the point
$vpptr_{el}[2]$	Pointers to viewpoints from which the point was seen
$rdptr_{el}[2]$	Pointers to readings by which the point was seen
s_{el}	Status

Table A.6: Data Elements of the "Elementary Point" Entity

Grouped Lines	
$elptr_{gl}[]$	Array of pointers to the elementary lines which form this group
s_{gl}	Status

Table A.7: Data Elements of the "Grouped Lines" Entity

Grouped Points	
$epptr_{gl}[]$	Array of pointers to the elementary points which form this group
s_{gl}	Status

Table A.8: Data Elements of the "Grouped Points" Entity

Confirmed Line	
a_{cl}	Angle of the line
$x_{cl}[2]$	X co-ordinates of the end-points of the line
$y_{cl}[2]$	Y co-ordinates of the end-points of the line
$sigx_{cl}$	Sum of the x co-ordinates of all contact points
$sigy_{cl}$	Sum of the y co-ordinates of all contact points
$sigx2_{cl}$	Sum of the squares of the x co-ordinates of all contact points
$sigy2_{cl}$	Sum of the squares of the y co-ordinates of all contact points
$sigxy_{cl}$	Sum of $x * y$ for all contact points
$cn_{cl}[]$	Array of contact points for this line
$glptr_{cl}$	Pointer to the originating grouped line
s_{cl}	Status

Table A.9: Data Elements of the "Confirmed Line" Entity

Confirmed Point	
x_{cp}	X co-ordinate of the point
y_{cp}	Y co-ordinate of the point
$sigx_{cp}$	Sum of the x co-ordinates of all contact points
$sigy_{cp}$	Sum of the y co-ordinates of all contact points
$cn_{cp}[]$	Array of contact points for this point
$gpptr_{cp}$	Pointer to the originating grouped point
s_{cp}	Status

Table A.10: Data Elements of the "Confirmed Point" Entity

Contact Point	
x_{cn}	X co-ordinate of the contact point
y_{cn}	Y co-ordinate of the contact point
$vpptr_{cn}$	Pointer to the viewpoint associated with the contact point
$rdptr_{cn}$	Pointer to the reading associated with the contact point

Table A.11: Data Elements of the "Contact Point" Entity

Appendix B

Test Rooms

Figures B.1 to B.8 show the test environments for the exploration experiments. Two figures are given for each environment. The first diagram shows the walls and objects in the environment. It also shows the positions and orientations from which exploration experiments were started. The second diagram for shows the 'ideal' free-space map which would result from complete knowledge of the objects in the environment.

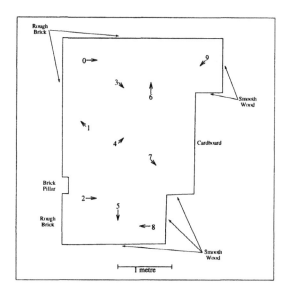

Figure B.1: A Diagrammatic Map of the 'Empty' Environment

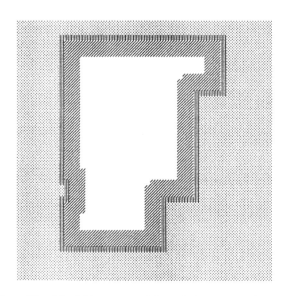

Figure B.2: The Ideal Free-Space Map of the 'Empty' Environment

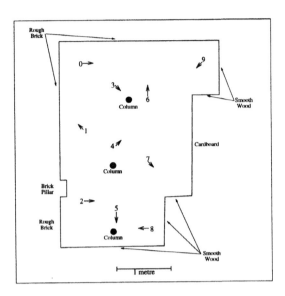

Figure B.3: A Diagrammatic Map of the 'Columns' Environment

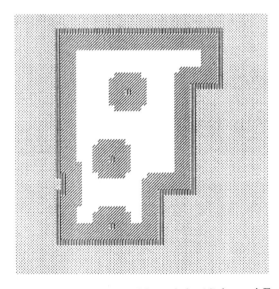

Figure B.4: The Ideal Free-Space Map of the 'Columns' Environment

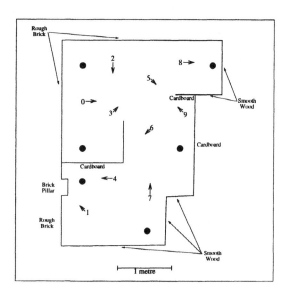

Figure B.5: A Diagrammatic Map of the 'Walls' Environment

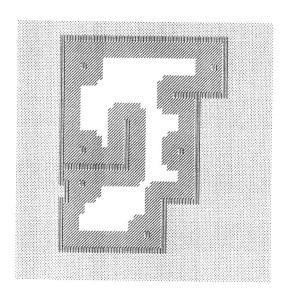

Figure B.6: The Ideal Free-Space Map of the 'Walls' Environment

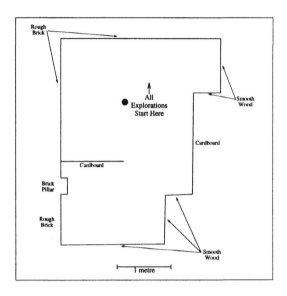

Figure B.7: A Diagrammatic Map of the 'Trap' Environment

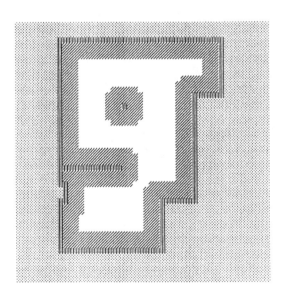

Figure B.8: The Ideal Free-Space Map of the 'Trap' Environment

Appendix C

Finding the Best-Fit Line

This Appendix gives the details of the calculations by which a line is fitted to a set of sonar observations.

It is initially necessary to distinguish two cases; the creation of a new confirmed line and the updating of an existing confirmed line. In both cases the confirmed line is fitted to a number of *contact points*, one for each sonar reading which corresponds to the line. The only difference is in the way the contact points are determined.

A confirmed line is created by 'upgrading' a cluster of elementary line segments. As explained in Section 7.1, each line segment has two contact points. Since segments are added to the cluster if they share a sonar reading with a segment already in the cluster, it is common for a single sonar reading to correspond to more than one segment. To avoid giving unnecessary weight to these 'multiple' readings, the confirmed line is fitted to a single contact point for each sonar reading. It is therefore necessary to calculate an 'average contact point' if the sonar reading corresponds to multiple segments.

If, on the other hand, the confirmed line is to be updated then the line already has a number of contact points and a new one is to be added. As explained in Section 7.3, a contact point is obtained by taking a point at the measured distance from the robot in a direction normal to the line.

In either of these cases, the line-fitting process begins with an array of n contact points, $cp_{cl}[]$, each of which has co-ordinates (x_{cp}, y_{cp}). (See Appendix A for listings of the attributes of the feature-map.)

The challenge of line fitting is to find a line such that the sum of the squared perpendicular distance from all the points to the line is minimised.

The best-fit line passes through the centroid of the contact points $(\bar{x}, \bar{y})$. Its gradient, g, is computed in stages. First, the variances and covariance are calculated:

$$\sigma_{xx} = \frac{1}{n} \sum_{i=1}^{n} (x_{cp}[i] - \bar{x})^2 \qquad (C.1)$$

$$\sigma_{yy} = \frac{1}{n} \sum_{i=1}^{n} (y_{cp}[i] - \bar{y})^2 \qquad (C.2)$$

$$\sigma_{xy} = \frac{1}{n} \sum_{i=1}^{n} (x_{cp}[i] - \bar{x})(y_{cp}[i] - \bar{y}) \qquad (C.3)$$

The gradient is then given by:

$$g = \frac{\sqrt{d^2 + 4} - d}{2} \tag{C.4}$$

where

$$d = \frac{\sigma_{xx} - \sigma_{yy}}{\sigma_{xy}} \tag{C.5}$$

There is, however, one remaining check to be made. In Equation C.4 one could choose the positive or negative value of the square root. One of these values gives the *best* fit line through the centroid and the other gives the *worst*. If one takes the positive root in Equation C.4 one can then check whether it is the best fit by evaluating:

$$h = \sigma_{xy}(2g^3 - 6g) + (\sigma_{xx} - \sigma_{yy})(3g^2 - 1) \tag{C.6}$$

If $h < 0$ then g gives the best fit, otherwise the gradient of the best fit line is given by g' where $g' = -1/g$. For the remainder of this Appendix, g will be taken to denote the gradient of the best fit line. The angle of the line, a_{cl}, is then arctan g.

The end-points of the line are found by projecting each contact point normally on to the best fit line. The normal from the ith contact point meets the best fit line at $(x_{int}[i], y_{int}[i])$ where:

$$x_{int}[i] = \frac{g(y_{cp}[i] - \bar{y}) + x_{cp}[i] + g^2 \bar{x}}{g^2 + 1} \tag{C.7}$$

and

$$y_{int}[i] = \bar{y} + g(x_{int}[i] - \bar{x}) \tag{C.8}$$

If the minimum value of $x_{int}[i]$ occurs when $i = i_{min}$, then $x_{cl}[1] = x_{int}[i_{min}]$ and $y_{cl}[1] = y_{int}[i_{min}]$. Likewise if the maximum value of $x_{int}[i]$ occurs when $i = i_{max}$, then $x_{cl}[2] = x_{int}[i_{max}]$ and $y_{cl}[2] = y_{int}[i_{max}]$.

Appendix D

ARNE's Standard Dialogue

The table on page 218 lists the input commands to ARNE's control software. The responses to each command are also listed.

Command	Meaning	Response
u	Ultrasonic Scan	(U *a d*) * 19 S 0
l *a*	Turn Left	S 0 H *pa*
r *a*	Turn Right	S 0 H *pa*
f *d*	Move Forward	S 0 (Move Successful) or S 1 (Obstacle Detected) or S 2 (Collision Occurred) D *pd*

Table D.1: Commands and Responses of ARNE's Control Software

Legend

a	Angle (degrees)
d	Distance (mm)
pa	Precision Angle (units of 0.1 degree)
pd	Precision Distance (units of 0.1 mm)

Notes

- Spaces are optional between the command mnemonic and its parameters.

- All angles are measured in the standard mathematical way: angles increase anticlockwise and zero degrees is directly in front of the robot.

- Angles returned by turn movements ('H *pa*') indicate the change in orientation caused by the movement.

- The ultrasonic scan moves in steps of 18 degrees. Only 19 values are returned because one reading is obstructed by the 'tail'.

Bibliography

Agre, P. E., and Chapman, D. 1987. Pengi: An Implementation of a Theory of Activity. In *Proc. American Association for Artificial Intelligence*, 268–272. Jul 1987. (Cited on page 15.)

AISB - Society for the Study of Artificial Intelligence and Simulation of Behaviour. 1994. *Models or behaviours - which way forward for robotics?*, University of Leeds, Apr 1994. (Cited on page 4.)

Ayache, N., and Faugeras, O. D. 1990. Maintaining Representations of the Environment of a Mobile Robot. In Cox, I. J., and Wilfong, G. T., eds., *Autonomous Robot Vehicles*. Berlin: Springer Verlag. 205–220. (Cited on pages 98, 106, 110.)

Baker, R. R. 1984. *Bird Navigation:the solution of a mystery?* London: Hodder and Stoughton. (Cited on page 16.)

Borenstein, J., and Koren, Y. 1991. Histogrammic In-Motion Mapping for Mobile Robot Obstacle Avoidance. *IEEE Transactions on Robotics and Automation* 7(4):535–539. (Cited on page 24.)

Borenstein, J. 1991. The Vector Field Histogram - Fast Obstacle Avoidance for Mobile Robots. *IEEE Transactions on Robotics and Automation* 7(3):278–288. (Cited on pages 23, 110.)

Bozma, O., and Kuc, R. 1992. Characterizing the Environment Using Echo Energy, Duration, and Range: the ENDURA Method. In *Proc. IEEE/RSJ International Conference on Intelligent Robots and Systems*, 813–820. Jul 1992. (Cited on pages 61, 110, 203.)

Brady, M. 1985. Artificial Intelligence and Robotics. *Artificial Intelligence* 26:79–121. (Cited on page 2.)

Braitenberg, V. 1984. *Vehicles:Experiments in Synthetic Psychology*. MIT Press. (Cited on pages 13, 14.)

Brooks, R. A. 1986. A Robust Layered Control System For a Mobile Robot. *IEEE Journal of Robotics and Automation* 2(1):14–23. (Cited on pages 3, 13.)

Brooks, R. A. 1990. Elephants don't play chess. In Maes, P., ed., *Designing Autonomous Agents*. Amsterdam: Elsevier Science Publishers B.V. 3–16. (Cited on page 37.)

Brooks, R. A. 1991a. Intelligence Without Reason. Technical Report 1293, MIT Artificial Intelligence Laboratory, 545 Technology Square, Cambridge, MA, 02139,USA. (Cited on page 38.)

Brooks, R. A. 1991b. Intelligence without representation. *Artificial Intelligence* 47:139–159. (Cited on pages 13, 24.)

Brown, M. 1985. Feature Extraction Techniques for Recognizing Solid Objects with an Ultrasonic Range Sensor. *IEEE Journal of Robotics and Automation*. (Cited on pages 67, 73.)

Burgess, N.; O'Keefe, J.; and Recce, M. 1993. Using hippocampal 'place cells' for navigation, exploiting phase coding. In Hanson, S.; Giles, C.; and Cowan, J., eds., *Advances in Neural Information Processing Systems.* San Mateo,CA: Morgan Kauffman. 929–939. (Cited on page 25.)

Cho, D. W. 1990. Certainty Grid Representation for Robot Navigation by a Bayesian Method. *Robotica* 8:159–165.   (Cited on pages 23, 24, 30, 32, 107, 109, 110.)

Chung, H.; Choi, Y. S.; and Lee, J. G. 1992. Path Planning for a Mobile Robot with Grid Type World Model. In *Proc. IEEE/RSJ International Conference on Intelligent Robots and Systems*, 439–444. Jul 1992.   (Cited on page 110.)

Connell, J. H. 1990. *Minimalist Mobile Robotics.* Perspectives in Artificial Intelligence. Academic Press.   (Cited on pages 15, 17, 39, 150.)

Connell, J. H. 1992. SSS:A Hybrid Architecture Applied to Robot Navigation. In *Proc. IEEE International Conference on Robotics and Automation*, 2719–2724. May 1992.   (Cited on page 15.)

Cox, I. J., and Leonard, J. 1991. Temporal Integration of Multiple Sensor Observations for Dynamic World Modeling: A Multiple Hypothesis Approach. In Schmidt, G., ed., *Information Processing in Mobile Robots.* Berlin: Springer Verlag. 23–34.   (Cited on pages 98, 110.)

Cox, I. J. 1991. Blanche - An Experiment in Guidance and Navigation of an Autonomous Robot Vehicle. *IEEE Transactions on Robotics and Automation* 7(2):193–204.   (Cited on pages 22, 34.)

Crowley, J. L. 1985. Navigation for an Intelligent Mobile Robot. *IEEE Journal of Robotics and Automation* 1(1):31–41.   (Cited on pages 13, 22, 37, 67, 72.)

Crowley, J. L. 1989. Dynamic Modeling of Free-space for a Mobile Robot. In *Proc. IEEE/RSJ International Conference on Intelligent Robots and Systems*, 626–633. Sep 1989. (Cited on pages 22, 98, 106, 110.)

Curran, A., and Kyriakopoulos, K. 1993. Sensor-Based Self-Localization for Wheeled Mobile Robots. In *Proc. IEEE International Conference on Robotics and Automation*, 8–13.   (Cited on pages 7, 98.)

Donnett, J. G. 1992. *Analysis and Synthesis in the Design of Locomotor and Spatial Competences for a Multisensory Mobile Robot.* Ph.D. Dissertation, University of Edinburgh. (Cited on page 18.)

Drumheller, M. 1987. Mobile Robot Localization Using Sonar. *IEEE Transactions on Pattern Analysis and Machine Intelligence* 9(2):325–332.   (Cited on pages 37, 72, 98.)

Dudek, G.; Jenkin, M.; Milios, E.; et al. 1991. Robot Exploration as Graph Construction. *IEEE Transactions on Robotics and Automation* 7(6):859–865.   (Cited on pages 15, 20, 40, 107, 110.)

Elfes, A. 1987. Sonar Based Real World Mapping and Navigation. *IEEE Journal of Robotics and Automation* 3(3):233–247.   (Cited on pages 23, 24.)

Elfes, A. 1989. Using Occupancy Grids for Mobile Robot Perception and Navigation. *Computer* 22(6):46–57.   (Cited on pages 23, 24, 30, 34, 97.)

Elfes, A. 1991. Dynamic Control of Robot Perception Using Stochastic Spatial Models. In Schmidt, G., ed., *Information Processing in Mobile Robots.* Berlin: Springer Verlag. 77–92. (Cited on pages 23, 41, 107, 109, 110, 128.)

Elfes, A. 1992. Dynamic Control of Robot Perception Using Multi-Property Inference Grids. In *Proc. IEEE International Conference on Robotics and Automation,* 2561–2567. (Cited on page 23.)

Engelson, S. P., and McDermott, D. V. 1992. Error Correction in Mobile Robot Map Learning. In *Proc. IEEE International Conference on Robotics and Automation,* 2555–2560. (Cited on pages 37, 107, 110.)

Etzioni, O. 1993. Intelligence without Robots:A Reply to Brooks. *AI Magazine* 14(4):7–13. (Cited on page 16.)

Gallistel, C. 1990. *The Organization of Learning.* Learning, Development, and Conceptual Change. MIT Press. (Cited on pages 14, 18.)

Gat, E. 1993. On the Role of Internal State in the Control of Autonomous Mobile Robots. *AI Magazine* 14(1):64–73. (Cited on page 14.)

Gelb, A. 1974. *Applied Optimal Estimation.* MIT Press. (Cited on page 102.)

Hallahan, S. 1994. The People's Revolution. *Computing* 18–18. August 11th 1994. (Cited on page 2.)

Hallam, J.; Forster, P.; and Howe, J. 1989. Map-Free Localisation in a Partially Moving 3D World: the Edinburgh Feature-Based Navigator. In *Proc. Intelligent Autonomous Systems,* 726–736. (Cited on page 98.)

Hallam, J. 1986. Analysing Specular Echoes in Active Acoustic Range Data. In Cohn, A., and Thomas, J., eds., *Artificial Intelligence and its Applications.* New York: John Wiley and Sons, Inc. 165–177. (Cited on pages 61, 62, 72.)

Hewlett-Packard. 1992. *Optoelectronics Designer's Catalog.* Hewlett-Packard Limited, Cain Road, Bracknell, Berkshire,RG12 1HN, U.K. (Cited on page 50.)

Iijima, J.; Asaka, S.; and Yuta, S. 1989. Searching Unknown Environment By a Mobile Robot Using Rage Sensor - An Algorithm and Experiment. In *Proc. IEEE/RSJ International Conference on Intelligent Robots and Systems,* 46–53. Sep 1989. (Cited on pages 43, 110.)

Kennedy, P. 1993. *Preparing For The Twenty-First Century.* London: Fontana Press. (Cited on page 2.)

Kleeman, L. 1989. Ultrasonic Autonomous Robot Localisation System. In *Proc. IEEE/RSJ International Conference on Intelligent Robots and Systems,* 212–219. (Cited on page 98.)

Koza, J. R. 1991. Evolution of Subsumption Using Genetic Programming. In Varela, F. J., and Bourgine, P., eds., *Towards a Practice of Autonomous Systems: Proceedings of the First Conference on Artificial Life,* 110–119. MIT Press. Dec 1991. (Cited on page 39.)

Kriegman, D. J.; Triendl, E.; and Binford, T. O. 1990. A Mobile Robot: Sensing, Planning and Locomotion. In Cox, I. J., and Wilfong, G. T., eds., *Autonomous Robot Vehicles.* Berlin: Springer Verlag. 450–458. (Cited on page 98.)

Kuc, R., and Viard, V. B. 1991. A Physically Based Navigation Strategy for Sonar-Guided Vehicles. *International Journal of Robotics Research* 10(2):75–87.   (Cited on pages 58, 61, 67, 72.)

Kuipers, B., and Byun, Y.-T. 1989. A Robust, Qualitative Approach to a Spatial Learning Mobile Robot. In *Sensor Fusion: Spatial Reasoning and Scene Interpretation*, 366–375. (Cited on page 18.)

Kuipers, B. J., and Levitt, T. S. 1988. Navigation and Mapping in Large-Scale Space. *AI Magazine* 9(2):25–43.   (Cited on page 20.)

Kurz, A. 1993. Building Maps Based on a Learned Classification of Ultrasonic Range Data. In Charnley, D., ed., *Intelligent Autonomous Vehicles*, 193–198. Apr 1993.   (Cited on pages 19, 20.)

Latombe, J.-C. 1991. *Robot Motion Planning*. Robotics:Vision,Manipulation and Sensors. Cambridge,MA: Kluwer Academic Publishers.   (Cited on page 29.)

Leonard, J. J., and Durrant-Whyte, H. F. 1992. *Directed Sonar Sensing for Mobile Robot Navigation*. Cambridge,MA: Kluwer Academic Publishers.   (Cited on pages 7, 22, 33, 58, 59, 60, 69, 72, 73, 77, 98, 107, 108, 110.)

Lim, J. H., and Cho, D. W. 1992. Physically Based Sensor Modelling for a Sonar Map in a Specular Environment. In *Proc. IEEE International Conference on Robotics and Automation*, 1714–1719. May 1992.   (Cited on pages 23, 24, 30, 109, 110.)

Lumelsky, V. J.; Mukhopadhyay, S.; and Sun, K. 1989. Sensor-Based Terrain Acquisition: a "Seed Spreader" Strategy. In *Proc. IEEE/RSJ International Conference on Intelligent Robots and Systems*, 62–67.   (Cited on page 122.)

Lumelsky, V. J.; Mukhopadhyay, S.; and Sun, K. 1991. Dynamic Path Planning in Sensor-Based Terrain Acquisition. In Elfes, A., and Iyengar, S., eds., *Autonomous Mobile Robots - Perception,Mapping, and Navigation (Volume 1)*. IEEE Publications. 530–541.   (Cited on pages 6, 43, 107, 122.)

Lynch, K. 1960. *The Image of the City*. MIT Press.   (Cited on page 18.)

Mali, A. D., and Mukerjee, A. 1994. Robot Behaviour Conflicts: Can Intelligence Be Modularized? In *Proc. American Association for Artificial Intelligence*, 1279–1284. Aug 1994.   (Cited on page 150.)

Manyika, J., and Durrant-Whyte, H. F. 1993. A Tracking Sonar Sensor For Vehicle Guidance. In *Proc. IEEE International Conference on Robotics and Automation*, 424–429. (Cited on page 203.)

Mataric, M. J. 1990a. A Distributed Model for Mobile Robot Environment-Learning and Navigation. Technical Report AI-TR 1228, MIT Artificial Intelligence Laboratory, 545 Technology Square, Cambridge, MA, 02139,USA.   (Cited on page 39.)

Mataric, M. J. 1990b. Navigating With a Rat Brain: A Neurobiologically-Inspired Model for Robot Spatial Representation. In *Proc. Simulation of Adaptive Behavior*, 169–175. Sep 1990.   (Cited on pages 19, 20, 25, 29, 39.)

Maybeck, P. S. 1990. The Kalman Filter: An Introduction to Concepts. In Cox, I. J., and Wilfong, G. T., eds., *Autonomous Robot Vehicles*. Berlin: Springer Verlag. 193–204. (Cited on page 98.)

McFarland, D. 1992. Animals as cost-based robots. *International Studies in the Philosophy of Science* 6(2):133–153. (Cited on page 123.)

McKerrow, P. J. 1991. *Introduction to Robotics*. Electronic Systems Engineering. Addison-Wesley. (Cited on pages 2, 3, 29, 87, 91, 201.)

Miller, D. P.; Brooks, R. A.; Chatila, R.; et al. 1989. Robot Navigation (Introductory statements for panel discussion). In *Proc. International Joint Conference on Artificial Intelligence*, 1672–1674. (Cited on page 6.)

Moravec, H. P. 1983. The Stanford Cart and the CMU Rover. In *Proceedings of the IEEE*, 872–884. (Cited on pages 3, 13, 22.)

Moravec, H. P. 1988. Sensor Fusion in Certainty Grids for Mobile Robots. *AI Magazine* 9(2):61–74. (Cited on pages 23, 24, 30, 31, 41, 106, 110.)

Moutarlier, P., and Chatila, R. 1991. Incremental Free-Space Modelling From Uncertain Data by An Autonomous Mobile Robot. In *Proc. IEEE/RSJ International Conference on Intelligent Robots and Systems*, 1052–1058. Nov 1991. (Cited on pages 42, 110.)

Nagashima, Y., and Yuta, S. 1992. Ultrasonic sensing for a mobile robot to recognize an environment - Measuring the normal direction of walls. In *Proc. IEEE/RSJ International Conference on Intelligent Robots and Systems*, 805–812. Jul 1992. (Cited on pages 59, 72, 73, 110, 203.)

Najand, S.; Lo, Z.-P.; and Bavarian, B. 1992. Intelligent Range Sensor Information Modelling for Autonomous Mobile Robots. In *Proc. IEEE/RSJ International Conference on Intelligent Robots and Systems*, 1025–1029. Jul 1992. (Cited on page 22.)

Nehmzow, U., and Smithers, T. 1991. Using Motor Actions for Location Recognition. In Varela, F. J., and Bourgine, P., eds., *Towards a Practice of Autonomous Systems: Proceedings of the First Conference on Artificial Life*, 96–104. MIT Press. Dec 1991. (Cited on pages 19, 39.)

Nehmzow, U.; Smithers, T.; and Hallam, J. 1991. Location Recognition in a Mobile Robot Using Self-Organising Feature Maps. In Schmidt, G., ed., *Information Processing in Mobile Robots*. Berlin: Springer Verlag. 267–277. (Cited on page 110.)

O'Keefe, J. 1990. A Computational Theory of the Hippocampal Cognitive Map. *Progress in Brain Research* 83:301–312. (Cited on page 25.)

Payton, D. W.; Rosenblatt, J.; and Keirsey, D. M. 1991. Plan Guided Reaction. In Elfes, A., and Iyengar, S., eds., *Autonomous Mobile Robots - Control,Planning, and Architecture (Volume 2)*. IEEE Publications. 184–196. (Cited on pages 15, 201.)

Peremans, H.; Audenaert, K.; and Van Campenhout, J. M. 1993. A High-Resolution Sensor Based on Tri-aural Perception. *IEEE Transactions on Robotics and Automation* 9(1):36–48. (Cited on pages 59, 72, 73.)

Piaget, J. 1956. *The Child's Conception of Space.* London: Routledge and Kegan Paul, Ltd. Translated from the 1948 French edition.   (Cited on page 18.)

Polaroid. 1991. *Ultrasonic Ranging System - User Guide.* Polaroid Corporation, Ultrasonic Components Group, 119 Windsor Street - 2B, Cambridge, MA, 02139,USA.   (Cited on pages 50, 58.)

Prescott, T. J., and Mayhew, J. E. 1992. Building Long-range Cognitive Maps using Local Landmarks. In *Proc. International Conference on Simulation of Adaptive Behaviour: From Animals to Animats,* 233–242. Dec 1992.   (Cited on page 25.)

PSI. 1991. *PSI Systems Mini-Module PSI-K100 Data Pack.* PSI Systems Limited, Unit 17/18, Chelmsford Road Industrial Estate, Great Dunmow, Essex, U.K.   (Cited on page 50.)

Rencken, W. 1993. Concurrent Localisation and Map Building for Mobile Robots Using Ultrasonic Sensors. In *Proc. IEEE/RSJ International Conference on Intelligent Robots and Systems,* 2192–2197. Jul 1993.   (Cited on page 98.)

Rumelhart, D. E., and McClelland, J. L. 1986. *Parallel Distributed Processing - Explorations in the Microstructure of Cognition.* MIT Press.   (Cited on page 24.)

Ryan, B. F.; Joiner, B. L.; and Ryan, Jr., T. A. 1985. *MINITAB Handbook.* Boston,MA: PWS-Kent Publishing Company, second edition.   (Cited on pages 124, 125.)

Sankaranarayanan, A., and Masuda, I. 1992. Senor Based Terrain Acquisition: A New, Heirarchical Algorithm And A Basic Theory. In *Proc. IEEE/RSJ International Conference on Intelligent Robots and Systems,* 1515–1523. Jul 1992.   (Cited on pages 44, 110.)

Sasaki, K., and Takano, M. 1992. Classification of Objects' Surface by Accoustic Transfer Function. In *Proc. IEEE/RSJ International Conference on Intelligent Robots and Systems,* 821–828. Jul 1992.   (Cited on page 203.)

Schlussel, K. 1983. Robotics and Artificial Intelligence Across the Atlantic and Pacific. *IEEE Transactions on Industrial Electronics* 30(3):244–251.   (Cited on page 2.)

Sharp, P. E. 1991. Computer simulation of hippocampal place cells. *Psychobiology* 19(2):103–115.   (Cited on pages 25, 109, 110.)

Shieh, J. S., and Calvert, T. W. 1992. View and route planning for patrol and exploring robots. *Advanced Robotics* 6(4):399–430.   (Cited on pages 43, 44, 110.)

Slack, M. G. 1993. Navigation Templates: Mediating Qualitative Guidance and Quantitative Control in Mobile Robots. *IEEE Transactions on Systems,Man, and Cybernetics* 23(2):452–466.   (Cited on page 16.)

Song, K.-T., and Chang, C. C. 1993. Ultrasonic Sensor Data Fusion for Environment Recognition. In *Proc. IEEE/RSJ International Conference on Intelligent Robots and Systems,* 384–390. Jul 1993.   (Cited on pages 67, 72.)

Speakman, A. 1987. Place cells in the brain:evidence for a cognitive map. *Science Progress* 71:511–530.   (Cited on page 25.)

Thrun, S. B. 1993. Exploration and Model Building in Mobile Robot Domains. In *Proc. IEEE International Conference on Neural Networks*, 175–180. Mar 1993. (Cited on pages 41, 106, 110.)

van Turennout, P., and Honderd, G. 1992. Following a Wall with a Mobile Robot using Ultrasonic Sensors. In *Proc. IEEE/RSJ International Conference on Intelligent Robots and Systems*, 1451–1456. Jul 1992. (Cited on page 39.)

Wilkes, D.; Dudek, G.; Jenkin, M.; et al. 1993. Multi-transducer sonar interpretation. In *Proc. IEEE International Conference on Robotics and Automation*, 392–397. (Cited on page 59.)

Worden, R. 1992. Navigation by Fragment Fitting: a Theory of Hippocampal Function. *Hippocampus* 2(2):165–187. (Cited on page 25.)

Zelinsky, A. 1991a. *Environment Exploration and Path Planning Algorithms for Mobile Robot Navigation using Sonar*. Ph.D. Dissertation, University of Wollongong. (Cited on pages 23, 24, 29, 204.)

Zelinsky, A. 1991b. Mobile Robot Map Making Using Sonar. *Journal of Robotic Systems* 8(5):557–577. (Cited on pages 7, 72, 73, 78.)

Zelinsky, A. 1992. A Mobile Robot Exploration Algorithm. *IEEE Transactions on Robotics and Automation* 8(6):707–717. (Cited on pages 23, 42, 110.)

Index

Individual exploration strategies are listed in *italics*.

Printed in the United States
By Bookmasters